Glimpses of Truth

JACK CAVANAUGH

Glimpses of Truth

The Wycliffe Translation

THE BOOK OF BOOKS

Book One

ZondervanPublishingHouse
Grand Rapids, Michigan

A Division of HarperCollinsPublishers

Glimpses of Truth
Copyright © 1999 by Jack Cavanaugh

Requests for information should be addressed to:

 ZondervanPublishingHouse
Grand Rapids, Michigan 49530

Library of Congress Cataloging-in-Publication Data

Cavanaugh, Jack.
    Glimpses of Truth / Jack Cavanaugh.
        p.   cm. — (The book of books)
    ISBN 0-310-21574-9
        1. Reformation—England—Early movements—Fiction. I. Title. II. Series:
Cavanaugh, Jack. Book of books.
PS3553.A965G55 1999
813'.54—dc21   98-51956
                                          CIP

All Scripture quotations are taken from the Authorized (King James) Version of the Bible of 1611. See the author's afterword.

Published in association with Alive Communications, Inc., 1465 Kelly Johnson Blvd. #320, Colorado Springs, CO 80920

Interior design by Sherri L. Hoffman

Printed in the United States of America

99 00 01 02 03 04 05 /❖ DC/ 10 9 8 7 6 5 4 3 2 1

To the memory of
Anne Askew
(1520–1548)
who at age 28 was burned at the stake.
Her crime? She read an English version of the Bible.

Hebrews 4:12

Forsothe the worde of god is quycke & spedy in wirchyng & more able for to peerse than al two eggide swerde & strecchyinge departide of soule & spirit & or ioyntours & merowis & the departer (or demer) of thoughtis & intenciouns of hertis.

WYCLIFFE'S ENGLISH NEW TESTAMENT (1380)

For the worde off god is quycke & myghty in operacion and sharper then eny two edged swearde: and entreth through, even unto the dividynge asonder of the soule and the sprete and of the joyntes, and the mary: and iudgeth the thoughtes and the intent off the herte.

TYNDALE'S NEW TESTAMENT (1526)

For the word of God is liuely, and mightie in operation, and sharper then any two edged sword, and entreth through, even vnto the diuiding asunder of the soule and the spirit, and of the ioynts, and the marow, and is a discerner of the thoughts, and the intents of the heart.

THE GENEVA BIBLE (1560)

For the word of God is living, and powerful, and sharper than any two-edged sword, piercing even to the dividing asunder of soul and spirit, and of joints and marrow, and is a discerner of the thoughts and intents of the heart.

THE AUTHORIZED VERSION OF THE BIBLE
("THE KING JAMES VERSION," 1611)

Wycliffe's England, 1384

FOREWORD ❧

B Y THE END OF the thirteenth century, no complete English Bible had ever existed. However, those attentive to the signs might have anticipated its soon arrival. There were several signs: earlier translations of the Psalter into English had been widely circulated; the church's grip on the Latin Bible was being loosened by such things as the Crusades, the spread of the new universities, and the conflicts between leading princes and the papacy; attention turned away from Rome, with its Latin literature and liturgy, and toward the "vernacular" languages of the rulers and the people as a variety of troubles engulfed Europe—the displacement of the papacy to Avignon (the so-called "Babylonian Captivity" 1309–77), widespread epidemics and famine (1313–17), the first phase of Hundred Years' War (1337–56), the Black Death (1347–50), and the "Great Schism" (1378–1414).

Amidst these upheavals, John Wycliffe (c. 1328–84), now called the "Morning Star of the Reformation," recoiled from the spiritual apathy and moral laxity of the clergy, and thrust himself into the limelight by voicing his conviction that papal claims were incompatible with the moral truth and with the paramount authority of the inspired Book, the Bible.

Much of Wycliffe's life revolved around his faith and his willingness to express it. At the age of thirty-eight, he became one of the king's chaplains (1366). He then earned a doctor of theology degree at Oxford (1372). While in France a few years later to negotiate a peace treaty, he met with papal authorities about filling ecclesiastical appointments in England—and after his return to England, he became a religious reformer. At the age of forty-nine, he published nineteen articles that challenged some of the church's doctrines; in response, the pope issued five bulls, accusing Wycliffe of heresy (1377). But Wycliffe could not be daunted. To the chagrin of many, he publicly denied the doctrine of transubstantiation (1382)—and paid the price. He was immediately relieved of his teaching and translation duties at Oxford and permitted to retire to Lutterworth. Two years later, after suffering a stroke, he died in communion with the church.

Perhaps what we remember most about John Wycliffe is his greatest accompliment: the translation of the Bible into English. Wycliffe was the first to set aside Latin as the language of the Scriptures and to reach the English people in their own tongue. Working from contemporary manuscripts of the Latin Vulgate, he sought "no strange English" but only the easiest, most common—albeit the most Latin-like—language possible. (Latin constructions and word order were preserved even where they conflicted with English idiom.) His work was used by the Lollards, a group of itinerant preachers ("poor priests") who went about preaching, reading, and teaching from the English Bible.

Wycliffite translations of the New Testament (1380) and Old Testament (1388), which was actually completed by Nicholas of Hereford, opened a new epoch in the history of the Bible. The English Bible continued to gain prominence. Eleven years after Wycliffe's death, John Purvey, formerly Wycliffe's secretary, revised the earlier Wycliffite translation by replacing many Latin constructions with native English idioms (1345). He also removed Jerome's prefaces (from the Vulgate) in favor of an extensive prologue. Purvey's rendition further weakened papal influence over the English people by moving even further from the liturgical Latin of the church.

The Wycliffite Bible, the first complete English Bible, was published, revised, and widely circulated long before the Council of Constance condemned Wycliffe and his influence by ordering his body exhumed, burned, and his ashes scattered on the River Swift (1415).

Wycliffe's translation is the centerpiece of the exciting story you are about to read, Jack Cavanaugh's *Glimpses of Truth*. Through the characters of Felice, Thomas, Bishop William Pole, and others he captures the drama, excitement, and flavor of the times with unusual insight and accuracy.

WILLIAM E. NIX,
DALLAS, TEXAS
JANUARY 1999

Glimpses of Truth

ONE ᣲ

"FELICE!"

It wasn't the sound of her name that startled her; it was the urgency of the cry, more like a chilling howl. She nearly dropped the basket of wet laundry lodged against her hip.

"Felice! Help me!"

She whirled around. Her throat clenched.

Her father lurched toward her, carrying his grown brother in his arms, a dozen bloody gashes marking the unconscious man's arms and chest. Her uncle's head lolled lifelessly from side to side with each halting step.

Clean linens spilled onto the dirt as Felice ran to her father's side.

"God have mercy! What happened?" she cried.

"Help me get him into the house."

Felice reached forward, not knowing exactly how she was supposed to help. Her father shook his head.

"I've got him. Run on ahead and warn Ertha. Prepare a bed."

Although Felice's father was a big man, he labored under his brother's gangly weight, his sweating brow and quivering thick black eyebrows registering the strain. Felice could feel his agony. She wanted to say something to comfort him but could think of no suitable words. She hesitated, praying that the words would come to her. They didn't. Lifting her skirt, she turned and ran toward the village. As she ran, she yelled for help.

Her uncle's house was not far distant. Roused by Felice's shouts, Ertha met her at the doorway. A short woman, Ertha barely filled the bottom half of the portal. Flour covered her hands up to her wrists like a white pair of gloves. She pushed back a wayward strand of wiry hair with the back of her wrist.

"Aunt Ertha! Something horrible has happened!"

The woman stared past Felice up the road. When Felice's father rushed into view, carrying Ertha's slashed and bloody husband like a baby, her mouth dropped open and she had to steady herself against the doorpost. "Lord, have mercy on us!" she cried.

While Ertha rushed to her husband's side, Felice hurried into the house. It was dimly lit. She took a few tentative steps and stumbled over a piglet that nearly sent her sprawling. The animal squealed shrilly and scampered to the far end of the dwelling's single room.

Leaning against the wall with an unsteady hand, she took a deep breath to calm herself, then made her way to the bed in the corner of the room and shooed two chickens off the mattress.

"Stand aside!"

At the sound of her father's voice, Felice jumped. With Ertha cradling her husband's head, together they lowered the wounded man onto the straw mattress. He gave a long, low groan.

"Ives! Who did this to you?" her father asked.

Less than half his size and probably a third of his weight, Ertha nevertheless shoved Felice's father aside to get to her husband. The wounded man stared up at them with unfocused eyes. His dirt-streaked arm dangled over the edge of the bed, the lifeless hand lying palm up in the rushes that covered the floor.

"Ives! Tell me—who did this to you?" Felice's father asked again.

"This is not the time for questions!" Ertha spat. Bending over her husband, she ripped open his shirt.

Felice felt the strangest mixture of sensations. Revolted at the sight of her uncle's wounds, she wanted to turn away. But she wanted to watch even more.

The worst gash cut across the large muscle of his left arm and continued across his chest. There were other cuts on his chest and arms and hands and a few on his upper legs, but none as bad as this one. The man's breeches were caked with dried and blackened blood. His hair was tangled with dirt and grass. His face bore fresh red bruises and abrasions.

"Ives! Can you hear me?" Ertha shouted.

Her husband's eyes fought to focus. It seemed a losing battle. He managed a single, breathy word.

"Howel. . ."

"I'm here," said Felice's father.

"Howel. . ."

"Yes, I hear you!"

"Brigands."

Howel nodded.

"Brigands!" the wounded man said again, exhausting himself with the effort.

"I heard you!" Howel shouted. He turned to Ertha. "We have to close that wound. Heat a knife."

"We need a surgeon!"

"There isn't time! He'll bleed to death unless we close it now!"

Ertha gaped at the wound. She shifted from foot to foot with indecision. Her hands worried her apron. Abruptly, she crossed herself three times and lunged forward, grabbing her husband's arm and clamping shut the wound. Ives wailed in pain. His head plunged back against the mattress. Undaunted, Ertha held the wound closed.

She prayed aloud, "In the name of the Father, Son, and Holy Mary. The wound is red, the cut deep, the flesh be sore, but there will be no more blood or pain till the blessed Virgin bears a child again."

Releasing her grip she stepped back. The wound yawned open. She clamped it shut a second time and repeated the prayer. The result was the same.

"I'll heat a knife," she said.

Howel nodded. He turned to his daughter.

The expression Felice saw on her father's face raised a lump of emotion in her throat. His eyes, normally so gentle and kind and warm were possessed by twin terrors, fear and pain. Not since her mother died had she seen this look in his eyes.

"We'll need hot water," he said.

"And a stone," Felice added.

How desperately she wanted to hug him and in turn to be held by him, to feel his massive ploughman's arms calm her shaking limbs. But there was no time. Death stood at the threshold, and they had to move quickly to prevent it from coming in.

Felice turned toward the door. In her haste she nearly bowled over her younger cousins, Leoma and Poppy, who had crept in quietly behind her. With straight blonde hair, bare feet, and dirty white tunics, the girls were nearly identical except that Leoma was four years older than her sister. Both of them stared at their father and his wounds with saucer eyes. Little Poppy's mouth was twisted in horror. Her chin trembled.

"Girls! Girls! I need your help!" Felice said. She turned them away from the bed and guided them toward the door. "We need a bucket of water and a stone. Can you help me get them?"

The girls' eyes drifted back toward the bloodied bed. Felice blocked their view and nudged them toward the door.

"Felice!"

She looked over her shoulder. "Yes, Father?"

"Send for Thomas."

Felice nodded.

She led the girls through the crowd of gawkers assembling at the door. Then, taking ten-year-old Leoma by the shoulders, she said, "Leoma, you're the oldest. I need you to do something very important. Do you think you can do something for me?"

The frightened girl managed a nod.

"Go to my house. Get Thomas and bring him back here. Tell him to hurry. And tell him to bring the cloth strips with him. The colored ones."

Leoma rubbed tears from her eyes. They were quickly replaced with fresh ones. Her gaze was fixed on the doorway of the house.

Felice's heart wrenched inside her. She had been four years younger than this when her mother died. Now she knew what that horrible ache looked like from the outside.

Getting down on her knees, Felice stroked the girl's cheek and hooked wet blonde hair behind her ears. She held Leoma's gaze with her own.

"You're a big girl now, Leoma. And your father needs your help. Can you do this? Can you get Thomas for your father?"

The trembling girl wiped her nose with a dirty forearm. After a moment, she nodded.

"What are you going to tell him?" Felice prodded.

"That father's hurt."

"That's right. What else?"

"To bring cloth strips."

"The colored cloth strips."

Leoma nodded. She repeated, "The colored cloth strips."

"Good girl. Now run! Hurry! Hurry!"

Felice watched as the little girl's bare feet thumped down the dirt path. She turned to the smaller girl. "Poppy, I need your help too. Do you know where your mother keeps the water bucket?"

Poppy nodded.

"Can you show me where it is?"

For a moment Poppy didn't say anything. Her eyes were enormous. Tears blazed fresh tracks down dirt-smudged cheeks. The small girl leaned toward Felice. She stretched skinny arms around her neck and squeezed. Felice held tight the trembling little body.

Fighting back tears of her own, she said softly, "You're right, Poppy. First we hug, then we get the bucket." Inwardly, she was grateful someone else needed a hug as badly as she did.

Hand in hand, Felice and Poppy hurried down to the stream with the water bucket. On their way back, they picked up a stone about the size of a man's head.

By the time they returned, the small crowd in front of the thatched-roof house had grown to be a large one. Suddenly, an unearthly scream escaped from inside. Several of those who were bunched closest to the door jumped.

Father had cauterized the wound.

Felice spied Leoma lurking near the door, her thin, twig-like fingers at her mouth.

"Did you get Thomas?" Felice asked.

There was no response.

Felice repeated the question.

Finally, Leoma nodded.

"He's bringing the strips of cloth?"

Leoma nodded again. In a barely audible voice, she said, "The colored ones."

"Good girl! I have to go inside. You two stay out here."

"Stay with us!" Poppy cried, tugging at her hand.

Felice scanned the crowd, looking for someone to help her. The crowd was mostly men. She kneeled next to Poppy.

"Leoma will take care of you," she said. "Won't you, Leoma? That's what big sisters are for."

The girls exchanged glances.

Felice gave each girl a hug. "Now you stay outside, do you hear me? No matter what happens, you stay out here!"

Both girls nodded.

Felice stood. She knew she'd taken too much time already, but she could not have left the girls without some sort of reassurance. With the water bucket in one hand and the stone cradled in the other arm, she shoved her way through the gawkers into the house.

The interior seemed darker than before. She thought at first it was because she had just rushed in from outside. But the feeling persisted beyond the time it took for her eyes to adjust. She realized then that it was not the absence of light she was feeling. It was the presence of death.

She glanced toward the doorway and saw that the people crowding there sensed it too. But their faces registered only disgust. To them, death was nothing more than an odious neighbor who had stopped by for a chat and a mug of ale before hauling off his next victim.

It was a complacency born of experience. How many houses had death visited in the past few weeks? Four Sundays ago, he was at the Haslett house, where he carried off Neda and her stillborn son. Soon after that he took the entire Lawton family when their house caught fire in the night. Later, death ambled down to the stream and the house of Thurmond Witt, the miller, whose belly had swollen to an enormous size. And just two days ago, death took the Irlaundes's baby daughter soon after she was bit in the head by a sow.

These deaths had been random and unrelated. They couldn't compare to the season of death that had swept through the village nearly two decades ago, when Felice's mother and older sister were taken, along with more than half the village. And though she was but a child, Felice remembered with remarkable clarity how her mother and sister had bloated and turned black just before they died.

She placed the stone in the fire and poured the water into a basin. She noticed that in her absence Ertha had sliced herbs into a small kettle of water, now boiling. Felice joined her father and Aunt Ertha beside the bed.

The sickening sweet smell of seared flesh wafted strong in the corner. Smoldering knife still in hand, her father stood over his brother, who was once again unconscious.

Ertha leaned forward and examined the arm wound. She nodded, satisfied that it was closed. Reaching for a cup of herbal medicine she'd prepared, she lifted it to her husband's lips. A tiny stream of liquid dribbled out of the corner of his mouth and down his chin.

By now the stone in the fire was scorched. With a lage pair of tongs Felice hauled it out and plunked it in the basin of water. Grabbing a towel, she carried the basin to the wounded man's bedside.

Ertha took the basin from her without comment. She dipped the towel into the water and bathed the bruises and abrasions on her husband's face. From another bowl she applied egg whites to his wounds as a balm.

Ives stirred. His eyelids fluttered. "Brigands," he whispered.

"Ives, what were they after?" Howel asked.

"Brigands," Ives said again.

Howel's forehead bunched with wrinkles. "Were you carrying Bromley's money again?"

"That's not your business!" Ertha spat.

The wounded man nodded, then groaned.

"Ives, how could you?" Howel cried. "The man is not to be trusted!"

Eyes half-closed, Ives said, "Must have been a dozen of 'em what jumped me. Gave as good as I got to one of 'em. A wicked slash across his cheek and eye. Shut his eye, I did."

Ives jerked and winced. Startled by the suddenness of his movement, Ertha recoiled.

"What happened?" Howel asked.

"The hand of death touched him!" she cried. "I felt it myself!"

No one doubted her. Death was close by. Felice could feel his presence in the room as clearly as any corporeal presence. The corner in which the wounded man lay grew dark and dank as though a shadow were falling over him. The air grew chilled.

"What's keeping Thomas?" Howel asked.

As though prompted by the question, the young man appeared in the doorway.

There was nothing physically remarkable about Thomas Torr's appearance. He was no shorter or taller than most men. A poor man's tunic covered bandy legs. He boasted no distinctive facial hair, his head was covered with an unruly, coarse black mop.

Yet there was a presence about him. Something spiritual. An air of confidence. Authority. Hope. It was noticeable in the way the crowd parted as though by invisible hands to let him through.

Howel stepped toward him. "Did you bring them?" he asked.

Thomas replied by holding up a fistful of colored cloth strips.

⋘ ⋙

BISHOP WILLIAM POLE'S CARRIAGE rattled down the rural road. He leaned forward to get a better look out the open window. England was greener than he'd remembered.

Odd. How could I forget a thing like that?

He inhaled the country air. Odors varied with the scenery. There was an earthiness from a recently plowed field, a hint of wet rocks and reeds from a running stream that paralleled the road, and the pungency of wool from a herd of sheep in a nearby field. The mounting nostalgia he felt surprised him. He sat back with a contented smile. He hadn't enjoyed these simple country pleasures since his days as Fearnleah's parish priest.

While his nostalgia was delightfully diverting, it didn't lessen the weight he felt over his impending mission. So much rested on his success. Ties between England and the Church, though currently strained, would be strengthened. A troublesome heresy that had sprouted up like a weed in England's fair garden would be rooted out. And a new era of church-state relations would unfold, one in which England would serve as a model for all the other nations.

Any bishop worth his vows would covet such an opportunity. But while Bishop Pole recognized the political value of his undertaking, he was driven by a much deeper incentive. A personal one. An incentive that eclipsed his ecclesiastical ambition.

Through the infinite mercy of the Almighty God, the bishop had been granted an opportunity to rectify a most grievous personal offense, a secret sin that had lain buried within him like a decaying carcass for years. During the course of this mission, he would have the chance to expunge this most heinous blot—though unknown to anyone but him—from an otherwise spotless record in his service to the Church.

He welcomed his penance. When he had left Rome, and then again when he had set foot on England's shore, he had vowed to God that nothing would stop him from rectifying this past indiscretion. Nothing.

The outskirts of Fearnleah came into view. Rustic homes sat a short distance back from the road. Each had its garden in front where cabbage, onions, parsley, and a variety of herbs were grown. Some of the houses, with their thatched roofs and rough walls, were neat and trim and in good repair. Others were dilapidated from neglect. How simple these structures appeared compared to the grand architecture of Rome, to which he had grown accustomed. The city's glorious marble columns, majestic spires, archways, and copulas never failed to inspire him. And how simple these villagers seemed compared to the citizens of the Holy City, who daily wrestled with the grand theological and political complexities of life.

He grinned, amused, as his carriage entered what might be termed the village proper of Fearnleah. A rustic fanfare greeted him: complaining cart wheels, squealing children, bawling hogs, the shouts of peddlers, the *clop, clop, clop* of horses, the ring of the smithy's hammer, and the incessant honking of gaggles of geese.

To think that his superiors—powerful cardinals in Rome, even Pope Urban himself—were anxiously awaiting his report regarding a certain young resident of this simple English village, one Thomas Torr.

≼§ §≽

"THOMAS! WHAT TOOK YOU so long?" Felice cried.

"Never mind that now," Howel interrupted. "Thomas, come here. Ives needs you." Signs of relief and hope appeared on Howel's large features as he ushered the boy with the cloth strips to his brother's bedside.

Felice felt it too. There was a solid self-assurance about Thomas. Villagers often remarked to her about the erect manner in which he carried himself, like nobility. There was a straightforwardness about him, a boldness uncommon for one so young and so poor.

Thomas handed the colored strips of cloth to Howel who cupped them in two hands, with the same care he would use to hold a baby chick. One by one, Thomas sorted through the strips. He would pick one, study it silently, replace it for another, then another.

From the bed the wounded man stirred. His eyes fluttered open and his gaze fell upon Thomas. A spark of recognition gave way to hopeful longing. Sitting on the bed's edge, Ertha paused in her ministrations. She stared too. In the doorway, the collected villagers wedged themselves into every available crevice in anticipation of what would happen next.

Thomas selected a dull tan strip of cloth then nodded. He'd found the one he was looking for.

The room fell silent.

Stretching the strip of cloth between two hands, Thomas raised it until it was inches from his eyes. He read, "'As the hart panteth after the water brooks, so panteth my soul after thee, O God. My soul thirsteth for God, for the living God. Why art thou cast down, O my soul? and why art thou disquieted in me? hope thou in God.'"

Ives closed his eyes as the words washed over him like a tonic. "These are truly God's words?" he asked weakly.

"Yes," Thomas replied.

With crusted lips the wounded man formed the words, "As the hart panteth after the water brooks . . ."

". . . so panteth my soul after thee, O God."

". . . so panteth my soul . . ."

"After thee, O God."

"These are truly God's words?" Ives asked.

"These are God's words," Thomas confirmed.

A smile formed on the wounded man's face and spread ear to ear. "I understand them," he mused. "God's words in my own house . . . and I understand them!"

Felice noticed something that caused her to raise a hand to her chest. She suppressed a soft gasp. She looked to her father. To Ertha. Did they see it too?

A light. A glow. A radiance. The kind that exists between a candle's wick and its flame. The corner of the room and everyone in it was bathed in a holy iridescence. Was she the only one who could see it?

No. Ives saw it too! With great effort he propped himself up on his least-injured arm and stared with open-mouthed wonder.

She wasn't imagining it!

Then, like a dying flame, the glow began to dissipate. This concerned the wounded man greatly. He cried, "Thomas, read me more of God's words! Quickly! I beg you, read me more!"

Thomas sorted through the jumble of strips in Howel's cupped hands till he found another he liked. Holding it close to his eyes, he read, "'Who shall separate us from the love of Christ? shall tribulation, or distress, or persecution, or famine, or nakedness, or peril, or sword? Nay, in all these things we are more than conquerors through him that loved us.'"

The glow intensified.

There was no visible source of the light Felice saw. The radiance was just there. Soft and white. It made no sense. But then who was she to try to understand such a wonderful, holy manifestation?

Contentedly, Ives lowered himself back onto the straw bed. He repeated the words, "Who shall separate us from the love of Christ? Yes, . . . yes, . . . these are the words of God." It was a statement this time, not a question. With his eyes reflecting the radiance, he spoke with unflagging assurance. Confirming, rather than seeking confirmation.

Also, as before, the glow began to fade. This time Ives didn't protest, but the next instant he was thrashing on the bed. Screaming. Tearing at his flesh as though to loose the grip of an unseen beast. His clawing and thrashing only served to open his wounds again.

Ertha jumped back. "Death has gripped him!" she cried. Turning to Thomas: "Help him! Help him! Command death to leave this house!"

Thomas stared at her blankly.

Howel shoved the strips of cloth into Thomas's hands. He went to his brother, pinning the wounded man's arms to the bed to prevent him from doing any further injury to himself.

"Do something!" Ertha screamed over the sound of her husband's wails.

Thomas fumbled through the strips of cloth. Felice stepped closer, offering her hands as a receptacle. With a quick glance, Thomas dumped the strips into her cupped hands. He found one he liked. To read it, he had to shout over the wounded man's wailing and Ertha's screaming. "'Come unto me, all ye that labour and are heavy laden, and I will give you rest.'"

Ives gave no indication he heard. Ertha grabbed Thomas by the sleeve and dragged him closer to the bed.

"Read it again!" she commanded.

Thomas looked hesitantly at Howel. The big ploughman gave him an encouraging nod. Thomas tried again: "'Come unto me, all ye that labour and are heavy laden, and I will give you rest.'"

As suddenly as the thrashing had begun, it stopped. Ives's chest rose and fell with heavy gasps. After a few moments, Howel tentatively released his brother.

Ives looked up at them. Between gasps, he said, "Don't blame yourself. You did all you could . . . not your fault. Howel, did you see the sky last night? The planet of black bile and melancholy was high. Not even you, brother . . . with your strong arms . . . could defeat such an adversary."

His head fell back. His eyes closed. His breathing was ragged.

"God's words," he murmured. "In my house . . ."

Ertha jerked Thomas forward. "Read the words!" she ordered. "Read!"

Thomas lifted the scrap of cloth. "Come unto me, all ye that—"

"Come unto me," Ives repeated.

"Yes," said Thomas.

"Come unto me," Ives repeated. "Yes, . . . so clear now, so clear . . . come . . . come . . . yes . . ."

His head fell to one side.

"Ives?" Ertha cried. "*Ives?*"

Howel leaned forward and laid his ear against his brother's chest. Looking at Ertha, he said, "He's gone."

Ertha stared at her dead husband with stunned disbelief. She shook her head. Turning to Thomas, she said, "Bring him back!"

"What?" Thomas stammered.

"Bring him back!" she shouted all the louder. "Bring him back! Bring him back!"

Thomas glanced helplessly about. "How?"

"With these!" She snatched the cloth from which Thomas had just read. "Bring him back with this!"

Thomas shook his head, "You don't understand."

"Are these God's words or aren't they?" Ertha shouted.

"Yes, they—"

"Then use them to bring him back!"

Thomas backed away. "These are passages of Scripture. They're not magical incantations! They have no power to . . ."

Ertha wasn't listening. With the cloth strip in her hand she climbed onto the bed next to her husband and pressed it against his deepest wound. Having done so, she turned to Thomas and shouted, "Now say the words! Say the words!"

"Saying the words won't—"

"Say the words! Say the words!" the woman ranted. She turned to Howel. "Make him say the words! Force the words out of him!"

Her brother-in-law looked upon her sadly. "If Thomas says there is no magic in the cloth strips—"

"He must invoke it!" she screamed. "Make him say the words!"

Howel looked pleadingly at Thomas.

With open palms Thomas insisted, "There's nothing I can do!"

With cat-like quickness Ertha lunged at Thomas. Shrieking. Clawing. Howel managed to pull her away and restrain her before she hurt him.

"There is magic in the cloth!" she screeched. "You saw it yourself! Don't deny it! He's your brother, Howel! Make this whelp bring Ives back to life!"

Howel looked bewildered.

"You saw it!" she shouted. "The light! You saw it yourself! And even before that, when he was holding the strips of cloth. He looked at them and knew the words without reading them! The words moved invisibly from the cloth to his mind! He's a sorcerer, I tell you!"

Thomas shook his head defensively. "There's nothing magic about that. I was reading the words silently."

Ertha's eyes were wild. She managed to free an arm and point an accusing finger. "Sorcery! We've all seen people read before! People read with their lips! But not you! You conjured up the words in your mind! Felice! You saw it too! Don't lie, girl! Tell your father you saw it too!"

Felice looked helplessly at Thomas, then her father.

"I can read silently!" Thomas protested.

Ertha flew into a rage and it was all Howel could do to restrain her. He looked at Thomas questioningly. Clearly, Ertha had succeeded in planting a seed of doubt in his mind.

Thomas insisted, "On my honor, I'm telling you the truth! These strips of cloth contain no magical powers!"

Felice watched with growing concern as a weariness descended upon her father like a great weight. The man was accustomed to overturning dirt and herding cattle. Solomon he was not.

With tired voice he said, "Go home. There is nothing else you can do here."

"No!" Ertha shrieked! *"No!"* She struggled fiercely to free herself, but she was overmatched by the ploughman's massive hands and arms. Rocking back and forth, he attempted to calm her as he would a child.

The villagers crowding the doorway parted to let Thomas and Felice through. They gave the couple a wide berth.

Felice handed Thomas the cloth strips. As she did, one fell to the ground. The three men closest to it jumped back as if it were an adder.

As Thomas bent to pick it up, he shook his head sadly. "It's only a strip of cloth," he said.

Still, no one was willing to get close to it.

Rising, Thomas took Felice by the arm and headed for home. They got no further than the edge of the crowd.

"Is the fool dead?"

The voice came from on high. Bromley, the town's bailiff, sat atop a powerful black steed that snorted contemptuously at the peasants around them. Beside him, mounted on a chestnut mare, was his son Kendall.

The black-haired bailiff appeared as menacing and dark as his horse. His tunic was made of flashing purple satin, while his outer cote-hardie was scarlet. Kendall, much fairer than his father, had light brown hair. He wore an equally fine tunic of reddish-orange with tan trim. The color and brightness of their apparel distinguished both men readily from the dusty earth hues worn by the village peasants.

With the sun directly behind the mounted official's head, Felice and Thomas had to shade their eyes when looking up at the bailiff.

"Ives is dead," Thomas reported.

"He was attacked by brigands," Felice added.

Bromley let loose with an unsympathetic snort. "And I suppose my money is gone as well," he groaned. His lips pursed, he acted as though he was the greater victim. "I never should have trusted the wretch," he concluded. Spying the strips of cloth in Thomas's hands, he asked, "What are those?"

Thomas started to answer. Before he could, Felice grabbed the strips from Thomas and held them behind her back. "Nothing of concern," she said. "Merely strips of sewing cloth."

The bailiff's eyes narrowed. "Let me see them," he said.

Reluctantly, Felice held out a fist with trailing edges of cloth spilling out from her grip. "Nothing of consequence. I assure you!"

"They are verses of Holy Scripture," Thomas said.

"Thomas!" Felice cried. She glared at him.

The bailiff chewed his lower lip. "Kendall, bring those pieces of cloth to me."

The younger man dismounted. He was of the same age as both Felice and Thomas. An attractive lad, and slightly taller than Thomas, his face had none of his father's fierce lines. As he approached Felice, he smiled slightly and looked at her fondly.

To Thomas, he gave a courteous nod. The two of them knew each other intimately. There had been a time when they were fellow students and the closest of friends. But when Thomas had begun to eclipse Kendall academically . . .

Kendall requested the cloth strips with an open hand.

Felice hesitated.

Thomas said, "Give them to him." To Bromley, he said, "The cloth strips are mine. Felice has nothing to do with them."

Bromley said nothing.

Kendall delivered the strips to his father. The bailiff examined one, then another, and read aloud the words, stumbling over some of the more difficult ones. His face clouded with anger.

Clenching the strips in his fist, he shook them at Thomas. "This is how you repay me? I took you into my house! I provided you shelter and an education! An education which you now use to perform this . . . this . . . heresy!"

Thomas replied, "My education suited your purpose at the time."

Enraged, the bailiff flung the cloth strips to the ground. The black steed trod them underfoot.

"Bromley!"

It was Howel. He stood in the doorway of the house. His shoulders spanned from side to side. A time-worn anger crossed his face, giving evidence of a long history of confrontation with the bailiff.

"Howel!" The name dripped from the bailiff's lips with disdain. "You're just in time to say good-bye to your young charge," he said. "I'm arresting him."

"For what reason?"

Bromley leaned forward in a condescending manner, his arm across the back of the horse's neck. "Why, even a miscreant like yourself knows that it is forbidden for laity to possess Scripture. Furthermore, it is forbidden to translate such works into the vulgar tongue. Thomas has violated both these laws."

Howel stepped out of the doorway.

"And should you unwisely contemplate interfering with his arrest," Bromley continued, "I will arrest both you and your daughter as accomplices."

Undaunted, Howel approached the bailiff. He was not intimidated by the man's bright clothing and elevated position.

Bromley's steed took a nervous step backward.

Howel said, "And surely you know that once I inform Lord Harborough of this, he will set Thomas free."

The two combatants glared at each other, neither one giving the other an inch.

Bromley scowled. "Sadly, I fear you will not have time to run off to Lord Harborough," he said. "I imagine you will have your hands full with other matters." Pointing to Ertha who now stood in the doorway with her daughters pressed against her, Bromley said, "I want them out of the house by nightfall. If they're not out, they will be charged with trespassing."

"What?" Howel thundered.

"I am fully within my rights," the bailiff sniffed. "I intend to sell your brother's holdings in partial repayment for the money he so freely relinquished to brigands today."

Howel was beside himself. "My brother gave his life protecting your money!"

"He didn't do a very good job of it, did he?" Bromley scoffed. "In fact, from the report I received, it seems as though your brother was in collusion with those men."

Howel repeated the word in confusion. "Collusion?"

"A secret agreement," Thomas explained quietly.

Howel's face colored at hearing the definition of the word. But before he could object, Bromley continued, "The way I heard it, your brother got greedy and attempted to betray his cohorts, which makes him a snake as well as a thief."

Howel charged the bailiff like a bull. Then, abruptly, he pulled up. Bromley was ready for him. With a flick of his wrist, he had produced a sword, its tip now poised just shy of Howel's neck.

The clattering of an arriving carriage disrupted their argument. All eyes watched as the carriage door swung open and a bishop appeared.

With a grunt, Bromley sheathed his sword. He dismounted and greeted Bishop Pole.

"Your Excellency," he said.

"Bailiff," the bishop replied. He surveyed the crowd with a sweeping glance. With his robe dusting the ground, he made his way into the center of the confrontation.

He sighed. "How many years has it been since I've been in Fearnleah?" he asked no one in particular. "Yet from all appearances, little has changed in my absence."

The bailiff stepped forward. In a perturbed tone, he said, "Simply doing my job, your Excellency."

"And what job is that, Bailiff?" the bishop asked.

"Arresting him," Bromley replied, pointing a finger at Thomas.

The bishop glanced at Thomas. "And the charge?"

"Illegal possession of Holy Scripture. See for yourself. Kendall, show the good bishop the evidence."

Kendall dutifully plucked several strips of cloth out of the dirt. He handed them to the bishop who shook the dust from them before lifting them up to the sun for examination. He read the words aloud, his eyebrows rising as he recognized them.

"Who wrote this?" he asked.

"The one in whose possession it was found," Bromley replied.

Bishop Pole approached Thomas. They were the same height. He studied the boy with a mixture of curiosity and amusement, circling him twice, looking him up and down. For Thomas's part, he endured the scrutiny with little or no visible emotion.

"You are Thomas Torr," said the bishop.

Thomas reacted with mild surprise. "Yes, your Excellency," he said, "I am."

The bishop nodded knowingly. Holding up the cloth strip, he said, "Is the charge true? Did you write the words on this cloth?"

"Yes, your Excellency."

Folds of skin bunched on the bishop's brow. "Why?"

"I am a poor man, your Excellency. Parchment is expensive."

The bishop examined the strip again. "Ingenious," he said. "And from what source have you copied these words?"

Thomas hesitated.

Bromley was quick to answer for him. "He's a student of the heretic Wycliffe."

The bishop nodded solemnly. "You say you copied these words," the bishop mused. "Can you read them as well?"

"Yes, your Excellency."

The bishop handed the cloth strip to Thomas. "Show me."

Taking the strip, Thomas read, "'As the hart panteth after the water brooks, so panteth my soul after thee, O God.'"

A pleased glint sparkled in the bishop's eyes. "And you say this is Dr. Wycliffe's translation?"

"No, your Excellency."

"No?"

"It's my own translation."

"From the Latin?" The bishop looked surprised.

"Yes, your Excellency. The Vulgate."

The bishop thought a moment. Then, his eyes brightened. He had a thought. To Thomas, he said, *"Undique totis usque adeo turbatur agris."*

Thomas smiled. He replied, "Yes, your Excellency. The countryside is in great turmoil. And I dare say, as a result, Rome is too."

The bishop laughed heartily.

"It is indeed, young man," he said. "And that is precisely why I have journeyed from Rome to meet you."

TWO ❧

$\mathcal{T}$HOMAS LAID HIS HAND on the rough wooden latch. It felt strangely coarse after having spent the day in the polished interior of Bishop Pole's carriage. Lifting it quietly, he crossed the threshold from a dark night into a darker cottage interior. He stepped softly on the freshly scattered straw so as not to wake anyone.

A low fire in the central hearth provided the room's only illumination. The flickering light cast long shadows up wattle-and-daub walls, black with soot near the arched beams and thatched roof. The lowing of a cow and rustle of chickens greeted him from the stall at the far end of the room. The animal sounds were accompanied by the familiar rumble of Howel's snoring.

A higher-pitched snore, like a persistent whistle, came from the opposite end of the room. It puzzled him. It was coming from behind the partition that separated Felice's sleeping area. As his eyes adjusted to the darkness, Thomas was further confounded by the sight of two tiny pair of feet protruding past the partition.

Then he remembered. Leoma and Poppy. Apparently Bromley had made good his threat to evict Ertha and the girls. In one way, it was a relief. The snoring was undoubtedly Ertha's. She was probably sharing Felice's bed.

With a silent yawn he made his way quietly to the livestock end of the room where a straw mattress awaited him beside Howel.

A sudden movement startled him. An arm appeared just beyond the hearth. A moan accompanied it.

Felice.

So she wasn't sharing a bed with Ertha. Rising up from her reclined position on the bench beside the fire, she looked at him with sleepy eyes.

"You came home," she said in a whisper.

"You're sleeping on the bench?"

Sitting up, Felice stretched gracefully. "Who can sleep with that noise?" she asked.

Just then, a double snort came from behind the partition followed by a moment of silence and the resumption of Ertha's whistle-snore.

Felice's eyes sparkled with merriment as she covered her mouth to stifle a laugh. Thomas too fought back the urge to laugh.

"Shhh!" Felice said with finger to lips.

The last thing either of them wanted was for Ertha to catch them alone at night in the dark. While Howel would simply cluck his tongue at them and warn them to behave themselves, Ertha would without doubt launch into one of her tirades.

How many times had they heard it?

"A girl needs a mother! I predict dire things for that one," she would say of Felice. "Plenty of diligent and silent work! That's the only way to deal with the foolish dreams that fill the head of that brainless creature!"

Thomas motioned to Felice that he was going to bed.

Her response was a protruding lower lip. "But I was waiting up for you!" she sulked.

Any resolve he might have had melted. In truth, when it came to Felice he hadn't much resolve to begin with, and what little he had was no match for her slightest sigh. And now that he got a good look at her in the firelight with her simple white nightgown draped over delicate shoulders, he was sufficiently stirred. Add to that the reddish-orange hair framing a face without blemish, two eyes that sparkled like azure gems, and coquettish lines punctuating the corners of her mouth and he was her slave.

"Well?" she said whispering. "Are you going to tell me or not?"

"Tell you what?" he whispered back.

"What happened today, silly!"

"Oh, that!"

Reluctantly, he dragged back the very thoughts that Felice's attractiveness had banished a moment earlier. In a whisper, he related to her his ride through the countryside with Bishop Pole and their conversation. As he talked, Felice reached for a wooden spoon and stirred the meatless barley frumenty she had been keeping warm over the dying fire. She dished up a helping into a wooden bowl, tore a piece of black bread to accompany it, and handed them both to Thomas. Scooting over, she patted the vacant space on the bench, inviting him to sit beside her. The flickering firelight highlighted the excitement on her face.

"What was it like to ride in a carriage?" she asked.

The sparkle that shimmered in her eyes halted Thomas midchew. He loved the way she looked at moments like this. Excited. Hopeful. Full of promise. Their life was full of hardship and drudgery, and her eyes didn't light up like this often. In some village women far younger than Felice, it had disappeared altogether. But for some reason known only to her, Felice refused to let the spark go out completely.

Thomas swallowed. Moving the flat of his hand smoothly on an invisible plane, he said, "Riding in a carriage is like gliding in the air three feet above the ground."

Felice closed her eyes and tried to imagine what it must feel like.

Thomas spooned a mouthful of meal. The sweetness of Felice's face was a spice that made even the bland barley taste good.

Felice's eyes shot open. "Did he talk of Rome?" She said it too loudly. Catching herself, she placed a hand over her mouth, then repeated her question in a whisper, "Did he talk of Rome?"

Thomas shook his head.

"Did he explain why he traveled all this way to meet you?"

Thomas nodded. Unhurriedly he scraped another spoonful of meal and with deliberate slowness lifted it to his mouth.

"Stop toying with me and tell me!" Felice cried with a constrained squeal. She gave his shoulder a playful shove. A blob of frumenty fell off the spoon and plopped on the front of his tunic.

Thomas stared dumbly at the mealy blob on his chest.

Felice covered her mouth with her hands in an unsuccessful attempt to cork escaping giggles.

Then, they both got to sniggering. The longer the blob lay unattended on Thomas's chest, the funnier it became. Soon, they were laughing so loud it disrupted Ertha's snoring. From behind the partition they could hear her stir. Attempts to hold back their laughter only resulted in teary eyes and explosive bursts.

As sure as anything, they were going to get caught. But Thomas didn't care. Let Ertha erupt. It was worth it.

But the expected scowling face never materialized from behind the partition. After a time, their giggles subsided and Ertha's whistle-snore resumed its normal rhythm.

"See what you did?" Felice giggle-whispered, wiping the errant blob from his tunic with her finger.

"What I did? You're the one who knocked my arm!"

Felice reached for a towel, wiped the frumenty from her finger, then finished dabbing what remained on Thomas's shirt. Thomas savored her closeness, the physical attention she was paying to his chest and the warm odor of her hair as she leaned close to him. His heart sank a little when she'd finished her task and sat back.

"Well, are you going to tell me or not?" She'd set aside the towel and was wiping the remaining tears of laughter from the corners of her eyes.

"Oh! Thank you."

A puzzled look formed on her face. "Thank you?"

"Thank you very much?"

She slapped his arm. "No! Why the bishop came to see you! Are you going to tell me or not?"

"Oh, that! He's interested in me. At least that's what he said."

"Did he mention your translating work?"

"He mentioned it."

"Well? What did he say?"

"He expressed his concern about translating the Bible into English."

"Concern? That's putting it mildly, don't you think? Maybe he's here to make more trouble for Dr. Wycliffe!"

Thomas shook his head. "I don't think so. Dr. Wycliffe has already appeared before an army of bishops at St. Paul's and at Lambeth Palace and at a synod at Blackfriars. What could one lone bishop do to him?"

"So you really think he's traveled all this way just to meet you?" she asked, gazing at him with admiration.

Thomas delayed his response. He fed off her gaze like a blossom drinking in the morning dew.

Finally, he said, "Is that so hard to believe?"

Felice glanced at the curtain behind which Ertha was sleeping. The snoring continued unabated. She whispered, "What else did you talk about?"

"The bishop was full of questions," Thomas replied. "He asked a lot of personal questions."

"Personal questions?"

"About my education, how I was raised, Lord Harborough's patronage, how I got started copying, then translating manuscripts—that sort of thing. He seemed to want to know everything about me."

A troubled expression clouded Felice's face. "Thomas, nobody could be more proud of you than I am. But bishops don't travel all the way from Rome to England just to make the acquaintance of a peasant boy. He must want something."

Thomas felt the sting of her bittersweet barb. Deep down he knew she was right, but he'd been so enthralled by the attention the bishop had lavished upon him that the thought hadn't crossed his mind. Now it disturbed him that he'd been so gullible. But he didn't want to admit that to Felice.

"All I know is what the bishop told me," Thomas defended himself, keeping his voice from rising. "He gave me no reason to doubt his word."

"What about the bailiff's charges and the strips of cloth? Did he say anything about that?"

Thomas brightened with the good news. "He did. He promised me he would persuade the bailiff not to pursue the matter."

She looked at him skeptically. "Can he do that?"

Thomas shrugged. "He said he could."

"Did he give you back the cloth strips?"

Thomas grimaced. Felice wasn't going to like this answer. "He destroyed them."

The bad news registered on her face.

"Destroyed them?" she cried, a little too loudly.

"The bishop's position regarding the cloth strips is a valid one," he said defensively. Dangling an imaginary piece of cloth between his thumb and forefinger, he said, "While we were in the carriage the bishop held up one of the strips like this and said, 'Thomas, do you honestly believe this is what God had in mind when He entrusted His Sacred Scriptures into our care?'"

Felice's eyes squinted in thought. "Was he referring to the cloth material or the fact that the words on the cloth were written in English?"

Thomas's arm dropped limply. "I don't know. He didn't say. I . . . at the time, I thought he was referring to the cloth, but I suppose he could have meant both."

"So then, are you going to stop working with Dr. Wycliffe? Stop translating?"

"Of course not!"

"But he can't be in favor of what you're doing. Maybe he came all this way to get you to stop translating!"

Thomas squirmed uncomfortably. Felice had managed to take all the shine off his once-glorious afternoon. "There's no use discussing this. He hasn't ordered me to stop translating."

"And if he does?"

"If he does . . . well, if he does, I'll decide then."

"He'll tell you to stop."

"You don't know that for sure."

"Yes I do."

Her tone, though restrained, was firm and unshakable. Thomas hated it when she was like this. He hated it because she was usually right. Felice had a wonderfully keen insight into people and their intentions, a gift that over the years Thomas had learned to appreciate—except when it ran counter to his opinion. Like now.

"If you ask me," Felice whispered, "Bishop Pole came to England with one goal in mind, and that's to stop you from copying and translating the Bible into English."

"That doesn't make sense," Thomas insisted. "Why me? I'm only one copyist!"

"Thomas, you're more than just a copyist! Dr. Wycliffe himself treats you differently from the other copyists! How many of them are doing translation work?"

It was a fact Thomas was extremely proud of. While Wycliffe had his close assistants, like John Purvey, Thomas alone among all the copyists seemed to merit the rector's special favor.

"And consider this," Felice continued, "Dr. Wycliffe is an aged man. You're young. And if Bishop Pole can stop your work, he might succeed in halting the spread of the English translation before it has a chance to take root."

A swirl of emotions churned inside Thomas. The idea that the Church might consider him important enough to take action against was immensely gratifying to a young man's ego; on the other hand, how could he enjoy the compliment without admitting that Felice was right?

"Nonsense," Thomas said, wondering if his protest sounded as feeble to her as it did to him.

"Just promise me you'll talk to Dr. Wycliffe about this."

"Of course I'll talk to Dr. Wycliffe."

"And tell him everything Bishop Pole tells you."

"I'll tell him."

"And promise me you'll listen to what Dr. Wycliffe has to say."

"Felice!"

She folded her arms in motherly fashion. "Promise me you'll listen to what Dr. Wycliffe has to say."

"All right! I promise!"

"And promise me—"

"Felice . . ."

". . . that no matter what happens, you'll never leave me."

Her eyes were moist as she spoke the words. She was serious. Did she really think that he would let anything—bishop, King, or even the Pope himself—come between them?

Thomas leaned close to her ear. He let his cheek brush gently across her cheek. "I promise," he whispered.

Pulling back only slightly, he gazed into her soft, inviting eyes. Their lips touched ever so slightly, separated, then touched again, this time with fervency.

Twin giggles startled them.

Two pair of tiny eyes peered at them from the dark recesses of the room. Leoma grinned and stared while Poppy sniggered and covered her eyes.

"You two should be asleep!" Felice scolded in a whisper.

"We were asleep," Leoma replied. "Your kissing sounds woke us up."

"Kissing sounds," Poppy echoed.

Felice looked helplessly at Thomas. "They're not going to go back to sleep as long as we're out here," she said.

Thomas frowned. "Then let's go outside."

"Outside? I'll freeze. I'm only in my nightgown!"

"Grab a blanket," Thomas said. "I'll keep you warm." He gave her a warm smile as a down payment on what was to come.

While Thomas lit a candle, Felice shooed the girls back behind the partition. She slipped on her shoes and threw a blanket over her shoulders.

Holding the door open for her, he shuddered. Not from the night air but at the thought of their forbidden rendezvous. Alone with Felice. In the dark. Huddling together to keep warm.

Placing his arm around her, they pressed into the night, a solitary candle flame leading the way. On one end of the house Howel had built a lean-to he used as a shed for his plow and tools. It also housed a desk and stool which he had built specially for Thomas. It was here Thomas practiced his letters and printed on the strips of cloth. A fresh pile of material sat atop the desk.

"Before all the commotion with Ives this afternoon, Father stopped by the tailor's shop and picked them up," Felice explained. "He thought you might be needing more."

Thomas acknowledged the strips with an approving nod, then shoved them aside with the back of his hand to make a place to set the candle. They maneuvered to share sitting space on his stool, which creaked a complaint under the double weight.

Felice lifted a corner of her blanket like a mother hen would lift her wing. Thomas took shelter beneath it. They huddled close together to get warm.

Their cheeks touching, Thomas nestled against her playfully. Felice cooed. Tenderly, Thomas traced her cheekbone with his nose, nuzzled her ear, then followed the line of her jaw to her chin, across her lips and back up her jaw to her neck. He settled beneath her hair, his lips against the warmth of her neck, relishing her scent and the softness of her skin.

Felice wriggled free.

"What's wrong?"

Her cheeks were colored. Her breathing heavy. "Maybe you should write something," she said.

"Write something? Now?"

Felice nodded. "It think it would be best." She was leaning away from him.

Thomas knew what she was doing. She was being cautious. He was tired of always being cautious. He wanted to cuddle up with her and lie beside her all night, to wake up in the morning with her in his arms.

Felice was fumbling for one of the fresh cloth strips. "Why don't you write down a verse from the Bible?" she said.

"It's too late for that," Thomas complained. "Besides, I don't feel much like writing. Can't we just sit here and enjoy being together and alone?" He reached for her waist.

She fended him off. "Just one verse," she insisted. She selected a strip of cloth from the pile, lifted the top of the desk that served as a lid to the compartment where Thomas kept his goose-feather pens and ink, and retrieved his writing instruments.

"I don't feel like doing this," Thomas complained. He refused the goose-feather pen she held out to him.

"Please! Do it for me. Write a verse of Scripture for me."

"What good would that do? You can't read! Besides, I'm not sure writing Scripture on pieces of cloth is such a good idea anymore."

"Looks to me like the bishop has already succeeded in stopping you," she said, challenging him to prove her wrong by holding out the pen to him.

"That's not it and you know it!"

"Then teach me to write and I'll do it!"

Thomas chuckled.

"What are you laughing at? I'm serious!"

"Teach you to write?"

"Sure! Why not?"

"We both know why you're doing this. You're just trying to keep me occupied so I won't—"

"Thomas, I'm serious!" Felice insisted. "Teach me to write and to read."

"That's crazy! Girls can't read and write!"

"Why not?"

"Well, because . . . there's no reason for you to know those things."

"I have a reason."

Now she was just acting like a child. Unable to keep the sarcasm from his voice, Thomas said, "Oh? What possible reason could you have to read and write?"

"If I knew how to read," she said, "then I could read the Scriptures that you translate into English."

She was so ready with her answer that Thomas knew this was no impulsive idea. She had been thinking about this.

Thomas shook his head. "I can read them for you."

Her eyebrows raised in triumph. Thomas had the uneasy feeling that he had just walked into a trap. And, like most helpless victims, by the time he realized it was a trap, it was too late.

"And what do you do when you can't read anymore?" she asked. "What happens when your eyes get so bad you can no longer see the words?"

Her words hit him hard. Already, his eyes were beginning to fail. Badly.

He had first noticed the problem one day when he was copying a passage from Paul's epistle to the Philippians. The tip of his pen had split and ink had splattered into his right eye. Though he did his best to rinse the ink from his eye, it seemed like one spot in the very center wouldn't wash away. Days later, it still had not gone away. He asked Felice to look at it, but she could see no ink spot on his eye.

Not many days later, an identical dark spot had appeared in the center vision of his left eye, and Thomas had reluctantly concluded that the splattered ink was merely a coincidence. His problem was not ink in his eyes. Something was seriously wrong with his vision.

Over the weeks and months that followed, the dark spot in the center of each eye gradually grew bigger and bigger and bigger. It became clear that it was only a matter of time before he would be blind.

"Come on, Thomas!" Felice purred. "It'll be fun! Think of me as your apprentice!"

Thomas shook his head. "It's not that easy."

"All the more reason to begin right now!"

Thomas continued shaking his head. He rubbed the back of his neck.

Felice said, "I already know some of the letters."

Thomas looked at her skeptically.

"Go ahead, test me!" she said.

Thomas accepted her challenge. He loaded his pen with ink and scratched a capital letter on a scrap of cloth. He sat back.

Felice was smiling even before the letter was complete. "That's a G!" she cried. "The first letter in the word *God.*"

Thomas's mouth dropped open. "How did you know that?" he cried.

Felice sniggered. "You taught me."

"I taught you? When?"

"About a month ago. Remember the day I watched you practicing your letters?"

Thomas nodded. "But you couldn't have remembered your letters just from that one day. Here, how about this one?"

He scratched out another letter.

Felice wrinkled her forehead and stared at the ink pattern. She shook her head from side to side.

"It's a capital D," Thomas said, confident he'd proved his point. He set out to prove it even further. "How about this one?"

He made another mark on the cloth.

"An L!" Felice said. "The first letter in the word *Lord!*"

Thomas was taken aback.

"Let me try to make a letter!" Felice squealed.

She reached for the pen. He moved his hand playfully out of her reach. Her lower lip protruded. She reached again, and again he moved his hand.

"Thomas! Don't be such a lout!"

He laughed.

A sharp jab in his side cut the laugh short and brought the pen close enough that Felice managed to snatch it from him.

"Not fair!" he cried, trying to grab back the pen. This time it was Felice who held it out of his reach.

"Teach me to write!" she insisted.

Feigning resignation, he gave a conciliatory nod. "Have it your way. I yield."

Cautiously, Felice relaxed her guard. Thomas grabbed for the pen. She was too quick for him. He grasped nothing but air.

"Thomas, I mean it! Teach me to write!"

He took a long look at her. She was serious. He conceded. "I'll teach you to write."

With a half-grin and suspicious eyes she cautiously relaxed her guard again. "No tricks? Promise?"

Thomas nodded. "Promise."

Hesitantly she positioned the pen over the desk and a waiting strip of blank cloth. Thomas reached for her hand. She pulled it away.

"You promised no tricks!"

"Not a trick. If you want me to teach you to write I have to guide your hand."

Her eyes squinted with skepticism.

"It's the only way I know to teach you. You'll just have to trust me."

Cautiously, Felice moved her hand and the pen within his reach. Thomas placed his hand on hers. He showed her how to hold the pen, then he guided her hand to the ink.

The sensation of her hand in his distracted him. Not only were their hands touching but their cheeks were close enough to each other that Thomas could feel her warmth.

The loaded pen touched the cloth. A black spot appeared and grew dramatically.

"Oh!" Felice cried, pulling away from the ugly black blot. "What did I do wrong?"

"Um . . . you have to learn to use the ink sparingly, especially with the cloth." In his distraction, he had not paid attention to how much ink the pen had drawn. Grabbing a rag, he wiped the tip of the pen. "Let's try again."

This time he helped her get just the right amount of ink on the tip of the pen. Then, moving her hand to the cloth he guided it down and across. An L appeared on the cloth strip.

"I did it!" Felice shouted. She dropped the pen to the table and clapped, bouncing on the edge of the stool and staring happily at the first letter she had ever written. "Now help me write a word! I want to write the word *Lord!*"

Pleased by her exuberance, Thomas picked up the pen and handed it to her. He said, "The second letter is a little harder because it's curved. It's an O."

"O," Felice said, matching the shape of her lips with that of the letter.

Once again Thomas placed his hand on hers and once again the warmth of her cheek next to his nearly made him forget what they were doing. Using all his willpower to concentrate, he managed to help her draw a circle.

When it was completed, he said, "L . . . O . . ."

The second letter received the same enthusiastic response from Felice as the first. She bounced happily on the stool and clapped.

Soon an R and a D were added to the cloth, completing the word. Felice gazed at her effort with pride.

"Let's dress the letters up a bit," Thomas said, warming to the role as her instructor. "With just a few additional strokes we can make them look like they're written for a king."

He reached for her hand as before, but this time it was unresponsive. When he turned toward her to see what was wrong, he found that there was barely any space between them. His nose and lips were nearly touching hers. Her eyes were soft and shimmering. He could feel her breath on his lips.

In that moment the universe was reduced to one man and one woman and the arousing, warm, glorious, indescribable attraction that pulled them together. Their lips brushed, separated, then brushed again. Parting, they met again and pressed fully, warmly. Felice closed her eyes with a gentle moan.

Suddenly, there was a loud cracking sound. The stool upon which they were sitting shuddered, cracked again, then gave way.

An instant later Thomas and Felice found themselves sprawled unceremoniously on the frozen ground. They exchanged stunned expressions. Then, when it was clear neither of them was hurt, they burst out laughing.

Lying in the dirt on their backs late at night they laughed until their sides hurt.

⋈

BISHOP WILLIAM POLE WOULD be the first to admit that he was a man of grand passions. There was little on this earth about which he did not feel strongly. He loved his architecture grand, his fields vast, green, and heavily populated with flowers, his sunsets rich with color, his conversation lively, his women beautiful though chaste, his hymns sung lustily, his ale strong, and his food savory and plentiful. He was enamored with the pleasures and possessions that came with wealth, though he rarely approved of the men in whose hands wealth so often resided. Such was the situation in which he found himself as the dinner guest of Gar Bromley, the Bailiff of Fearnleah.

With clasped hands, the bishop eagerly greeted the steaming pie that was set before him. As the aroma of the pastry shell fresh from the oven rose to meet him, he closed his eyes in a silent prayer of gratitude for the experience.

"Do you like Lombard chicken pasties, your Excellency?" Bromley asked. The bailiff sat at the head of an enormous oak table, which was itself dwarfed by the immensity of the stone hall that it occupied. Bishop Pole sat with his backside warming to a fireplace ten feet wide. Opposite him sat the young man Kendall, Bromley's son. Identical pies had been placed in front of each of the three diners.

In answer to his host, the bishop leaned forward and savored the butter-brushed pastry with several unhurried inhalations. He gazed with amorous eyes at the glistening brown crust and said, "I love food, my dear host."

It didn't escape the bishop's notice that Kendall was eyeing him with amusement. An unguarded chuckle slipped past the boy's lips, which brought a swift rebuking glance from his father.

"You say there is a chicken lying in wait beneath this glorious crust?" the bishop asked.

"Yes, your Excellency," replied Bromley. "Please, do us the honor of taking the first bite."

With his nose still poised within an inch of the pie, the bishop raised a patient hand. "In good time, my dear host. One doesn't ravish a dish as lovely as this. It deserves a few moments of adoration." With plump, delicate fingers he rotated the pie, slowly savoring and sniffing, sniffing and savoring.

The other two diners watched and waited.

After a time the bishop surfaced. With a contented sigh he reached for his knife. Delicate cuts were made in the crust, incisions that would have made a surgeon envious. In time the crust was laid open. The bishop gasped. His face bore the expression of a child unwrapping a gift.

Throwing his arms wide, he shouted, "Bacon!"

Indeed, beneath the crust two strips of bacon crossed a tender white chicken breast. The bishop excised a generous portion of both meats and laid them ever so tenderly on his tongue. With many moans and sighs, he chewed.

At the head of the table the gaunt and bony bailiff sniffed and picked at his pie, shoving bits of meat and crust from one side of the dish to the other, giving the impression he was using them to play chess. In short order he commanded a servant to take his plate away. The bishop watched with mournful eyes as his host's largely uneaten pie was carried from the room.

Kendall ate with a young man's appetite yet without letting his meal divert his attention from the bishop's display.

The bishop noticed the boy's attention and saw it as an opportunity to expound on his theology of eating. Laying aside his knife, he interlaced plump fingers over a good-sized paunch, as was his custom whenever he spoke of matters of great significance. It was not uncommon for these same interlaced fingers to flap like butterfly wings as he paused in his discourses to think.

"My boy, the ability to take pleasure in one's food is a gift granted exclusively to mankind," he expounded. "You will not see a bird of prey savoring its kill, nor will you observe a lion seasoning his meat. Man alone has this capacity to combine pleasure and eating, and this from God.

"You see, son, the key to happiness in this wretched world is to learn to enjoy the simple blessings of God. In His goodness, God has given us appetites which serve as appreciators of life. For example, our appetite for beauty is satisfied when we slow our journey enough to admire the pale afternoon sunlight as it filters through the leaves in the forest.

"So too our other senses. Songs pleasure our ears. Freshly picked wildflowers pleasure our sense of smell. The warmth of the spring sun on our flesh following a hard winter pleasures our sense of touch. And food—properly prepared and seasoned and received with relish—pleasures our sense of taste.

"These simple graces are afforded every man, whether king or nobleman, prelate or peasant. Happy is the man who recognizes this and enjoys them lustily. So, my dear boy, that is why I eat as I do. It is out of praise to God for the appetites and pleasures He has so graciously afforded me."

To reinforce his teaching, for the remainder of the meal the bishop played the appreciative audience to the chef's gourmand performance. He clapped when the spit-roasted venison steaks with pepper sauce were served. He cheered the golden steamed custard. And when a chalice of fig and raison creame was placed before him, he all but swooned.

Apparently, the bishop's little theology lecture took, for Kendall began following his example. Hesitantly at first, then lustily and with good humor when his father made no effort to rebuke him. As for Bromley, the bailiff's stony presence remained unchanged.

Not until the last morsel was consumed and the last drop of liquid refreshment drained did the bishop's exuberance flag. He resisted the urge to lick the creame that coated the inside of his chalice, a concession to manners he would not have made had he been dining in any lesser abode.

All too quickly thereafter he found himself in a far less enjoyable setting. No sooner had the base of the bishop's empty chalice touched the wooden table than Bromley's wooden chair scraped against the floor, announcing the meal's conclusion.

Servants swarmed liked flies over the remnants of the meal as they hastily cleared the table. Kendall dismissed himself with a ritual parting and disappeared up a long flight of stairs while Bromley ushered his guest into an adjoining room.

A lively fire awaited them. As the bishop followed his host, he was led past an enormous tapestry that covered an entire wall. Its powerful scene, strong with motion and color, dominated the room. Mounted armored men on horseback raised flashing swords; row after row of taut bows launched deadly missiles at an opposing force of men on foot wearing peasant dress and armed only with wooden staves. Fallen peasants littered the ground beneath the pounding horses' hooves. Each of the bodies was pierced with many arrows. Some were missing arms or legs or heads. Others bore slashing red wounds. Yet for all their various wounds they had something in common—without exception their faces were portraits of agony.

"Have a seat, your Excellency," Bromley said. He motioned to one of two high-backed chairs situated on a rug in front of the fire.

With a nod of gratitude the bishop took his seat. Bromley remained standing, using the back of his chair as an armrest. To look at his host the bishop had to twist in his seat. The tapestry served as a grim backdrop.

"Now tell me," Bromley began, "exactly what brings a bishop from Rome to Fearnleah?"

The bailiff went straight to business. No after-dinner chatter. No sharing of gossip. This was the Gar Bromley the bishop remembered. To men such as he, sumptuous dinners were nothing more than formalities to be endured. Business was their meat and potatoes.

The bishop said, "Do you find it so unusual that a cleric would visit his former parish? Must I have a reason other than sentiment?"

A gleam as hard as flint flashed in Bromley's eyes. "My good bishop," he said, "let us dispense with the usual parrying and get to the point. I am the bailiff of this land. It is my duty to be informed of all persons and events that would threaten the peace."

Pole smiled. "A threat to peace? Surely you don't perceive me, a simple bishop, to be such a threat?" It was another parry. The bishop couldn't resist. He had never cared much for Bromley. Theirs had always been a relationship of verbal banter and sidesteps. And, to this point at least, the two men had always managed to keep out of each other's affairs. The bishop meant to keep it that way.

Bromley laughed a low, soft laugh. It was an unsettling sound like the rumbling of a crouched lion in the bush. "No, bishop," he said, "I cannot imagine that you would ever be a threat to me."

Pole wasn't sure how to interpret this remark. Was it a statement of goodwill, or had the bailiff just shooed him aside as he would a bothersome insect?

Bromley continued, "It is what you represent that poses the threat. Or have you forgotten the grisly fate of the Archbishop of Canterbury?"

A pool of fear swirled inside the bishop's stomach. He hadn't forgotten. It had been the archbishop's murder at the hands of peasants that had prompted Pole's first audience with the Pope. Upon hearing the news, the Holy Father had sought an Englishman's explanation to the uprising, and Bishop Pole, serving already in Rome, had been the handiest Englishman. Pole had been caught completely off guard. He hadn't yet heard of any insurrection. And he had found himself in the unenviable position of having to defend his native land to the Pope while not excusing the actions of a lawless rabble. It had been an altogether regrettable experience.

Bromley continued, "Lord Harborough and I were in London when the peasants mobbed the streets. They burned the manor of Savoy to the ground. Prisoners they had loosed from Fleet Prison ran wild in the London streets. We saw the archbishop's head on a stake at London Bridge. A disagreeable sight, I assure you."

The bishop bowed his head. He had known Simon Sudbury before he'd ever been appointed primate. A likable fellow. It was unsettling to imagine him coming to such a ghastly end.

"Lord Harborough was quite shaken by the whole affair," Bromley said. "Consequently, rarely does he venture far from his manor anymore. He fears the countryside is no longer safe."

Pole hadn't heard this news about Harborough, but it had a ring of truth. He knew Harborough to be a sensitive Christian man.

"The seeds of this uprising," Bromley concluded, his voice rising as he spoke, "are being sown by John Wycliffe and his traveling preachers. They challenge established institutions, spread anti-clerical sentiment among the peasants, and stir up the countryside to insurrection. So, your Excellency, you can appreciate my concern. The very presence of a bishop from Rome this close to Lutterworth could incite an uprising. For the good of Fearnleah it is imperative that I know your intentions."

The bishop hung his head. "Of course," he said softly.

He felt ashamed. He had allowed his personal feelings for Bromley to overshadow the greater good.

Rising from his chair, he faced the bailiff squarely. "My mission is to prove England's loyalty to the Church and to His Holiness the Pope by thwarting John Wycliffe's efforts to translate and distribute the Scriptures in the vulgar language."

"And you see young Thomas Torr as the key to your effort."

"Why, yes!" the bishop cried, surprised at Bromley's insightfulness.

Bromley sniffed. "I agree. Wycliffe is not well and his movement draws its strength from him. If he were to die tonight, his work would be forgotten within a year's time."

The bishop nodded. "Wycliffe is no fool. This is why he trains the men he calls Lollards to go throughout the land, spreading his heresy."

"But the Lollards are a loose confederation at best," Bromley added. "Strike the shepherd—"

"—and the sheep will scatter."

The two men stared knowingly at each other. They were of one mind.

Bromley said, "We must also insure that before he dies Wycliffe does not pass the torch of leadership on to another—someone who has a leader's charisma and who can oversee the translation process."

"Who himself is not a cleric, so that the peasant masses will accept him—Thomas Torr," the bishop said.

"Thomas Torr," Bromley agreed.

Walking over to the tapestry, Bromley looked at it and said, "Thomas must be removed from the equation."

"Perhaps not," the bishop countered.

Pole's deviation from the expected course brought Bromley's black eyebrows together in a most threatening way.

Defending his logic the bishop raised a postulating finger. "What if," he said, "what if instead of removing Thomas, we were able to convert him?"

The frown remained, but Bromley was listening.

Pole said, "Imagine the response if Wycliffe's hand-chosen disciple sees the error of the English Scriptures and boldly speaks out against them."

A slow, thin smile spread across Bromley's face. "An interesting plan," he mused, "but one not easily attained."

It was the bishop's turn to smile. "It may be easier than you think. All we have to do is give Thomas what he wants."

"And just what is it he wants?"

The bishop interlaced his fingers on his paunch. While fat fingers flapped like butterflies, a smug grin graced his lips. "I spent the afternoon with him in my carriage. During that time I observed him carefully. Asked him questions."

"And from a single afternoon ride in the countryside you know the boy's heart?"

The bishop's grin widened. "I assure you it was not difficult to assess. He wants what every idealistic young lad wants who is interested in spiritual things."

"And that is?"

"Praise. Recognition. He dreams of standing before crowds and kings and popes proclaiming to them the ways of God. He fantasizes men and women sitting at his feet, marveling at his great insight and uncommon wisdom."

A chuckle escaped Bromley's lips. "My dear bishop, I do believe you're right."

"I know I'm right," Pole boasted. "I recognized it immediately. It's exactly what I dreamed of when I was his age."

"I foresee two obstacles," Bromley said abruptly. His expression and posture reverted to one of control.

"Obstacles?"

"First, Howel's daughter. He desires her too."

"A peasant girl. She poses no threat."

"Don't dismiss her so readily. She's a peasant girl with a quick wit and a sharp tongue. More importantly, the boy's in love with her. He listens to her. If she senses a threat, she could be a problem."

"What do you propose?" the bishop asked cautiously.

Bromley read the concern on the bishop's face. "Nothing harmful to the girl, I assure you, my good bishop," he said. "But our plan would have a greater chance of success if she were out of the way."

"Out of the way?"

"Women are fickle, are they not? Let's say she marries another man, a man who can keep his wife in her place. Given that development, she would no longer have any influence over the boy, would she?"

The bishop smiled his approval. "Is there a rival for her hand?"

Bromley sighed. "We can arrange it. My own son, Kendall, for one. He's been in love with the silly girl since they were children."

"Kendall?" Bromley's answer surprised the bishop.

"I know what you're thinking, and you're right," Bromley cried in exasperation. "A bailiff's son deserves better. But it would make the boy happy, and it would solve our problem."

But that's not what the bishop was thinking. What took him aback was the quickness with which Bromley was willing to use people, to alter the course of their lives, merely to suit his own purposes. The man was offering to marry off his own son just to gain an advantage.

The proposal weighed heavily inside the bishop's gut, like an undigested bit of beef. But he could think of no acceptable reason to object to the bailiff's plan.

"We must also consider Lord Harborough," Bromley mused. "He might become an obstacle."

"How so?"

"He's still protective of the boy," Bromley said. "Has been from the beginning. It took me years to regain Lord Harborough's favor after I kicked the boy out of my house."

"Thomas told me he had once been Kendall's academic study partner. What happened?"

"The boy was disruptive and a general nuisance. He robbed Kendall of all desire to learn. I only took him into my home as a favor to Lord Harborough in the first place. But I couldn't keep him here at my son's expense."

The bishop nodded to indicate that he was listening, but he wasn't. There was good reason why Lord Harborough acted as he did toward the boy. The bishop's mind wandered back nearly twenty years.

❧ ❧

IT WAS NIGHT. POLE, Fearnleah's parish priest, had just secured the outer doors of the church when someone fell upon them, banging furiously. Pole opened the doors.

"Lord Harborough!" he exclaimed.

A sobbing Lord Harborough burst in and collapsed on the floor. At first the priest feared that he was injured in some way. But the man's heaving chest and screams were driven by internal, not external, injury. Just seeing this physically and socially powerful man distraught in this way—sobbing convulsively, repeatedly cursing himself, pounding large fists against the church floor—caused the priest great anguish himself.

Kneeling beside him, Pole managed with tender, consoling words to convince the man to turn over. Lying on his back, his face heavenward, wet with tears, Harborough begged God to forgive him.

"What is it?" Pole asked.

Harborough closed his eyes. With palms pressing against his temples until Pole thought the man would crush his own skull, he screamed for relief, so badly did he want to excise the agony from his mind.

"For God's sake, confess your sin, man!" Pole pleaded.

Harborough wailed. "I have sinned! I have sinned! I have sinned! I have sinned!"

"Tell me your sin, my son!"

The man's face bunched, his lips trembled, his whole head shivered. With great effort, he managed to speak his sin in a single word.

"Callie."

"Your house servant?" Pole asked.

Grimacing, Harborough managed a nod.

"Ah," said the priest. With one word he understood. He sat next to the penitent lord and waited for him to regain control of himself. As he waited the image of a young, vibrant woman came to his mind. Fairer than any he had ever seen before in his life. Callie.

"It was an unguarded moment," Harborough muttered. He remained on his back, staring up at the ceiling, a forearm covering his eyes.

"Go on," Pole said.

"It was me," Harborough insisted. "I want you to know that. It was all me. She did nothing to entice me or tempt me, other than simply being Callie. Sweet. Alluring."

Pole nodded. He understood. Maybe too well.

"At first," Harborough continued, "she resisted. But by then I had given in to my passion. It consumed me, controlled me. It was madness, I knew it, but I didn't care . . . I didn't care. Ultimately, she yielded." He laughed bitterly. "What else could she do? I am her lord."

"Where is the girl now?" Pole asked.

"Outside."

This gave Pole a start. "Outside? She's outside, alone in the night?" He jumped to his feet.

Harborough grew animated. He scrambled to his feet. Grabbing the priest's robes, he restrained him. "Not until I'm gone!" he cried. "I beg you, don't bring her in until I'm gone! I couldn't bear to look on her again in my shame!"

Pole looked down on the cowering figure in disdain. The proud Lord Harborough, model ruler and Christian, reduced to blubbering in guilt and shame. All because he could not control his passions.

But judgment belonged to the Lord.

"Return to your manor," Pole said.

"You'll take care of Callie?" Harborough asked. "I knew you would. That's why I brought her here."

"I'll take care of the girl."

"Please understand, she can no longer stay with me," Harborough cried. "Not only could I not bear the shame, the constant reminder of my sin, but I fear that, another time, in another moment of weakness . . ." He didn't finish the sentence. He didn't need to.

"You'll see that she is given food and shelter?"

"Yes," Pole said, ushering Harborough out a side door.

"And another means of living! She has suffered enough because of my sin."

"Yes, yes, I'll find her another means of living. Now be on your way."

Harborough whirled back around. "Whatever expenses you incur, I will quickly repay," he said.

"Understood. Now go!"

"Wait! My forgiveness!"

With an exasperated sigh, the priest replied, "Consider yourself forgiven!"

"And my penance?"

"We'll take care of that later! Right now my concern is for that poor waif you deposited outside the doors of the church."

Lord Harborough sobered. "Yes, of course. How selfish of me. Please, Father, go to her. Convince her that I am truly repentant."

Pole finally managed to shut the door and latch it. His footfalls echoing in the empty church, he hurried to the front door, unlatched it, and threw it open.

He found the girl huddled at the base of a tree a short distance away. She had covered herself with a shawl. Bending down, Pole assisted the girl to her feet and led her into the church. Once they were safely inside, he latched the door.

"There, there," he said to the frightened girl. "You're safe here. This is God's house."

She remained hidden beneath her shawl.

Gently, Pole reached toward her and uncovered her head and face. As he did, he felt his heart rise in his throat. Even in the dim candlelight of the church interior, even with a face wet and red from her tears, she was stunning. Never before had he seen a woman as beautiful and naturally alluring as this woman.

❦

"YOUR EXCELLENCY, DID YOU hear what I said?"

A scowl on Bromley's face chastised the bishop for letting his mind wander.

"You were speaking of Lord Harborough," the bishop replied, as though he'd been listening all along.

"I was speaking of Lord Harborough's obsession when it comes to this boy. Do you have any idea why Lord Harborough protects him so?"

The bishop cleared his throat. "Leave Lord Harborough to me," he said.

"But he *favors* Wycliffe! And many other nobles look to him for direction. And it is he who introduced the boy to Wycliffe in the first place."

The bishop waved a hand, unconcerned. "I believe I may be able to convince our Lord Harborough that Thomas is destined for greater things than serving as a copyist for a heretic. Leave Lord Harborough to me. He wants the best for the boy. I'll convince him that the boy's future lies in Rome, not Lutterworth."

This seemed to satisfy the bailiff. "Then our business is concluded," he said. His heels clicked rapidly as he crossed the floor to the doorway. This man knew nothing of transitions.

"I suppose it is," said the bishop, amused at the bailiff's abruptness.

As Bromley ushered the bishop to his waiting carriage, he said, "So it's agreed. You take care of Thomas and Lord Harborough, and I'll take care of the girl."

The bishop nodded. It was agreed.

As Pole climbed into the carriage, he gave his host one final nod. Icy black eyes met his. The bishop shivered as the carriage plunged into the darkness. But that was to be expected; the night was dark and cold.

THREE ❧

"HOMAS?"

With a moan, Thomas stirred, goaded by the sound of his name. He scrunched his closed eyes tighter and rolled over, tucking the warm blanket around his neck. Slumber reclaimed him.

He dreamed he was showing a completed English Bible translation to Bishop Pole. Thomas stood at the bishop's elbow, explaining his translation of a difficult passage. The bishop was pointing to the verse with a sausage-like finger, perplexed at Thomas's reasoning. A low groan tumbled from his mouth, a dissatisfied rumble.

"Thomas?"

The bishop in his dream was looking at him, expecting some kind of answer to a question that had never been asked. Thomas was puzzled. The sound of his name did not come from the bishop's lips. And what was it about the verse the bishop didn't understand? It seemed clear enough to him.

"Thomas? Thomas!"

There was his name again. Still the bishop's mouth remained immobile as a low rumbling sound came from him.

Then, the bishop began shuffling his feet. Why was he doing that? Thomas looked down. He saw the bishop's sandaled feet moving back and forth on a straw-covered floor. No, not feet, hooves.

"Thomas!"

Another rumbling sound. Thomas stirred as the sounds of the outside world began to overshadow his dream. He blinked open unwilling eyes only to be greeted by an enormous black nose with cavernous nostrils just inches from his face.

"What . . . ," Thomas cried.

He reached up and shoved the cow's nose away from his face. As his faculties stirred awake, his heart gave a start. What time was it? Wasn't he supposed to be at Lutterworth today? He threw off his blanket.

No, wait. He wasn't supposed to be in Lutterworth until tomorrow.

"Thomas!"

This time the voice he heard calling his name was clear and recognizable. He pulled the blanket back and covered himself.

A grinning Felice stood across the room with a wooden spoon in her hand. She was flanked by Leoma and Poppy. Both girls gripped the folds of Felice's dress, half hiding behind them.

"Get up!" she said. "Can't you hear him? Father's calling for you!"

From somewhere beyond them, outside the house, he could hear Howel's low, rumbling voice calling his name.

Thomas threw off his blanket as Felice turned the girls away. He pulled his breeches on beneath his night shirt. Then, slipping the nightshirt off, he ducked into his shirt and pulled on one shoe then the other, hopping across the floor to the door.

"You'd better take some kind of covering," Felice said. "It's cold."

Grabbing his coat from a peg beside the door, Thomas lifted the latch with one hand while shoving the other in the coat. He stepped outside into the frosty morning air.

As the door closed behind him he could hear Ertha's complaining voice: "Does Howel *always* let that boy sleep half the day away like this?"

The eastern horizon blushed rosy red at the imminent appearance of the sun. Felice was right about the cold. It sought out every crack and crevice in his clothing, looking for the slightest opening that it might penetrate his defenses and chill his flesh and numb his bones. Within seconds, the wind had smacked red his exposed cheeks and hands.

Thomas crunched through icy mud to the side of the house. Patches of snow dotted the ground.

"Ah! There you are, Thomas!" Howel cried. His massive plough-man's hands hoisted a broken stool in one hand and splintered leg pieces in the other. "Do you know what happened here?"

There was no anger in the question. Howel was not the sort of man who felt compelled to fix blame, nor did he embrace the common fault of valuing possessions over people. He was merely inquiring into the stool's fate since he would be the one to fix it.

"The stool!" Thomas said, chuckling. He was stalling, trying to give his still-groggy mind an extra moment to ascertain how much of the previous night's rendezvous with Felice he should reveal.

The crunch of footsteps behind him gave him a welcomed and momentary reprieve. Felice appeared from around the corner of the house, her shoulders hunched against the cold.

"Breakfast is almost ready," she said to the men. Then, seeing her father with the stool in his hands, she shot a glance at Thomas. The corners of her mouth twitched, fighting back a grin.

It was infectious. For now Thomas found himself struggling to suppress a resurgence of giggles.

Howel cocked his head and stared at them.

Thomas said, "I was . . . um, working last night, just for a short time, and . . . um—" Each *um* swallowed a guffaw that was busting to come out. "Well, while I was working, and . . . um, sitting on the stool, when all of a sudden the leg . . . um, gave way, and . . . well . . . it simply gave way. Must have been rotten, or weak, or . . . something."

"Working?" Howel said. "It was freezing last night!"

"Yes, um . . . it was cold . . . ," Thomas stammered.

Felice jumped in, "Actually, Father, I brought Thomas out here to show him the new cloth strips you picked up from Mr. Riggs." She pointed to the multicolored pile on the desk.

"Yes!" Thomas cried. "The new cloth strips. I want to thank you for picking them up for me. That was very kind of you. Picking them up for me, that is."

Howel stood and waited. He still didn't have an explanation for the broken stool.

"And since we were out here," Felice continued, "I asked Thomas to show me how to make letters. See? These are my letters!" She ran to the desk and sorted through the stiff cloth strips. Finding the right one, she held it up.

Howel moved closer to the desk to get a look at the cloth.

Thomas grinned in admiration. Felice was diverting her father's attention from the stool.

"See? I made these letters!" she cried excitedly. "This is an L . . . and this one is an O . . . and an R . . . and a D! It spells *Lord!* I wrote that! Well . . . with Thomas's help."

Howel stared in wonder at the markings on the cloth strip. "You did that?"

Felice beamed.

"It's not that difficult," Thomas said. "I could teach you how to do it too!"

The ploughman seemed unable to take his eyes off the printed letters. He shook his head slowly. "No . . . no, I'm only a commoner."

"Sure you can!" Thomas cried. "Here . . ." He retrieved the pen and ink from the belly of the desk, only to discover that the ink was frozen.

Thomas's heart sank. Felice's face registered the disappointment he felt. Then, she cried, "Wait right here!" Her hurried footsteps crunched in the ice and snow. She disappeared around the corner of the house. A moment later she returned sheltering the flaming end of a fiery brand with a cupped hand.

With a pleased grin, Thomas held the ink pot over the flame until it took its familiar liquid shape.

"There! Now we're ready. We'll start with an easy letter." He scratched a capital T onto a clean cloth.

"It looks like the cross of Christ," Howel said.

"It does, doesn't it?" Thomas replied. "Now you try it."

Thomas offered the pen to Howel. The ploughman shook his head.

"Go ahead, Father!" Felice urged him. "Try it!"

Howel stared tentatively at his daughter, then Thomas. He looked to the corner of the house and behind him, checking to see if anyone was around. Then, with a mischievous smile, he set aside the stool and splintered leg. He brushed his large, rough, heavily scarred hands on the front of his clothes before reaching for the pen. Thomas showed him how to hold it. The moment Thomas released the pen, however, it went awry and tumbled from Howel's fingers.

Howel stepped back from the desk as though the pen had bit him. "See? I'm just a commoner," he said.

"Don't be afraid to grip it," Thomas said. "Here, try again."

Howel stared uncertainly at the pen.

Felice said: "Please, Father? One more try?"

Wiping his hands a second time on the front of his tunic, Howel inched toward the desk. He extended his right hand for Thomas to place the pen in it.

"Firmly, but gently," Thomas said.

This time the pen remained secure in Howel's massive paw. He grinned in triumph.

Holding the man's wrist, Thomas moved his arm to the ink reservoir and helped him load the pen. Felice, who had been warming a cloth strip, set it in front of her father.

Thomas talked him through the making of the letter. "The stem of the letter is a simple straight line from top to bottom," he said. "Think of it as the trunk of a tree."

With Thomas holding the cloth securely in place and with Felice leaning anxiously over her father's shoulder they watched as Howel moved the pen uncertainly in a downward line. The result was a crooked mark.

He pulled his hand away and frowned. "Looks like a diseased stump," he said.

"No! It's a good start!" Thomas cried. "Now this time, you'll do the same thing, only sideways. Make a line across the top of your tree. It's called 'crossing the T.'"

This time as Howel positioned the pen, his tongue appeared, firmly clenched between his teeth. The resulting mark was slanted upward and it didn't quite touch the top of the stem, but his effort resembled the letter T.

"You did it!" Felice cried, clapping her hands.

Thomas congratulated him too with a hearty slap on the back.

Howel set the pen atop the desk reverently and stepped back, staring at his handiwork. He cocked his head to one side as he examined his letter. "Maybe I would do better," he said, "if Thomas and I were sitting next to each other on the stool. What do you think?"

Felice covered her mouth and blushed. Color warmed Thomas's cheeks.

Howel laughed. "Do you think I'm so old that I've forgotten what it is like to be young?"

Partly to change the subject and partly because he loved his newfound role as teacher, Thomas took up the pen and drew the ploughman's attention back to the letter he'd just made.

"Howel, look at this. By adding additional letters . . ." Two new letters appeared beside Howel's T. Thomas stepped back. ". . . you can make a word. T-h-e. 'The.'"

He wasn't finished.

Bending over the desk again, he said, "And if we add Felice's word . . . L-o-r-d . . ." He stepped back and held up the cloth strip. ". . . we have, 'The Lord.'"

Felice mouthed the letters of the second word, declaring that it indeed was her word.

"Finally," Thomas said, dipping his pen several times in the ink as he appended additional words, ". . . if we add these words, we have Scripture."

Finished, he displayed a completed sentence. He read it aloud: "The Lord is my shepherd."

Felice smiled as she stared at the new letters, attempting to recognize some of them.

Thomas looked at Howel. The expression he saw on the ploughman's face concerned him. The man's large features were drained of all color. His eyes were wide. His lips trembled.

"These are words from the Bible?" he gasped.

Thomas nodded, though he didn't understand Howel's reaction. "One of King David's psalms," he said.

"O my," Howel said, his voice quivering. His eyes glazed with tears. "And that's my letter."

"Yes. That's the T you wrote."

"My hand printed Scripture?"

"Yes."

"Father, are you all right?" Felice asked.

Howel didn't respond. His eyes were fixed in awe at the letters on the cloth strip. Tears spilled onto his cheeks. "Say the words again," he asked.

Thomas shot a questioning glance to Felice. She nodded, but only hesitantly.

Thomas read slowly, "The Lord is my shepherd."

Softly, reverently, Howel repeated the words. "The Lord is my shepherd." He closed his eyes and said the words over and over. "The Lord is my shepherd. The Lord is my shepherd. Oh! What a grand thought! And it begins with my T!"

Felice laid her cheek against her father's arm. When Howel opened his eyes, Thomas handed him the cloth strip. The ploughman held it in his oversized hands as though it was a splinter of the cross of Christ.

With raspy voice he said, "Never could I have dreamed that I would be part of something so wonderful. God's Word ... in my house ... by my hand!"

Ertha's grating voice rounded the corner before she did. "Felice! Felice, where are you?" It was an unpleasant intrusion on a sacred moment.

Her wrinkled face appeared. "Ah! There you are! I thought I sent you out here to call the men to breakfast." She pulled up short and stared at them with the suspicious look of a mother who had just caught one of her children doing something naughty. "What in the ..."

She spied the cloth strip in Howel's hands. Her face turned as dark as a thunderstorm.

"Good heavens, man!" she cried. "Didn't your brother's death teach you anything? Some things are not to be meddled with!"

"Ertha ...," Howel said.

She wasn't listening. Her hands raised high, she shook her head emphatically from side to side. "That does it! I will not keep my girls in a house of sorcery, where there is no regard for sacred things or the laws of England!" She whirled and disappeared around the corner.

Howel followed her. "Ertha ..."

"Next thing you know," her voice continued, "they'll be consorting with demons directly. Not me! I'll go to Coventry and live with Mady before I'll spend another night in this den of—"

Her tirade was cut off by the slamming of the door, although they could still hear the garbled snarl of her ranting.

Thomas looked at Felice and shrugged. "I'm sorry," he said. "I know how much Leoma and Poppy mean to you."

Felice returned his shrug with one of her own. "If it wasn't this, it would be something else."

Thomas cleaned the tip of the pen with a cloth and placed the writing utensils inside the desk. When he turned around he saw Felice standing behind him with the pieces of the broken stool in her hand. A silly grin graced her face.

He chuckled. Then laughed.

She said, "Do you suppose father will build one that will support us both?"

❦

ON HER KNEES IN the snow, Felice pressed Leoma against her with one arm and Poppy with the other. Even with them bundled up, she could feel how skinny they were beneath their coats.

"I'm going to miss you so much!" she whispered to them, fighting back her tears. She kissed first one then the other on their red, chapped cheeks.

Leoma began to cry. "When I grow up, I'm going to come back and live with you!"

Felice glanced up at Ertha.

A scowl indicated she'd heard. "Leoma. Poppy. Come!" she snapped. "The day is wasting away." Not waiting for them, she started down the road without so much as a farewell.

"Felice, I want to stay with you!" Poppy cried. Her little arms clenched tightly around Felice's neck.

Felice returned the hug. "Your mother needs you now," she said softly. "She'd be sad without you."

Ertha turned and hollered at the girls, threatening them with whacks if they didn't catch up with her soon. To Howel, she added, "And mark my words! That girl of yours is coming to no good! You'll wish you'd listened to me. You'll see. Diligent and silent work is the only way to deal with the foolish dreams that fill the head of a brainless creature like her!"

Though the words were directed at Howel, they were intended for Felice to hear. Because Howel was accompanying her on her trip,

Ertha would have all day to tell him what a bad father he was and how Felice would come to no good.

After one last hug Felice pried the girls off her neck. "Hurry and catch up with your mother!" She gave them a little shove to get them started.

Hand in hand, the two sisters walked down the road after their mother, but not without turning back frequently. Each time they did Felice smiled and blew them kisses, though her heart was breaking.

Howel stood close by at the business end of a hand cart burdened with Ertha's possessions. "I don't like leaving you alone," he said. "Are you sure you'll be all right? Maybe you'll reconsider and go stay with—"

"It's just one night, Father," she assured him. "I'll be fine."

Thomas emerged from the house wearing his traveling hat and coat and shoes; he carried a stuffed leather bag. Although he could not have heard Howel's comment, he said, "Felice, I've been thinking. Maybe it would be better if you stayed with—"

"I'll be fine! Believe me, I'll be fine!" Felice insisted. "Now both of you, go! Especially you, Thomas Torr. You're late and I told you I'll not let you use me as an excuse for your tardiness to Dr. Wycliffe."

To Howel, Thomas said, "I can stay an extra day and go to Lutterworth tomorrow."

A warm tide of anger rose up the back of Felice's neck. "Thomas Torr!" she cried. "I'll not have you standing there talking about me like I was some kind of farm animal. I'm fully capable of taking care of myself! Now both of you, stop it this instant and be on your ways!"

Thomas and Howel exchanged glances. The younger man said laughingly, "Pity the poor man who should cross her in our absence."

"He wouldn't stand a chance," Howel deadpanned. "She'd string him up in the rafters like so much cheese."

Felice felt like taking a switch to both of them when a horse and rider appeared.

"What's he doing here?" Thomas grumbled.

Howel too glared at the approaching rider. When the rider came within earshot, Howel shouted: "Hold and state your business!"

The rider continued toward them.

Howel set the cart down. Walking toward the rider, he raised both hands over his head. "I said, *'Hold!'*" he shouted.

The rider reigned his chestnut mare to a stop.

"Now, state your business!" Howel shouted.

The rider, Kendall, smiled: "It is not business that brings me here."

"Then what?" Thomas barked, matching Howel's less than hospitable tone. He dropped his bag and stood shoulder to shoulder with Howel.

"I'm here on a social matter," Kendall said.

Felice watched from a distance. What social business could Kendall possibly have with Howel?

"I stopped by to wish Felice a fine day," Kendall said.

Felice felt her face flush. Her father and Thomas turned to look at her. Clearly, neither of them was pleased.

A mix of emotions stirred inside her. Though she knew Kendall was partial to her, he had always kept his distance, stealing glances at her from afar. To think that he'd ridden all this way simply to wish her a good day was flattering. Yet the animosity his presence evoked from her father and Thomas was strong and unmistakable.

Howel returned his attention to the rider. "Very well," he growled. "Say your peace, then be on your way."

"Father!" Felice cried. "Don't be rude! If Kendall took all this time to ride out here—"

Thomas interjected, "Then the sooner he says his piece and begins his return journey, the sooner he'll be home."

"Honestly!" Felice cried. She strode toward her two protectors. She'd had enough of them running her life for one day. "It's the two of you who should be on your way! Father, if you don't hurry, Ertha will be in Coventry before you reach the halfway stone. And Thomas, you're already late for Lutterworth."

Neither man made a reply. Nor did they make any effort to move.

"Go on! Be off with you!" Felice insisted. She shooed them both with the backs of her hands.

Reluctantly, Howel returned to the cart. With a grunt that was more displeasure than effort, he lifted the handcart and set its wheels in motion. He started to say something. Felice cut him off.

"Have a good trip, Father!" she said.

Thomas leveled one last scowl at Kendall before retrieving his bag. Walking backwards at first, then turning around and glancing over his shoulder he made his way down the road toward Lutterworth. In due time both men were out of earshot; a short time later, out of sight.

"My apologies, Kendall," Felice said. "I don't know what got into them."

Kendall grinned. If he was offended, he gave no evidence of it. He dismounted his horse. His blue satin tunic caught the early morning sun's rays in dramatic fashion, reminding Felice of her own simple, coarse clothing. She felt very much the commoner.

"I trust," Kendall said, "your father's anger is directed more at my father than at anything I have done."

Felice took a fresh look at the bailiff's son. Strange that such an outwardly kind person could be the son of a man so expert at generating ill will among the village peasants. "Do you get a lot of anger that should be directed at your father?" she asked.

"I try not to take it personally."

Felice looked away and said nothing, giving him the opportunity to say what he came to say. But from the corner of her eye she could see that Kendall stood with his head cocked to one side, staring at the ground, then toward the house, then at the sky, and worrying the leather reins in his hands.

The silence grew embarrassing and uncomfortable, like an ill-fitting garment at a festival. Felice wanted to ease their mutual discomfort, but she didn't know what to say. She stared at the snow-patched ground. Even Kendall's mare shifted from foot to foot with impatience.

She ventured a glance at Kendall and caught him staring at her. The moment he saw her look at him, he looked away and chuckled nervously.

Finally, Felice cleared her throat to break the silence, then followed it quickly with words lest the silence take hold again. She said, "I must tend to my chores."

"Can I help you?" His eyes were bright, his voice eager.

"Well . . ." She looked at the house and thought of the breakfast dishes strewn across the table, the animal pen that needed fresh straw, laundry piles here and there, candle wax and wicks waiting to be joined together, and spinning to do. All that was inside. Besides the conventional wisdom that warned against being alone with a young man inside your house, she would have been embarrassed for him to see the conditions in which she lived.

"I need to collect some firewood," she said.

That was marginally safe, as long as no one came riding by and saw them together. And if they did, at least she wouldn't have to hear a lecture from Ertha.

"I can help you gather firewood!" Kendall said eagerly.

Felice looked at his spotless clothes and smooth, white hands. These did not belong to a man accustomed to gathering wood.

For his part, Kendall had already tied his horse to a tree and was walking toward her. "Where do you normally gather your wood?" he asked.

"This way." Felice led him to a thick patch of woods a short distance from the house, acutely aware of his nearness.

In the woods, they worked in silence. Felice stooped and picked up dead branches that had fallen from the trees. Kendall was quick to follow her example. Soon he was clutching a small bundle of branches against his chest with one arm while he gathered with the other. The twigs and branches tore at his clothing and dirtied them. Kendall gave no indication that he cared.

Felice watched him out of the corner of her eye, wondering what it must be like to live in a house where such finery was commonplace. It was a familiar fantasy, one she'd harbored since she was a little girl.

In those earlier days, she had talked freely about someday living in wealth. Ertha and other women of the village had been quick to chide her for such foolishness. "You were born a peasant, you'll die a peasant," they'd told her. "To think so highly of yourself is a sin!"

Their scolding hadn't stopped Felice from dreaming, only from verbalizing her dreams. She'd been reluctant to give them up. Her dreams gave her hope, especially when the days grew hard. Besides, Thomas had proven that a man could rise above his station in life, hadn't he? An orphan boy, translating Scripture with the learned Dr. Wycliffe! If Thomas could rise above his station, why couldn't she?

She glanced at Kendall, who was searching the ground but finding nothing. There had been a time when he had figured into her dreams. What easier way to escape poverty than to marry a rich man? But that was before her feelings for Thomas had awakened.

Kendall put down his bundle of branches and tried to rip down a dead branch still attached to a tree.

"What are you doing? Don't do that!" Felice cried.

He stopped. "Why?"

"It's illegal, that's why! We can gather only the wood that's on the ground. Anything in the trees is the property of Lord Harborough."

"I know," Kendall said, jumping again. This time he managed to grab hold of a branch. Its cracking echoed through the forest.

Felice was aghast. "Stop!" she cried.

Kendall stood with the limb in his hand as proud as any hunter displaying his game. He placed his foot on it and cracked it in two. "It would have fallen soon," he reasoned. "Besides, it'll make a fine fire, don't you think?"

Glancing nervously in every direction, Felice said, "But what if someone were to see you? What if you were caught?"

Kendall grinned. "So? Do you think my father is going to arrest his son over a dead tree limb?"

His logic was convincing. Still, the thought that Kendall had just done something illegal prompted her to look over her shoulder again to see if anyone had seen. There was no one in sight.

Kendall gathered up his bundle of wood, as much as he could carry. "Is this enough, or do you need more?"

What he'd done for her was sweet, the kind of thing powerful people could do simply because they were keepers of the law. And by doing it for her, he seemed to be elevating her above her rightful level of society.

"Does your father know you've come here to see me?" she asked, not sure whether she wanted to know.

"It was his idea."

"*His* idea?" Felice was shocked.

Kendall grinned. He looked as pleased as she was shocked. "I don't pretend to understand it either," he said. "It's the first thing we've agreed upon in years."

Felice felt her face flush. She was flattered and perplexed and confused. To think that Bailiff Bromley and Kendall were even talking about her numbed her mind. But that the bailiff had sent his son to visit her—that was simply beyond comprehension.

Back at the house, Kendall offered to carry the wood in for her, but Felice refused. He placed it beside the door. Standing in the doorway, she self-consciously wiped her hands on her dress. Then, realizing what she was doing, she attempted to brush her dress clean. It was unnerving to have someone as finely attired as Kendall standing outside a peasant's dwelling.

"I'll be on my way now," he said. "If I stay too long, tongues might wag. And I wouldn't want to cause you any discomfort."

He seemed more confident than when he'd arrived. He turned to leave. Stopped. Hesitated. Then turned back toward her. In that brief amount of time, the uncertain, shy Kendall returned. "Um . . . ," he stammered. Reaching into his cote-hardie he produced a scarlet silk scarf.

"Here. This is for you," he said, thrusting it at her.

Felice stifled a gasp. The scarf was magnificent. Especially next to the drab surroundings of her home: rough wooden shutters, a thatched roof, daub-and-wattle walls, and a muddy pathway. For whatever reason, the scarf fluttered brightly, like a flaming torch in the night.

"Oh Kendall!" Felice cried. "I could never accept—"

"Sure you can! It's a gift. We want you to have it."

"We?"

He shrugged sheepishly. "Again, it was my father's idea. He gave the scarf to me to give to you. I don't know what you did to gain his favor as you have, but whatever it is, I'm certainly glad you did it."

With trembling hands, Felice fondled the scarf as Kendall draped it over her hands.

Oh, the sensation! She had seen such finery but had never felt it. It was unlike anything she could have imagined. Light and airy, it was as though someone had captured a pocket of mist and ironed it into this delicate garment.

"Do you like it?" Kendall asked.

Felice was rendered speechless. Not only by the scarf but by Kendall's question. How could men be so blind? Could he not see that she was overcome by the gift?

"Of course I like it!" she cried. "I love it!"

She touched the scarf to her cheek and closed her eyes. It felt like the breath of an angel.

"Thank you, Kendall. And thank your father for me."

With a grin too wide for his mouth, Kendall mounted his horse. "I couldn't help overhearing that you'll be alone tonight," he said. "I'll ride by later to check on you. Just to make sure you're all right."

His comment broke the spell that the scarf had conjured. She was once again standing in the mud in front of her daub-and-wattle house and feeling rather vulnerable.

"That won't be necessary," she said. "I'll be fine. It's only one night."

"Are you certain?"

She nodded.

"Well . . . good-bye, then," Kendall said.

With one last look at her, he rode off.

⋙ ⋘

FOR THE REMAINDER OF the day Felice carried the scarlet silk scarf with her. No matter what she did, it was nearby. She paused frequently to admire it, to weave it between her fingers, or to brush it against her cheek. She owned nothing else in the world like it. Nothing so lovely or so costly.

As night fell, she checked the shutters and bolted the door. It seemed strangely quiet and still in the house that night, especially considering that for the past few nights their number had doubled with Ertha and the girls. Remembering, Felice grinned. She didn't know who had been noisier—two little giggling girls or Ertha, who prattled constantly with that nasal whine she called a voice. Now, the only sounds in the room were the crackle of the fire, the rustle of chickens, and the occasional stirring of the cow.

Just then, she heard the snort of a horse. Someone was outside the house!

Jumping to her feet, she stood by the fire, her eyes darting around the room looking for a weapon. Panic took hold of her, radiating signals of alarm to every limb. She trembled; her breathing became short and shallow, her every sense keenly on edge.

Staring at the door, she expected at any moment to hear someone pounding on it from the other side. But no pounding came. Strange. And suddenly, no pounding was scarier than pounding. She listened harder. Still nothing.

Her heart thumped wildly. She pulled a shawl tightly around her shoulders and listened . . . listened . . .

Mooooooo!

The lowing of the cow behind her nearly made her jump out of her skin. A hand flew to her breast in a feeble effort to quiet a heart racing out of control. She took several ragged breaths, trying to calm herself.

Knowing that she wouldn't be able to settle down until she knew for sure whether someone was still outside, she tiptoed to a shutter. With great care she lifted the latch. Praying that the shutter wouldn't creak when she opened it, she gently pushed.

It didn't open. She pushed again. It wouldn't budge. She examined the rough wood. The shutters could be swollen or frozen.

She tried again, this time harder, knowing that if the shutters gave way suddenly, anyone outside would hear them. At this point, she didn't care. She had to know if someone was outside her house. So she pushed.

There was a cracking sound. She let up. It wasn't loud, but she could hear chips of ice falling away outside. She tried again.

Success! The shutters broke free, at least partially. But that was all she needed. She peered through the open crack as the cold night air streamed in, numbing her face.

The narrow view the shutters offered was enough. In the darkness, she saw the horse. And the rider. They were a fair distance from the house. The rider was hunched against the cold. The horse's reins drooped in the snow. The rider was clearly waiting for something or someone. But who? And why was he waiting in front of her house?

The rider moved. Stretched. He lifted his face toward the sky. The moonlight highlighted his features.

Kendall!

He sniffed and hugged himself to keep warm. Despite her telling him not to, he had returned! But why? She watched him for several minutes. Then, it came to her. He was guarding the house! A rich boy was sitting outside her house in the freezing night air protecting her!

For a long time Felice leaned against the window sill and stared at Kendall through the thin opening. As she did, she touched the scarlet red scarf to her cheek and smiled.

FOUR ❧

No OTHER MANOR CELEBRATED the Christ child's birth with as much extravagance; and no other lord welcomed peasants into his household with as much zeal as Lord Harborough.

In other parts of the country, the winter celebration began with peasants storming the doors of the their local manors. The lord of the manor's expected response was to invite the peasants in and offer them the best his manor had to offer—the best food, the best ale, and the best music. If he refused, then the peasants were within their rights to perform some mischievous trick, usually destructive. As the song of the season promised:

> "... then down will come butler,
> bowl and all."

In Fearnleah, however, Lord Harborough adroitly avoided both mischief and manor-storming by hosting an elaborate celebration on the eve of Christ's Mass for all who would attend. In keeping with the spirit of tradition, he dressed in peasant's garb and personally served his guests, down to the lowliest beggar, as though they were all nobility.

Thomas, having returned from Lutterworth for the holiday, leaned against the massive stone wall of the great hall and moaned. He rubbed his protruding belly and wished he'd had the good sense to keep from eating that last piece of mince pie. But how could he? Even now he seemed unable to take his eyes off the tables laden with roasted boar, slices of beef, frumenty, gallons of posset, and an array of pies and desserts, including his seasonal favorite—Yule dolls made of gingerbread.

His discomfort was real, his senses dulled. After all, he'd eaten more food in one night than he'd eaten in the last two weeks. He moaned again, but the small sound of his complaint was lost in the greater din of shouts and screams and squeals of celebration.

The hall was alive with the tide of human celebration. All around him heads flew back with raucous laughter; bodies twirled in dance; drunks shouted to be heard; hands were a blur as they strummed string instruments; women balanced on men's laps, alternately teasing them and pushing them away. An army of people with drinks in hand gathered in front of the Yule log, warming themselves against the nighttime chill that lay beyond the walls and watching as each flying spark from the fire promised the birth of an animal in the village come Spring.

"There you are, Thomas!" Felice ran up to him breathlessly. She grabbed his hand and attempted to pull him away from the wall. "Come along! They're playing hoodman's bluff!"

Thomas smiled. She looked so beautiful when she was happy. Her face was flushed with excitement, her eyes sparkled with blue joy, her mouth framed a smile that made his heart jump with excitement. His queasy belly, however, overruled any excitement she mustered within him.

He waved her off. "I can't," he said.

"Come on! It'll be fun!"

"No. It's my stomach. I ate too much."

"This will help you work it off! You'll feel better!"

Scrunching his face into a miserable expression, he moaned and lowered his head and shook it.

"Please, Thomas? Please?" She bent down into his field of vision and stared up at him. "Please?"

It was the eyes that did it. What was it about this woman's eyes that held such mastery over him? All she had to do was to get him to fix upon her eyes and she could have her way with him. Every time. And she knew it too!

With a reluctant smile, Thomas allowed himself to be pulled away from the wall.

"You'll have fun!" she said.

He doubted it.

At the far end of the hallway a young peasant boy was being fitted with a blindfold. He couldn't have been more than eleven or twelve years of age, which made Thomas question his decision to play this game. He didn't want to play with a bunch of children! Then, as the game began, he saw that most of the other players were his age or older, and he recalled that he was about twelve when he was first allowed to play. He remembered how exciting it had been to intermingle with the adults, especially the young female adults. The remembrance gave him an idea.

Thick locks of black hair spilled over the boy's blindfold as he was turned around and around and around. When he was let loose, he staggered a bit, dizzily, before lunging in the direction of a particularly loud gaggle of peasant girls.

Like geese they scattered every which way, avoiding his touch. The blindfolded boy circled around with arms extended and tried a different direction just to the right of Thomas and Felice.

Felice backed away from the boy, stifling a squeal. She bumped into Thomas. The boy swung in her direction. She managed to elude his grasp again. The boy turned a different direction.

Thomas planted his feet securely. He poked Felice in the ribs. She squealed. Hearing the squeal, the boy turned back and lunged at her. Felice tried to get away, but she ran into Thomas and the blindfolded boy touched her. Her arms slumping in resignation, she leveled a challenging scowl at Thomas.

In order for the boy to win, he had to guess whom he had caught. Folding his arms in studied concentration, he tilted his head back slightly. It was an ancient trick that fooled no one. He was peeking out the bottom of the blindfold.

"Um . . . Felice!" he shouted.

A cheer went up. The boy ripped off the blindfold, his gap-toothed grin acknowledging the applause. His flashing eyes indicated his pleasure at having caught an attractive young woman. No one chided the boy for peeking. In such games, festivity overruled chicanery. Felice instead turned on Thomas.

"You did that on purpose!" she cried.

"I don't know what you're talking about! You backed into me! What else was I to do? Don't be such a mewling kid!"

Her wagging finger warned him to be on guard. She would be looking for an opportunity to get even. For Thomas that meant that the evening's fun was far from over. Meanwhile, Felice took her turn at being blindfolded—which gave Thomas the chance to carry out the second part of his scheme.

As soon as the blindfold was in place, Thomas made his way through the thick circle of players and found a vacant spot against the wall. There, he leaned contentedly and watched the others play.

No sooner had Felice been spun around than she headed straight for the spot he had recently vacated. Thomas grinned. She was a sly one. She'd undoubtedly counted the number of turns and was now attempting her revenge. Only, she didn't know he was no longer playing.

People scattered madly as a grinning Felice reached blindly. Thomas was enjoying himself. Since Felice was the active participant in the game, he could stare at her openly—nor did he have to worry about her catching him, because she was blindfolded. And he didn't have to worry about what others thought of his staring, because she was the center of attention.

She was a beautiful, vibrant, quick-witted woman. Their future together looked promising. If events continued to unfold as it appeared they might, by this time next year he and Felice might very well be married. The thought that next Christ's Mass they might attend the feast as a married couple amused him.

A cheer went up, drawing Thomas's attention back to the game. Felice had caught someone, which meant his reprieve was nearly over. Once the blindfold came off, she would surely pull him back into the game.

With a sigh he pushed himself from the wall to see who had been so cloddish as to get himself caught. Probably some half-drunk farmer.

He stepped to one side to get a clear view. He spotted Felice at once, still blindfolded, still smiling. Her captive remained hidden to him. Stepping to one side to get a better look, he spied the culprit. At that instant, Thomas could have sworn he felt hackles rise on the back of his neck.

Kendall!

Felice had her hands on his shoulders. His knees slightly bent, Kendall gave the appearance of being a little shorter than he actually was. This bit of deception was part of the game and the crowd was enjoying it immensely.

"Hmmmm. Not too tall. Just my size," Felice said.

A ripple of laughter passed through the crowd.

Her hands moved to his face. Kendall grinned, obviously enjoying the moment. He was enjoying it far too much for Thomas's taste.

Felice traced a hand across his open mouth.

"He has all his teeth! That's always a good sign!" she cried.

The celebrants roared.

"I wonder . . . ," Felice said, her voice cooing like a lovebird. "Could it be?"

Thomas's face grew warm. Warmer still with each person who sought him out in the crowd to catch his reaction to the game.

She reached for his hand and felt the palm. "Mmmm. No calluses here. These are not the hands of a laborer. More like those of a scribe, maybe?"

Thomas understood now. Felice mistakenly thought she'd succeeded in capturing him! Should he cough? Make a noise to warn her? No. It was only a game.

"Yes," she purred. "I think I might be able to guess who this is."

Then, to Thomas's horror, Felice leaned forward and gently kissed Kendall on the lips.

The room erupted with laughter and applause.

"It's my Thomas!" Felice cried, lifting the blindfold.

But instead of seeing Thomas, she saw a blushing but happy Kendall.

Again the crowd roared.

Felice stepped back, her face crimson, her hands to her mouth. She scanned the crowd until she located Thomas. Her eyes locked with his.

"I thought it was you!" she cried. "Honestly, Thomas, I thought it was you!"

All around him people were laughing and pounding his back good-naturedly. Thomas did his best to smile. It was a weak effort.

"You were wrong," he said. "You have to play again."

Felice tried to surrender the blindfold to someone else, but the crowd insisted the rules be followed. She was blindfolded again, but not without first taking another glance at Thomas. A pleading glance.

Thomas didn't know who she captured on her second turn. He didn't stay around to find out. He gravitated back to the food table.

❧ ❧

"LORD OF MISRULE! LORD of Misrule!"

The chant echoed to the hall rafters. Everyone's attention gravitated toward a wooden stairway leading to a balcony at one end of the room. It was here that candidates would be presented and the vote for the Lord of Misrule would be cast.

"Are you still angry with me?" Felice asked, holding Thomas's arm. She cuddled next to him on a bench against the wall, watching the festivities from the party fringe.

"I told you, there's nothing to be angry about. You thought it was me, didn't you?"

"Of course, I thought it was you!" She sounded hurt by the question.

"Then it would be foolish of me to be angry with you, wouldn't it?"

"I suppose."

Thomas could feel her looking up at him. He sensed she needed reassurance, but for some reason he couldn't find it within himself at the moment to give it to her. The image of Felice kissing Kendall was stamped on his mind and he couldn't see past it. He kept his eyes forward, pretending to be interested in the proceedings as one candidate after another was proposed as this year's Lord of Misrule.

Two aspirants stood on the hallway steps. Odell the beggar scratched an explosion of unruly hair and pulled at his rags self-consciously. He'd been shoved up the steps against his will. He never lifted his gaze. Squeezing his eyes open and shut with exaggerated effort, he fought to keep from looking at anyone directly—a nearly impossible task, given his vantage point overlooking a sea of faces.

The second candidate was Pyn, a skinny student from Cambridge. Unlike the beggar, this scrubbed and groomed nominee interpreted his place on the steps as a great honor. With arms widespread, he played the fool. A small band of fellow students congregated below him and cheered on his puerile act.

A third and final candidate took his place on the lower steps to a decidedly mixed reaction of cheers and hisses. He was a robust man with wide shoulders, curly red hair, and a ready, if not winning, smile.

"Who is that?" Felice asked.

"Cayle, a carpenter from Crick," Thomas replied. He squinted his eyes in thought as he observed the man. Cayle's presence on the steps disturbed him. Why would a man like that allow himself to stand with a beggar and an obnoxious student for such a dubious title as Lord of Misrule?

"Why are people hissing at him?"

"Rumor has it he runs with a band of brigands. From what I heard he was prominent in the uprising a few years ago."

"Well, that doesn't make sense. Why would he want to be Lord of Misrule?"

Thomas wished he had an answer to her question.

As the three candidates were individually presented to the crowd a final time, Thomas noticed an odd movement among the crowd. A handful of men were circulating among the people whispering in people's ears. The return glances they received were not pleasant ones.

Thomas leaned forward, attempting to hear what one of them was saying. Just then he received a blow to his shoulder, forceful enough to cause him to knock heads with Felice.

Wincing, Thomas glared in the direction of the blow and came face-to-face with a burly man about three times his size, sporting a bandage on his left cheek and eye. He jabbed a filthy finger in Thomas's face.

"When the vote is taken," he said, "I want to hear you shouting loud and clear for Cayle. Understand?"

Thomas opened his mouth to say something. Before the first word was uttered, a stubby finger rammed into his chest.

"This ain't a request!" the man said. With one final shove, he moved on to another couple and repeated his threat.

"Thomas," Felice whispered. "What are you going to do?"

The circumstances were indeed unusual. The election of a Lord of Misrule was more a title of ridicule than of honor. So what were Cayle and his followers up to? Thomas would have shrugged them off as a band of overzealous ne'er-do-wells if it weren't for the fact that his chest still throbbed where it had been poked.

The voting for the Lord of Misrule began. Barnaby Riggs, the village tailor, held his hand over the beggar's head. All who wanted to elect Odell the beggar as the Lord of Misrule were instructed to voice their approval.

Thomas stood and shouted with all his might, along with several others in the crowd.

His vote earned Thomas a murderous glance from the burly man, but nothing more. At least for the moment.

A hand was held over the head of the student. Pyn. There was a smattering of cheers and claps. With the exception of a patch of fellow students directly beneath the candidate, the response was significantly less enthusiastic than the vote for the beggar.

Riggs held a hand over Cayle's head. The carpenter encouraged people's votes with outstretched hands. A sizable cheer rose from the crowd. He had a significant following.

Having clearly received the least number of votes, Pyn was eliminated from the competition. The cheerful grin vanished. As he descended the steps he made an obscene gesture toward the crowd, who in turn voiced their disapproval over his lack of sportsmanship.

This left two candidates. Announcing that he was unable to choose a clear winner from the previous round, Barnaby Riggs declared that a deciding vote would be needed.

Throughout the hall Cayle's supporters jumped into action, grabbing arms, muttering threats, and wagging fingers. The burly man worked his end of the room feverishly but was unable to reach Thomas and Felice before the vote was taken.

A hand was raised over Odell's head. Thomas yelled at the top of his lungs. Felice added her voice to his. Their shouts died of loneliness in the great hall.

Then Riggs held his hand over Cayle's head. A loud, but less than enthusiastic roar elected him Lord of Misrule.

Although Thomas was curious as to what would happen next, his first concern was the possible return of Cayle's burly promoter. While the large man had his back to them, Thomas grabbed Felice by the hand and led her through the throng to the other side of the hall. Spotting Howel, they joined him.

The large ploughman was shaking his head as they approached. "What do you make of that?" he asked.

On the balcony a mock crown was placed on Cayle's head; a purple robe was placed on his shoulders; and he was handed a wooden staff as a scepter.

"I'm not sure," Thomas said.

Howel took a swig from his mug and said, "Aren't you glad we don't choose our real leaders by popular vote? It would be sheer folly!"

Cayle stood with arms outstretched as he received the cheers of a crowd that seemed eager to embrace a festive mood once again. For the rest of the evening Cayle was their king. He would rule over the festivities.

Lord Harborough appeared next to the newly crowned Lord of Misrule. It had been his custom over the years to enter into the spirit of the season by placing himself at the elected ruler's disposal for the remainder of the evening.

Harborough matched the rogue carpenter in height and size, though his regal bearing made him appear taller. His black hair was combed neatly; his thinly styled beard neatly trimmed. His fine features were all the more prominent as he stood before Cayle barefoot and dressed in a peasant's tunic.

A hush fell over the crowd while a spark of realization flashed in Thomas's mind. "I'll bet that's what he's after," Thomas muttered.

Lord Harborough took Cayle by the hand. The lord of the manor knelt and bowed. Loud enough for all to hear, he said: "I acknowledge you as my liege lord for the remainder of this evening of festivities. Your wish, your desire, is my command."

The wide-shouldered Cayle now towered over the man who knelt before him. All traces of levity and celebration drained from his face. In a voice strong and loud, he said, "Indeed, Lord Harborough, the day will come when you and all other English nobles will kneel before the common people, not just for a night but for all of time!"

I knew it! Thomas said to himself.

A hush fell over the crowd as collectively they held their breath.

Astonishment lined Lord Harborough's face as he looked up at the peasant Cayle. His regal features hardened. He stood. The two men stared at one another for what seemed an age. Then, Lord Harborough turned toward the assembled peasants below.

"Let the festivities continue!" he shouted.

Slowly at first, like an old man stretching stiff joints, the music and games resumed. Soon they matched the volume and gaiety that had characterized the earlier part of the evening. However, in every corner of the hall there was an underlying buzz of serious discussion. While some debated Cayle's motives and what he hoped to gain by such a demonstration, others spent the remainder of the evening predicting Lord Harborough's response.

While Thomas was thus engaged in discussion, a servant touched his arm and whispered in his ear, "Come with me, quietly. Lord Harborough requests your presence."

⋙ ⋘

LEAVING THE SOUNDS OF celebration behind him, Thomas followed the bobbing head of a brown-haired servant up one corridor and down another until he was turned around. He wondered if he could find his way back to the great hall without assistance should circumstances require it.

His disorientation was partly his fault. He'd allowed himself to be distracted by the servant who preceded him. The man had the most unusual bald spot on the back of his head. It was a good-sized fleshy patch, clean as a whistle, and—what made it so unusual— off-center, to the left of the man's crown. Thick hair surrounded the spot and flowed to the servant's shoulders which made it stand out all the more in the dimly lit corridors.

Thomas couldn't help but wonder if the spot was naturally occurring, or if the man for some reason had shaved his head in such an unusual way, and if so, why?

The bobbing bald spot slowed. The click of a door latch in the servant's hand echoed loudly up and down the corridor.

"Wait in here," the servant said.

As Thomas stepped past the servant, he had the strongest urge to inquire about the man's bald spot. But how does one go about bringing up such a topic without risking offense?

"Lord Harborough will be with you shortly," the man said. He stared past Thomas with disinterested eyes.

A moment later the latch on the door sounded again and Thomas found himself alone in a room that was easily three times the size of his house in height as well as length and width. The vast, empty echoing sound from a scuffed step or a cleared throat resembled that in a cathedral.

The expansive walls were papered with a swirling design, yellow set against a red background. A variety of heraldic shields rimmed the room: a green lion rampant on a pure yellow field; a fierce-looking griffin with uplifted sword set against three red bars on a silver field; a quartered black-and-white field with a black fleur-de-lis set against a white upper right quadrant; a sneering reindeer bound by collar and chain.

Thomas cocked his head at this. What knight would be intimidated by a sneering reindeer? And a captured one at that? He wondered what family was unfortunate enough to have to defend this crest to generation after generation.

"There you are, Thomas!"

Lord Harborough breezed through the same door Thomas had entered, held open by the same servant that had let him in.

"Let's sit over there, by the fire. I'm freezing!"

Rubbing his hands together, Lord Harborough headed straightway toward a blazing fireplace. Thomas followed him. He didn't think the room was that cold.

He stood off to the side while Lord Harborough hunched over the fire, palms facing the flame. For some reason, he looked smaller than he did from a distance—maybe because he was hunched over and wearing a peasant's tunic. Or maybe it was because up close, his imperfect humanity—wrinkles, stray hairs—was more evident, while at a distance he managed to appear more lordly.

"Aren't you cold, Thomas?"

"No, your lordship."

Lord Harborough studied him with an appraising eye. He seemed pleased at what he saw.

"Take a seat, my boy." He motioned toward a stuffed, high-back chair with a nod of his head.

Thomas moved toward the chair uncertainly. Custom dictated that he shouldn't sit while Lord Harborough remained standing. Was his lordship testing him?

"Sit! Sit! Sit!"

"Yes, your lordship." Thomas sat.

Lord Harborough turned around. This seemed to satisfy two necessities. First, he could address Thomas face-to-face; secondly, he could warm his backside.

"Are you enjoying the festivities?"

"Yes, your lordship."

"Are Howel and his daughter . . . what's her name . . ."

"Felice."

"Yes, Felice! Are they enjoying the festivities?"

"Yes, your lordship."

"Good . . . good."

Lord Harborough straightened with a stretch, luxuriating in the fire's warmth. He had aged since the last time Thomas had seen him up close. Thin streaks of gray lined his coal-black hair. The streaks were noticeable in his mustache and beard as well.

"That was a rather nasty bit of politics played by Cayle a few moments ago, don't you think?"

"It was, your lordship."

"Inappropriate. Rude. Took me by surprise, it did. Wouldn't have thought that Cayle would use a seasonal tradition as a medium for his rebellious views. I should have known he had an ulterior motive when he allowed himself to be nominated as a candidate for Lord of Misrule."

"He was wrong to take advantage of the season and your hospitality the way he did."

"Quite right," Lord Harborough harrumphed. "Goes against the very reason for the celebration."

"How so, your lordship?"

"Why, it's a celebration of peace and goodwill, Thomas! You see, my boy, it has been my experience that this one night of generosity and celebration puts the villagers in a more harmonious mood the year round. Why, with all the discord and unrest among the masses in the countryside, one night of generosity in return for a year of goodwill is quite a bargain indeed. You'd think that other men of nobility would recognize its benefit and follow my example."

Like a clapper striking a bell, Lord Harborough's words struck a recent memory, causing it to resonate in Thomas's memory. It was something Cayle had said: "*. . . the day will come when all English nobles will kneel before the common people, not just for a night . . .*"

"Well, let's not travel any further down that unpleasant road," Lord Harborough said. For a second time Thomas felt the appraising gaze of his lordship. His voice grew soft and friendly as he said, "Of course, you wouldn't know this, Thomas, but there is a lot of your mother in you."

Thomas didn't know how to respond, so he simply smiled.

Lord Harborough looked upward as he did some mental calculations. "What? It's been nearly two decades since her passing, hasn't it? But I can still see her scurrying through the hallways here. She was always pleasant. Always cheerful. Always faithful to her duties." His voice trailed off.

"I wish I could have known her," Thomas replied. "Or at least had some kind of picture of her so I could know what she looked like."

Thomas's statement seemed to unsettle his lordship. With downcast gaze, Lord Harborough said, "She was a beautiful woman, Thomas. Full, auburn hair that curled at her shoulders. An eggshell white complexion without blemish. Blue eyes that were as enchanting as a quiet lake on a sunny afternoon. Once you looked at them it was next to impossible to look away."

He seemed lost in her memory for a moment before catching himself.

"But as attractive as your mother was, her real beauty was internal. She was spring incarnate. Bright. Happy. Joyful." Like the sudden appearance of an untimely storm, his lordship's face darkened. "Her death was a cruel injustice. She deserved better than the short, tragic life she lived."

"From what Howel told me, she gave her life protecting me," Thomas said.

"Yes, she did. And I find it particularly distressful that she was alone when she died."

"That's something I've never understood," Thomas said. "I know that she was at the parish church when her labor pains began. Why did she go off by herself?"

Lord Harborough shook his head sadly. "I don't know. I wish I had an answer for you. She must have had her reasons. And we're not sure how long she was dead before Howel happened upon you. It's a miracle you survived."

"Howel told me that when he found her she had a stick in her hand, perhaps to beat off animals."

The fire crackled. Lord Harborough took a step away from it and stood silently, lost in thought. Then, with a single clap, he broke the silence.

"Well, Thomas. To the matter at hand."

"Yes, your lordship?"

Another clap. Thomas hadn't realized it until now but Lord Harborough used a single clap as his personal fanfare. It meant he was about to make an announcement.

"Thomas, you are a wonder! In a very short time you have gained considerable attention! First with Dr. Wycliffe and most recently with Bishop Pole."

"It was you who introduced me to Dr. Wycliffe, your lordship."

"So I did. But it is your work that has impressed him. On more than one occasion he has expressed to me his pleasure with your work and dedication. He has done so in most glowing terms."

"Thank you, your lordship." Thomas knew Wycliffe was satisfied with his work. In the time he had gotten to know the aged scholar, Wycliffe had never been stingy with his compliments. Still, it warmed Thomas to hear that good things were being said of him to others.

"And then as recently as yesterday, you were the subject of much discussion when Bishop Pole called on me. He too is highly complimentary of your aptitude and future."

Thomas glowed inside.

"It is an unusual person who garners praise from two opposing camps, young man. I wonder if you fully appreciate your position."

For once, wisdom won out over youthful exuberance. Thomas refrained from replying, allowing Lord Harborough to spell it out for him instead.

"Bishop Pole is a brilliant man. And I believe he is correct in his assessment of you," Lord Harborough began. "You are destined for great things, Thomas. However, I disagree with him over the course your life should take to fulfill that promise."

Thomas was so pleased he could barely concentrate on what Lord Harborough was saying. The fact that nobility and bishops and scholars were discussing his future went beyond his dreams.

"Thomas, are you listening to me?"

"Yes, your lordship."

There was a flicker of displeasure in Lord Harborough's eyes. It disappeared the moment he began speaking again. "Now, whereas Bishop Pole would have you enroll in Oxford where you might receive a formal education . . ."

Oxford! The very thought of attending Oxford made Thomas's head spin excitedly.

". . . I have concluded that you will reach your fullest potential in your current position."

"My current position, your lordship?" For one brief instant, he was enrolling in Oxford. Then, just as suddenly, Lord Harborough was snatching it away from him. Thomas tried to swallow his disappointment.

"I want you to continue working at Lutterworth with Dr. Wycliffe."

It wasn't that he didn't enjoy his work with Dr. Wycliffe. But this was a chance to attend Oxford! How often had he dreamed of Oxford—the studies, the reading, the lectures from learned men—only to dismiss it as an unattainable dream? To be surrounded by men who loved and cherished the same things he did! He had dreamed of the expressions he'd see on people's faces someday when he told them he'd been accepted at Oxford. Thomas Torr going to Oxford? No! Really? Our Thomas? Nobody from Fearnleah has ever attended Oxford!

"Thomas!"

Startled, Thomas looked up into the hardened gaze of Lord Harborough.

"I understand the lure Oxford must be for an ambitious lad like you."

Were his thoughts so transparent?

"But hear me out!"

"Yes, your lordship."

"The reason I want you to remain with Dr. Wycliffe is because his health is failing. It is uncertain how many more years the man has left."

"Yes, your lordship."

"You, Thomas, have it within you not only to see that his work continues, but according to Dr. Wycliffe you have the ability to refine it."

"Refine it, your lordship?" The very idea was difficult for Thomas to imagine.

"Yes, to improve upon his translation. To make it more readable. This is Dr. Wycliffe's plan for you. Has he not spoken to you of these things?"

"No, your lordship."

Lord Harborough shook his head. "Maybe I'm speaking out of turn. Anyway, it is imperative that you remain at Lutterworth. Wouldn't you agree?"

Thomas fidgeted. It was flattering that Dr. Wycliffe thought so highly of him, but in his estimation of things Oxford still seemed to be the brighter gem.

"In addition, I want to commission a Bible from you."

"Your lordship?"

"You heard me correctly, Thomas. I am commissioning you to oversee the production of an English Bible based on Dr. Wycliffe's translation with your refinements."

Thomas was stunned. A multitude of thoughts and details flew by so fast in his head that, try as he might, Thomas was unable to capture them. There was the scope of the project itself. Years of work. Translation. Inscription. Drawings. Materials. Then there were the implications. What about the sanctions against the English Bible? How would the other nobles respond? Parliament? The King?

"The Bible is not for me," Lord Harborough hastened to say.

"Your lordship?"

Lord Harborough moved away from the fire and took a chair opposite Thomas. It was the way he moved that caught Thomas's attention, as though in an instant the man had aged a hundred years.

"When you are finished with the project, Thomas," he said, "together we will travel to London where, in a private audience with King Richard, you will read aloud portions of the text you have translated. And together we will present the Bible to His Highness as a gift."

The images that came to Thomas's mind rendered him dumb. Thomas Torr standing before the King of all England? Thomas Torr reading from the Bible, in English, to the royal court! Thomas Torr demonstrating the spiritual impact and efficacy of God's written Word spoken in a manner that both King and ploughman could understand!

Suddenly, attending Oxford became a poor second to what Lord Harborough was asking him to do. Hundreds of men could lay claim to having attended Oxford, but how many of them could say they had been given a chance to persuade the King of England to embrace an English translation of the Bible?

"The King has agreed to receive us?"

"Several of his closest advisors have indicated he would not be disagreeable to a private audience."

Lord Harborough's words didn't strike Thomas as an open invitation to the King's palace, but then Lord Harborough knew better than he the ways of the royal court. So, if he said they would gain an audience, it was good enough for Thomas.

In a sobering move, Lord Harborough moved to a chair close to Thomas. His face was serious, his tone heavy.

"These are critical times, Thomas," he said. "Wycliffe has enjoyed the protection of Parliament and the nobles while the Church has called for his head. When the Pope sent three bulls to England—one to the Archbishop, one to Oxford, and one to the King—instructing them to take immediate steps to silence him, John of Gaunt, myself, and others protected him. And when he was brought to trial at Lambeth Palace, it was the Queen Mother herself who forbade the bishops to pass sentence on the man. Up to this point it has suited England's purpose to act in this manner. However, times are changing, and it is getting increasingly difficult to protect Wycliffe.

"Thomas, many believe Wycliffe's itinerant preachers are behind the recent peasant uprisings. The nobles are frightened and Parliament is increasingly edgy. That is why this Bible I am commissioning from you is so important! We must use it to prove to the King that an English translation of the Scriptures does not promote rebellion. And we'll do that by letting him hear the words for himself! I believe with all of my heart that this is the very purpose for which you were born, Thomas, so that God might bring good from bad."

There was a knock at the door. The servant with the bald patch hurried in and whispered something in Lord Harborough's ear. His lordship nodded. When he spoke again, his voice was light and festive as though it had been that way all along.

"So what do you say to our little project, Thomas?" he said cheerily. "Is it something you can sink your teeth into?"

"I only wish tomorrow weren't Christ's Mass, your lordship," Thomas replied. "I should like to get started as soon as possible."

◄§ §►

WHEN THOMAS RETURNED TO the great hall, Felice was nowhere to be found. He was spilling over with excitement, wanting to share his good news with her. Not finding her among the revelers, he bundled up and wandered outside. A blast of cold night air assaulted him.

After a short time of searching he found her standing in the center of two intersecting paths that divided the vast snowy expanse in front of Lord Harborough's manor into four equal sections. She was not alone.

A broad-shouldered man stood opposite her. He reached toward her. She shied away. He laughed.

The man's identity was not difficult to assess, even in the dark and from a distance. There was only one man that night who wore a crown, a cape, and carried a staff for a scepter.

Cayle.

Felice spotted Thomas. She ran to him. "Where have you been?" she cried.

Cayle looked at them with an amused expression. Deep crevices framed grinning lips.

"Ah! The ever faithful brother!" Cayle cried.

"Thomas is not my brother," Felice replied.

"Not your brother? Yet, he lives with you?"

Felice flushed. "I don't know who you've been talking to, but that is not your business!"

To Felice, Thomas said, "Let's find Howel and head for home." He turned her back toward the manor. When she was beside him, he whispered: "Where is Howel?"

"He's walking Widow Meriweather home," she whispered back.

Cayle called after them, "I was just warning this lovely young maiden of the dangers of the forest. Who knows what lurks in the dark shadows at night? Travel alone is not advisable. Even small groups are unwise."

"Thank you for your concern," Thomas said over his shoulder. "But we'll be fine."

As though to contradict him, five ragged, husky men appeared from nowhere and stood between them and the manor. In the center was the burly man with the bandaged face, the one who had pressured Thomas to vote for Cayle.

"Like I was saying," Cayle laughed from behind them. "It is dangerous to travel at night. That is, unless you have adequate protection."

"What's going on here?"

The voice thundered from the dark. Howel emerged from the shadows and white mist that rose from the ground. Covering the distance between them quickly, the huge ploughman put a protective arm around his daughter. He glared alternately at Cayle on one side and the five thugs on the other.

Cayle, a large man himself, looked small next to the larger ploughman. But if he harbored any uncertainty, it dissipated quickly. "Only doing my duty," he said. With a cocky step he strode toward them.

"Duty? A fool has no duty," Howel said.

Cayle laughed. Swirling breath vapors appeared with each guffaw. His eyes sparkled merrily. He gazed at Felice with an interest that disturbed Thomas.

"As I was telling this boy here, I was simply warning this fair maiden of the dangers of the forest. It is easy to be deceived by the brightness of the goodwill and music and food aplenty that are to be had so freely within those walls. But this side of the walls lies nothing but darkness and fear and want. Be assured, come tomorrow those huge wooden doors will be shut tightly with a single intent—to protect those inside. And no amount of pounding will gain you entrance or assistance."

All manner of levity was gone from his face. An instant later it reappeared.

Cayle said: "Just a friendly Yuletide message from the Lord of Misrule himself! Now, if you'll excuse me, I must lead my band of merrymakers through the streets of the town." With a wink at Felice, he added, "It is one of the heavier burdens of my elected office."

As he left them he was greeted by shouts and drums and music and horns by the drunk and merry who would extend their reveling well into the night.

FIVE ❧

UER NATUS EST NOBIS, et filius datus est nobis:
cuius imperium super humerum eius.

Resonating among the lofty arches of the cathedral in Coventry, the musical introit welcomed the worshipers into God's presence as they came to celebrate Christ's Mass. Thomas closed his eyes. He invited the music to reverberate within him, to fill his heart and nourish his soul. He could feel the emotion of the season welling up inside him as the words painted images in his mind.

A child is born to us, a son is given to us,
his shoulders shall bear princely power.

A sharp nudge in his ribs made him wince.
"Wake up!" Felice whispered.
Thomas grunted from the unexpected blow. "I wasn't sleeping."
An impish grin indicated she didn't believe him.
"I wasn't sleeping!" Thomas insisted.
His protest was cut short as the congregation began to sing:

Kyrie eleison.
Christe eleison.
Kyrie eleison.

With a scowl Thomas joined them, perturbed at Felice for spoiling his worship with her rude poke. He tried to shrug if off and regain the mood.

Lord, have mercy.
Christ, have mercy.

Lord, have mercy.

Another song followed: "Gloria in Excelsis Deo," the song the angels sang to the shepherds when they announced the birth of the Christ child.

As he sang, Thomas imagined what it must have been like on that dark hillside so long ago. In his mind he saw pockets of ragged shepherds littering the hills, feeble campfires their only light. Then, suddenly, the darkness was no more, everything was white with light. Shepherds lifted tired eyes toward the source of the radiance, their fearful faces bathed in the glory of heaven. Oh, how their hearts must have soared as they heard words such as man had never heard before! "Glory to God in the highest . . ."

The second jab in the ribs was harder than the first.

"You're sleeping again!"

"I'm not sleeping!"

"You don't fool me, Thomas Torr. You're sleeping!" Felice's eyes sparkled playfully. She truly believed she'd caught him dozing off during Christ's Mass.

Her whimsical spirit worked as an irritant on Thomas's mood, elevating the level of his anger. "I'm trying to worship!" he hissed. "Leave me alone!"

His words hit their mark. All levity vanished from Felice's face. Howel leaned toward them and, just as he had done when they were children, shook a scolding finger.

With a single cross comment, Thomas had managed to anger both Felice and Howel and spoil the mood for the service.

He sighed. The Service of Readings began, with its musical responses.

He tried to catch Felice's eye to attempt a silent apology. Her gaze and demeanor were frozen, fixed on the priest as he read Old Testament Scripture from the Latin Vulgate. Thomas poked her arm. She ignored him.

With a heavier sigh, Thomas settled back into his seat. He would have to make up with her during the walk home.

A reading from the Gospel of Luke, also in Latin, was followed by a sermon. To Thomas's surprise—though, thinking about it afterward, he wondered why he'd felt surprised—Bishop William Pole was introduced to deliver the Christ's Mass sermon.

The priest gushed as he presented the bishop to the congregation. "Rarely are we granted the honor to have such a humble yet mighty man of God in our midst," he said. "A product of the English nation, and this region in particular, Bishop William Pole is truly one of God's chosen servants. For unto him has been granted the high calling to serve in the Holy City during these dark and troubled days. And yet our nation's suffering has proved to be our blessing, for it has brought this great man of God back to us to bless us with his unique spiritual wisdom during this high and holy season."

In keeping with the theme of the introduction, Bishop Pole moved slowly and reverently to the side pulpit with bowed head. His message was brief; he emphasized the need for all men to live in a spirit of peace throughout the year while performing acts of goodwill.

If the expressions of the people at the end of the sermon were any indication, his message had been well received—due, undoubtedly, to its brevity rather than its content.

After the sermon, the congregation stood and sang the Credo, the statement of faith. Thomas sang lustily, his faith bolstered as the words formed on his lips. There was no other feeling like it in the world. This was Christ's Mass, second only to the Easter celebration in its importance.

Yet all around him, people sang hollow-eyed and without conviction, like wooden marionettes mouthing words not their own. This perplexed Thomas. How could these people be so passionless about something so vital? Didn't they realize the significance of the words they were singing? Didn't they understand—

No, of course not. They *didn't* understand! Or more accurately, they'd forgotten the meaning of the words they'd once learned. As children, they had been taught the meaning of the Latin words, but like tarnish on silver, time had dulled the shine!

It was different for Thomas. He knew Latin. For him, the words still sparkled with meaning.

How horrible for them! While they sang in forgotten code:

Gloria patri, et filio, et spiritui sancto;
sicut erat in principio, et nunc et semper,
et in saecula saeculorum. Amen.

He sang:

Glory to the Father, and to the Son, and to the Holy Spirit;
as it was in the beginning, is now,
and ever shall be through all ages! Amen.

Thomas turned to Felice. He wanted to translate for her. Right now. To pull back the curtain so that she might see the wondrous glory of God!

But Felice, apparently still angry, refused to look at him.

Thomas glanced at Howel. Like all the other congregants, the ploughman's lips moved but there was no light of awe or reverence in his eyes.

Thomas remembered how Howel had wept when he'd heard the simple words of Scripture in English in his own tool shed. How much more would he be moved if he understood the words and music of the Mass! In this majestic cathedral, who could help but lift his eyes and heart and soul heavenward and be transported into the very presence of God?

A nudge jabbed him in the ribs for the third time that day. Eagerly this time, Thomas turned toward Felice. Unsmiling, angry, she shooed him along. It was their turn to proceed to the altar and partake of Communion.

Thomas was more determined than ever to make it up to her. This afternoon, alone with Howel and Felice, he would open their eyes to the meaning of the Mass once again. He would help them to see the things he saw, to understand as he understood.

Felice would forgive him once he explained to her what the Mass meant to him. Besides, today was a holiday and Felice had already spent several days preparing the food for a festive afternoon. And she was, Thomas knew, particularly anxious to make the afternoon special, since this was the first year she had prepared the meal without Ertha looking over her shoulder and telling her what to do.

In previous years, Ives and Ertha and the girls had joined them in celebrating Christ's Mass. The two families would eat and sing and tell stories and sometimes exchange gifts. But with Ives dead and Ertha and the girls gone, this year it would be just the three of them. And Felice had made it clear that she wanted her first Christ's Mass dinner to be a memorable one. So, for the sake of the holiday, she would forgive him. Of this he was confident.

Thomas knelt at the rail and received Communion. It was served to him by Bishop Pole. Their eyes met. The bishop gave him a familiar nod.

As Thomas received the host, it occurred to him again: If only everyone knew what he and the bishop knew. How much more meaningful worship would be! He would speak to the bishop about the Mass. Maybe it, like the Bible, could be translated into English!

If the Mass was translated into English, then every time the people sang the Credo they would know exactly what they were pledging to God! It would all make sense!

He could barely contain himself as he walked back to his place in the congregation. Why hadn't the bishops and priests thought of this already?

After the entire congregation had shared the presence of Christ, the deacon dismissed them. He sang:

Ite missa est.

The people replied:

Deo gratias.

Felice ducked out of the cathedral before Thomas could catch her and was soon lost in the throng of people filling the steps and open courtyard. The entire expanse buzzed with festive chatter and laughter.

Thomas stood on the top step and shielded his eyes against the bright sunlight as he attempted to locate Felice in the crowd. Though the sky was clear, it was frigid. And people were bundled up, making it harder for him to single her out. A cheer distracted him.

Lord Harborough, heavily robed in silks and furs and adorned with jeweled pendant and rings, emerged from the cathedral. Good wishes were tossed in his direction like flowers. The lord of the manor waved graciously with cupped hand to the ragged peasants, then disappeared into his waiting carriage.

As the nobleman's carriage rattled down the road a trail of well-wishers followed behind. Intent on finding Felice, Thomas waded into the crowd, where most of the conversation was about the food and drink and dancing and games of the night before. He couldn't help but think that, were Cayle hearing these comments, the rebel doubtless would have been disappointed. His antics as the Lord of Misrule seemed to have made little impression on the people. No one seemed to share his discontent with the nobility.

Thomas spotted Howel. The oversized ploughman stood out readily in the crowd. Thomas only hoped Felice would be nearby. She was. But, Thomas noted with a frown, she was not alone.

Kendall stood opposite her. The two were engaged in conversation. Felice was smiling. Then, laughing, she reached out and touched his arm.

Plunging into the crowd, Thomas worked his way through the mass of people with all the urgency of a salmon swimming upstream. When he was about a dozen feet away, Felice and Kendall noticed his approach at about the same time. Kendall's reception was the only cordial one.

"Thomas!" Kendall cried. "I trust you enjoyed the Mass."

Felice turned aside and lowered her eyes, refusing to look at Thomas. Her response did not go unnoticed by Kendall. It brought a half-smile to his lips.

Thomas said, "You'll have to excuse us, Kendall. Felice has prepared a wonderful holiday meal and we must be on our way."

Felice was the one to answer him. "You go on ahead, Thomas," she said. "I'll catch up with you and father after I'm finished talking to Kendall."

"But your father is waiting for us," Thomas lied. "I'm sure Kendall understands."

For emphasis he looked in the direction of Howel, hoping the ploughman would appear even remotely ready to head for home. He was in luck. Howel was motioning to them.

"Perhaps," Kendall offered to Felice, "I could walk with you part of the way home."

"We wouldn't want to inconvenience you," Thomas replied.

Kendall smiled. "No inconvenience."

"I think I'd like that," Felice replied sweetly to Kendall.

Thomas knew she was just getting back at him, wanting him to suffer. He bit his lower lip. "Felice, we need to talk," he said solemnly. "I need to explain some things to you. And I want to share some thoughts with you that came to me during Mass."

Felice gazed at him indifferently. "I'm sure whatever you have to say to me can wait," she said. For added measure, she took Kendall's arm. "Shall we go?"

Thomas felt two raging emotions fomenting inside him: anger and desperation. It was a volatile mixture. Felice was being unreasonable. In the first place, he hadn't meant to hurt her feelings. Secondly, he was trying to apologize. She was just being stubborn. More than stubborn. She was using Kendall to strike back at him. To hurt him.

Her tactic was working.

Before any more could be said, a commotion arose behind him. It wasn't a commotion of noise; in fact, it was just the opposite. It was a hushing. Where once was noise and merriment, there was quiet. It began in the distance and crept toward them. Thomas turned to see what was causing such an extraordinary effect.

He saw the crowds parting like the sea did before Moses. The person parting the masses was Bishop Pole. There was no meandering in the cleric's course. It led him straight to Thomas.

The bishop's white miter floated above the crowd. His golden shepherd's staff drew as much attention as his personage. Many of the assembled peasants dropped to one knee and crossed themselves. Others stared open-mouthed in awe at the sight of a bishop from Rome walking among them.

It was so quiet you could hear the bishop's robes rustling as he walked. They grew silent when the bishop stopped just a few feet from Thomas. For a long moment he didn't speak, while observing the three young people before him. With studied deliberation he looked at Kendall, then Felice, then Thomas.

"Greetings to you all," he said. "Greetings, Thomas."

"Your Excellency," Thomas replied.

"Thomas, I was hoping to prevail upon you."

"Anything, your Excellency."

"Would you be so kind as to spend this Christ's Mass afternoon with me?"

An audible gasp rose from the crowd so impressed were they at hearing such an invitation.

Before Thomas could respond, the bishop added: "I couldn't help but notice how moved you were during the Mass by the music."

Thomas shot a glance at Felice. Here was his vindication! Her expression was neutral.

"It became apparent to me," the Bishop continued, "that we share a common love for the music of the Church. I was hoping we might spend the afternoon discussing it. That is, unless you have other arrangements." He looked to Felice.

Thomas hesitated. What to do? Felice had worked so hard to make this a memorable Christ's Mass meal. But then, hadn't he just prayed for a chance to speak with the bishop about his worship revelations? And how could he turn down the bishop's offer without insulting him in front of all these people? Look at the way the people were staring at him! Yet he wanted to patch things up with Felice. And leaving her alone on this day of all days . . .

"Forgive me," the bishop said. "It was imprudent of me to make such a request at this late date. You obviously have plans with this lovely young lady."

"Forgive him, your Excellency," Felice said. "Thomas is being rude. He would love to spend the afternoon with you."

Thomas turned to her. "Are you sure?"

She smiled sweetly and nodded. But Thomas wasn't fooled. She'd said the words, but she didn't mean them.

"Your Excellency," Thomas said, "if I could first see that Felice arrives safely home . . ."

It was the bishop's turn to appear to be in a quandary. "Hmm . . ."

"Thomas!" Felice scolded. "Where are your manners? Really, your Excellency, there's no need . . ."

The bishop's eyes brightened with an idea. "Here's a thought. Maybe Kendall would be so kind as to help us out here! Kendall, dear boy, is it possible that you might escort this fair lady home?"

Kendall grinned readily. "It would be my pleasure to see Felice home, your Excellency."

"A perfect solution!" Felice cried. But again, her eyes betrayed her.

"Then it's settled!" the bishop exclaimed. "Thomas, come with me!"

Troubled, Thomas followed in the bishop's wake. That hadn't gone well at all. His hesitation had cost him the chance to make the decision himself—and had only resulted in throwing Felice and Kendall together. But then, had he made the decision himself, the result would probably have been the same.

How had all this come about? The day had started with such great promise! Then, one cross word had led to misunderstanding, which had led to a tiff, which had led to retaliation and then anger and things said and done that never should have been said or done. Could things have turned out any worse? Of one thing Thomas was sure, however. Felice would not be speaking to him for a long time.

Thomas shivered alone in the carriage for more than half an hour as the bishop changed from his robes into his traveling clothes. Meanwhile, the courtyard cleared as the last of the celebrants straggled home. Many who passed the bishop's carriage couldn't help but take a curious peek, only to be startled at finding someone sitting inside.

As the last of the voices died away, Thomas was left watching the swirls of his own breathing and listening to the snorts of impatient horses and the persistent cough of the barefooted boy who was holding the reins.

Finally, he heard voices. Two, both male. One he easily identified as the bishop. The other voice sounded familiar, but spoke so few words, and those at a distance, that he was unable to recognize him.

The carriage door swung open, letting in a swirl of glacial air.

"Bailiff Bromley!" Thomas cried.

There was no return greeting as the bailiff fell into the seat opposite Thomas. Bishop Pole was right behind him. Thomas scooted over to give the prelate the ample space he would need. The carriage rocked crazily to one side and never fully recovered even after the bishop had gained his seat.

"The good bailiff has invited us to join him for dinner," the bishop explained. With a friendly pat on Thomas's arm, he added, "But I assure you, Thomas, it will not interfere with our scheduled afternoon activity. I am looking forward to it immensely."

Thomas hazarded a glance at the bailiff. The man's expression was as dark as his black clothing and as cold as the stable boy's bare feet. "It's been quite some time since you've dined at my house, Thomas," he said. There was a mocking undertone to the comment which was not lost on Thomas.

The bishop signaled the driver. The three men were jolted simultaneously as they got underway.

The ride to the bailiff's manor was silent. The bishop seemed content to watch the passing countryside, frosted by the recent arrival of winter. The sky was blue, the air was clear and fresh with a healthy bite to it. At one point the bishop declared the sunny day to be God's gift in celebration of His Son's coming to earth.

Thomas smiled and mumbled his agreement, wishing the bishop would cover the window. He was freezing. The bailiff said nothing, nor did his expression change. But then Bailiff Bromley had always looked stiff and frozen. His black empty eyes were fixed on Thomas.

From past experiences Thomas knew well how the man's mere presence could evaporate joy; it could take the zing out of spring and drain the happiness from a host of celebrants. Thomas could swear that candles dimmed as the man passed by. But these were experiences from Thomas's past, and he was more than content to leave them there. He knew all too well what it felt like for this man to suck the passion and vitality from a life.

"Ah! Thomas! There's your lady friend," the bishop exclaimed, pointing out the carriage window. "And your son, bailiff!"

Thomas leaned forward to get a better look as the carriage passed by Felice and Kendall. The two were walking side by side down the road. Kendall's horse trailed behind them. They were so engrossed in their conversation they didn't seem to notice the carriage.

Further down the road the carriage passed Howel. He was walking alone. A dark cloud seemed to cover his face when he caught sight of the carriage and its occupants. Clearly, he recognized them. A flash of pain twisted his face when he saw Thomas with Bromley.

Thomas slumped back in his seat. He closed his eyes, wishing he could tell Howel that he hadn't known Bromley would be accompanying them. The last thing he would ever want to do was to hurt Howel. What a lousy holiday this must be for Howel. His daughter was shoulder-to-shoulder with the son of his enemy, while the boy he'd taken in out of the goodness of his heart was riding to dinner with the enemy himself. Thomas felt miserable.

When Thomas opened his eyes, Bromley was still staring at him. He was grinning.

The carriage pulled up to the entrance of the bailiff's impressive stone manor. Thomas followed the two older men inside. No sooner had he stepped through the door of the manor than a rush of old feelings greeted him, none of them good.

The entryway, the halls, paintings, and tapestries were disturbingly familiar. Even the air—musty, moldy, chilly, and damp— was as he remembered it, was as he loathed it. Apparitions of earlier days haunted him at every turn. He had not stepped foot in the manor since the day he ran away from it.

More than ever, Thomas wished he'd gone home with Felice and Howel.

❧ ❧

BARELY THREE WORDS HAD passed between Felice and her father since they'd arrived at home and Kendall had ridden away. Howel had said he was going outside to chop wood for the fire, though there was an ample supply stacked against the side of the house. Alone with her thoughts, Felice busied herself preparing the meal—a meal that had originally been planned for three. She tried not to think about that, since thinking about it only made her angry.

Taking her prepared mixture of lean cooked pork, salt, and currants, she placed small portions at the end of pastry strips, then rolled them up and pinched the ends to keep the mixture in. These she cooked by dropping them into boiling salt water. In another pot she stirred a sauce of strong chicken stock that would be poured over the pork rolls just before serving them.

When everything was ready, she called her father, then sat at the table alone and stared at the settings and the food while he took his time washing up.

They sat on opposite sides of the table. In silence, Howel picked at the pork rolls on his trencher. The sauce was still steaming.

"Ouch!"

He stuck a burned finger in his mouth.

"Let it cool!" Felice cried. "Don't be in such a hurry."

"But I'm hungry now," Howel growled. He picked apart a hot roll, which he stuffed into his mouth. He chewed it gingerly.

"You're going to burn your mouth," Felice said. "That is, if you haven't already."

Howel ignored her. He washed down the first roll with a swig of ale and reached for another one.

Silently, Felice chastised herself. She was sounding like her Aunt Ertha. She knew she shouldn't be acting like this toward her father. She wasn't angry with him; she was angry with Thomas. First, for chastising her in the cathedral, then for choosing to spend the holiday with the bishop instead of her. Sure, she had made it difficult for him, but he should have insisted on coming home with her! The empty seat beside her at the table shouted his choice.

"What special treat did you make for us this year?" Howel asked. The man's plate was devoid of pastry and almost all trace of sauce. From the grin on his face, the food in his belly had revived his usual good-natured demeanor.

"What makes you think I made anything special?"

"You always make something special for Christ's Mass."

Felice stood and gathered up the plates and utensils, though she had hardly touched her meal. She went to the larder and returned a few moments later with a tray bearing three cream-custard tarts. Howel's eyes lit up appreciatively. With eager, childlike fingers, he selected one. It was gone in a couple of bites. While Felice took one, Howel eyed the third.

"Do you think Thomas will mind if I ate his?" he asked.

"Of course he'll mind," Felice said. "Help yourself."

Howel grinned. He did.

Her father was finished with his second tart before Felice took a bite of hers. She reached across the table and brushed crumbs from his chin.

Howel rose. Going to the door he pulled on his coat. "Think I'll take a walk," he said. "Isn't often we get a clear day like today on Christ's Mass."

Before Felice could respond, the door slammed behind him and he was gone.

"No," she said to herself. "It isn't often we get a day like today."

With the weariness that comes with disappointment, she cleared the table, washed the dishes, and then looked around for something to do. There was always mending. And knitting. Their supply of candles was getting low. And the animals needed fresh straw.

Normally, on the afternoon of Christ's Mass the house was alive with sounds. Howel and Ives would sit in a corner and talk. Thomas would join them for a while. Leoma and Poppy would settle into a corner and giggle and play, while Ertha and Felice cleared the table and cleaned the dishes.

Then Ertha would pick an argument with her husband—her way of involving herself in the men's conversation. Felice would play with the girls for a while. Then, she and Thomas would catch each other's eye and announce that they were going to take a walk. Naturally, this provoked a lecture from Ertha regarding the immorality of two young people left to themselves. So she would bundle up and follow them at a distance.

This was Thomas and Felice's Christ's Mass gift to the rest of the family—getting Ertha out of the house so the others could enjoy themselves.

But today, the only sounds in the house were ones Felice made herself. She didn't blame her father for leaving her alone. He missed his brother.

Felice tried not to think of what Thomas was doing. Even so, visions of an abundance of rich food, music, and entertainment filled her mind. While she was spending the afternoon all alone, Thomas was undoubtedly surrounded by merrymakers.

A new thought occurred to her: Couldn't she expect this same thing to happen more and more as Thomas moved up in social position? Wasn't this, ironically, exactly what they had been hoping for? After all, who better to help Thomas advance than a bishop from Rome? This was a good thing, wasn't it?

Another thought, this one chilling: Yes, this *was* a good thing for Thomas, but was it good for her? Today was a step upward for him, but he was taking it without her. While Thomas Torr was socializing with bishops and nobility and who knows who else, she was sitting alone in a peasant's house.

What guarantee did she have that it would ever be any different for her? They were not married, nor did they have any definite plans to marry. They had talked about it. Generally. But how much could she depend on that which was less than a promise? What if, along the way, Thomas met a woman more in keeping with his new position? Someone more attractive? A woman of background and culture?

Another thought, another chill, this one colder than before: Maybe that was all for the best. After all, she was not an asset to Thomas's ascent—more like an anchor around his neck. The best thing he could do for himself would be to cut her lose.

Ambling over to her bed, Felice reached beneath her pillow and retrieved the red scarf Kendall had given her. Sullenly, she worked it between her fingers and rubbed it gently against her cheek. Its silky surface soothed her.

Reclining in a rocking chair, she caressed her hands and face with the scarf. It was the only pleasant experience she'd had all day.

Soon she fell asleep.

❦

"THE KEY IS THE octave," Bishop Pole said excitedly. "Also called the Law of Seven. It is this law that governs the time succession of events."

There was excitement and energy in the bishop's eyes as he spoke. Thomas sat beside him in an alcove off the cathedral. Several pages of music lay draped across the bishop's lap. With one hand he held them in place; his other hand moved excitedly in the air as he spoke.

The dinner at Bromley's had gone about as Thomas had expected, with one exception. The cavernous dining area had remained unchanged since he'd been there last. The servants looked as if they hadn't changed one iota over the years. Their clothes, their expressions, their service were exactly as he remembered them. And if they remembered him, their faces didn't show it.

The only thing different was Bishop Pole's entertaining presence as he clapped and cheered and cried out exultantly with each new dish. By the time the last of the trenchers and cups were removed from the table, the bishop was crying tears of joy, nearly exhausted from his animated style of eating.

There had been only the three of them in the entire hall. A fourth place had been set for Kendall, who had arrived midway through the third course. Citing his tardiness, his father refused to allow him his place at the table. After a quick glance at Thomas, Kendall left the great hall. He didn't appear to be disappointed over missing the meal.

During the carriage ride back to the cathedral, Bishop Pole slept rather soundly and Thomas feared the entire afternoon would prove to be a waste of time.

But once inside, the music revived the bishop. It did more than revive him—it filled him with life and enthusiasm nearly matching that which he had displayed over the food. It was infectious. The more the bishop spoke, the more enthused Thomas became.

"The concept of the Law of Octaves is formative in the development of civilization," the bishop explained. "It is the pattern for the architectural arrangement of temples, the organization of ceremonies, and the composition of literary works. It is even the very basis for the arrangement of Mass!" His free hand emphasized each word.

"I didn't know that," Thomas said.

Pole's eyes gleamed with pleasure at Thomas's obvious interest. He resettled himself on the bench before continuing. "The organization of the Eucharistic ceremony follows the octave in an orderly progression that takes the assembled worshipers from their entrance into the church to divine union with Christ. The only two necessary ingredients are the faith of the participant and the absolute grace of God."

Thomas nodded to indicate he understood.

"It is a spiritual and emotional time, not an occasion for the intellect. There are other times for that. But during the Mass we evoke the mysterious presence of God through acts of praise and thanksgiving. And, unless I was mistaken earlier today, you are already a willing participant. While your eyes were closed I was watching you. And from the expression on your face it was evident that the music was moving you, calling you to worship, calling you closer to God."

Thomas felt vindicated. Why hadn't Felice seen what the bishop had?

"The Mass begins with an introit, or entrance song. Instead of announcing, 'Today we will remember and celebrate the birth of Christ,' we sing:

Puer natus est nobis, et filius datus est nobis:
cuius imperium super humerum eius."

The bishop had a wonderful tenor voice. Clear. Unwavering. Thomas translated:

"A child is born to us, a son is given to us,
his shoulders shall bear princely power."

"In Latin," the bishop prodded. "Sing it with me."

With a raised hand, Thomas begged off. "I'm one who *appreciates* music. I can't perform it."

"Nonsense!" cried the bishop. "That's the beauty of the chant. Anyone can do it. Besides, it's purpose is not to perform or entertain; it's purpose is to resonate within the person and thus bring them in tune with the Almighty God! Try it! Sing with me!"

The bishop sang the phrase again. Haltingly, Thomas attempted to join him. He felt foolish. Embarrassed at the sound of his voice.

"Again!" the bishop encouraged, his expression a portrait of encouragement and excitement. Thomas made a second attempt. Then a third. By the fourth try, he was beginning to feel comfortable with it. On the seventh attempt, he began to feel the words and the music resonating within him in a way he had never felt before.

"Now try this one," the bishop said.

Sancte deus, sancte fortis,
sancte misericors salvator,
amarea morti ne tradas nos.

Thomas stumbled through it, doing his best to match the words with the tones.

"Translate it."

"Holy God, holy strong one,
holy and merciful savior,
do not betray us to bitter death."

"Excellent! Now sing it."

Following the bishop's lead, Thomas sang the phrase over and over again until his head was swimming in the tune as his spirit was lifted higher and higher. He closed his eyes.

Nothing else existed save him and God and the pool of worship in which he floated. Each phrase, each tone drawing him closer and closer into the mysterious presence of God.

⋘ ⋙

"WHAT IS THIS!"

Felice awoke to the thundering fury of her father standing over her. It was late. The room was dark. There were only glowing coals in the hearth to light the room, just enough to highlight the rage on Howel's face.

"I asked you a question!" Howel shouted. "What's this?"

Her head hadn't yet cleared. Her eyes fought to bring everything into focus. At first, she saw only a red blur. Then, she recognized it.

"It's a silk scarf."

"Don't get smart with me," Howel warned. "Of course it's a silk scarf. Where did you get it?"

Felice struggled to sit up in the chair. Her joints ached. Her head pounded. None of this was making sense. The man standing over her was not acting like her father. Rarely had she ever seen him angry. Never before had his anger been directed at her to this degree. The man's face was quivering with rage.

"Answer me! Where did you get this?"

"Kendall gave it to me."

The answer only made him angrier. He glared at the scarf until his arm shook. It was as if he was holding evil itself in his hand and he didn't know what to do with it.

Walking over to the hearth he grabbed a piece of firewood and poked the coals alive.

"No, Father!"

He gave no sign that he heard her.

"Father! No!" She jumped out of the chair.

The fire leaped to life.

"Please don't!" Felice screamed. "It's only a scarf! Kendall didn't mean anything by it!"

Howel thrust the scarf into the flames, so far, in fact, that surely he burnt himself before releasing it. Within seconds the scarf shriveled, turned black, and became nothing more than a prune-sized wrinkled clump.

Now Felice felt rage too. It swelled in her chest and narrowed her eyes; it squeezed tears from her eyes that she had fought to restrain. Her jaw was so tight she couldn't speak.

Howel squatted beside the fire with his back to her. His shoulders slumped as the scarf was consumed. He said, "You are never to accept a gift from Kendall again."

Felice was not quick to answer. Feelings of rebellion churned inside her that she thought she'd outgrown years ago. "How dare you . . ." She bit off the sentence, having thought better of it. She tried again. Still, her words were clipped lest the seething tide of anger within her spill out with them. "That was my scarf. A gift to me. You had no right to do what you did."

Howel stood and turned toward her. Felice was surprised at how quickly her father's emotions had changed. Gone was the rage. His jowls hung mournfully beneath teary eyes. Powerful, long arms fell limp at his sides.

"You're right," he said. "But you don't understand."

"Then help me understand," Felice pleaded. What was happening to them? This was so unlike them. Thomas this morning, now her father. Other families fought like this, but not this family. The three of them had always gotten along. What evil forces were at work to set them at each other's throats now?

Slowly Howel moved toward her. He backed her into the chair and sat on the floor at her feet. Felice couldn't remember the last time her head was higher than her father's. It was such an unusual perspective to be looking down upon him.

"What did Kendall tell you when he gave you the scarf?" Howel asked.

Felice didn't want to get into this, afraid that talking about it would only serve to ignite their anger once more. But there was something about her father sitting on the floor looking up at her that eased her fear.

"He told me it was a gift. Something he wanted me to have."

"Did he tell you it was once given as a gift to your mother?"

Felice didn't reply. This was news to her.

"And that she refused it?"

"Father, I know how you feel about Bailiff Bromley. But that was a long time ago. Besides, mother chose you . . ."

"Whose idea was it to give you the scarf?"

The questioned stunned Felice. How could he have known?

"Kendall said it was his father's idea."

Howel nodded.

"And was it Kendall's idea to come visit you?"

Again, her father's insight into things he couldn't have known amazed her.

"That too was his father's idea. In fact, Kendall expressed surprise that his father had suggested it."

For a long time Howel said nothing. He was lost in thought. Felice gave him the time and silence he needed.

Clearing his throat, Howel said, "I don't doubt that Kendall has feelings for you. But he is not to be trusted."

Felice shook her head. "We have nothing to fear from Kendall, Father. He would never do anything to harm us."

Howel took this in and seemed to chew on it awhile. Then he said, "Intentionally."

"What do you mean?"

"Kendall would never do anything to hurt you intentionally."

"What are you getting at?"

"I don't know the boy well enough to interpret his actions. You know him better, so I'll take your word regarding his character. But I know his father. All too well. He is not above using people to work his will."

"His own son?"

"Bromley has done worse than that."

"But that doesn't make sense. The man is wealthy. What could we possibly have that he would want?"

Howel looked up at her.

"You," he said.

"Me?"

Tears filled her father's eyes. "What better way to get even with me than to take away the one person I love more than life itself?"

THE BISHOP OFFERED THOMAS a ride home in his carriage, but Thomas insisted on walking. Especially tonight. As he walked along the road, the canopy of stars became his cathedral, the trees of the forest its pillars. His heart and mind were still filled with music and worship and praise that begged to be released in some form of expression.

It had been a glorious afternoon of worship. Never before had Thomas met a man who loved the same things he loved, and as deeply as he loved them too.

Today had been far and away the best Christ's Mass he had ever spent. Possibly the best day in his life. Bishop Pole was astounding. Unlike other clerics who kept their knowledge of the things of God secret, for fear that sharing them with commoners might somehow smudge them, this man shared openly his knowledge. And when he spoke of God and of the Church, one got the impression he was speaking of a beloved mistress.

The creak of the front door hinges brought Thomas back to the reality of his common life. He crossed the threshold and closed the door behind him.

He had hoped Felice would be waiting up for him, like she had the day Bishop Pole first arrived. But the bench on the far side of the hearth was empty.

The cluck of chickens and rustle of the cow in the pen reminded him of his station. He'd been born and bred a peasant in an insignificant little English village. But all that would soon change. Of that, he was certain.

What mere peasant has a Bible commissioned of him by the lord of the manor? And what mere peasant's company is sought by a bishop from Rome? And what mere peasant spends Christ's Mass day being tutored by that same bishop?

Thomas was more certain than ever that his destiny lay beyond the daub-and-wattle walls of this little cottage. Someday he would stand next to Lord Harborough and present a Bible to the King of England. And, although the offer had not been made, he was sure that someday he would stroll with Bishop Pole through the city of

Rome and possibly even have an audience with the Pope himself! Ah, life was good!

He glanced again at the empty bench, disappointed that Felice had not waited up. There were so many things he wanted to tell her. Then, as he made his way across the dark floor he remembered she was angry with him. *Well, that explains it,* he thought.

To the sound of Howel's gentle snore, Thomas slipped out of his clothes and into bed, promising to make amends with Felice first thing in the morning. There were events taking place all around them that would change their lives forever. Someday she would understand as even now he understood.

"Of that, I'm sure," he muttered.

He closed his eyes to sleep. Instead, he heard music. Glorious music.

Puer natus est nobis . . .

It was several hours before the music died away and Thomas fell asleep.

SIX ❧

NO OTHER PLACE ON earth was as sacred to Thomas as a scriptorium. Though he had never beheld Constantine's Basilica in Rome, nor stood at the tomb of Saint Peter, nor sat in the cathedral at Canterbury, nor walked a Jerusalem street, he doubted that any of these could stir his soul as deeply as a scriptorium.

It was here God spoke to him.

> *Draw not nigh hither: put off thy shoes from off thy feet, for the place whereon thou standest is holy ground.*
> *Thou shalt love the LORD thy God with all thine heart, and with all thy soul, and with all thy might. And these words, which I command thee this day, shall be in thine heart: And thou shalt teach them diligently unto thy children, and shalt talk of them when thou sittest in thine house, and when thou walkest by the way, and when thou liest down, and when thou risest up. And thou shalt bind them for a sign upon thine hand, and they shall be as frontlets between thine eyes. And thou shalt write them . . .*

And write them he did, from the moment the sun's rays filtered through the northern window beside his desk until dusk was too dark to do justice to his holy task. On the days he was in Lutterworth, he was the first scribe to arrive and the last to leave. On the nights he stayed over, he would read on his cot by candlelight until he could no longer keep his eyes open for the pain.

Not all who worked in the scriptorium with him shared his fervor. Wrote one scribe, "Writing is excessive drudgery. It crooks your back, dims your sight, twists your stomach and your sides. Three fingers write, but the whole body labors."

Thomas was well acquainted with the pain of the task. His passion for the work did not make him immune from the backache. He knew all about wrenched guts. And, increasingly, daily, he was reminded of the toll the task took on his eyes.

But no other work was as lofty or as noble as the work of a scribe. The very words uttered by the lips of God were entrusted to his care. And while other men labored to provide food and clothing for the body, the scribe provided them with the bread of heaven; he clothed them with the armor of God.

The room in which Thomas carried out this sacred trust was a long one, with seven desks set beside seven windows. Two scribes shared each desk. The room was a wing on the larger complex of buildings that was Wycliffe's church at Lutterworth.

With even greater anticipation than was usual for him, Thomas prepared his desk for the day's work, his mind forming the words he would use to inform Dr. Wycliffe of Lord Harborough's desire to commission a copy of the English Bible.

He checked the point of his quill pen, which was made from the primary wing feather of a goose. With a knife, he carved a broad edge, then cut a tiny slit to allow ink to flow whenever pressure was brought to bear upon it.

Next he set out his awl, stylus, ink pot, lead weights, and pounce. The pounce was a concoction of brewer's yeast, flour, and powdered glass which had been left to rise and baked into small loaves. This was used for the final smoothing of the writing surface.

He placed the Latin Vulgate into a reading frame that held the book open. He was the only person in the scriptorium who had been assigned to translation. Everyone else was busy copying pages of Dr. Wycliffe's 1382 translation for use by the Lollards. It was a work Wycliffe had begun while at Oxford and completed these last two years after leaving behind his duties as an Oxford don and returning to Lutterworth to serve as rector.

Other scribes began to enter the scriptorium to begin the day's work. Thomas nodded as each one passed his desk. They did not speak. Silence was a scriptorium rule—a burden for some, who found creative ways to express themselves, such as writing comments in the margins that would soon be lost, embedded in the binding of the book. Comments such as:

"Thin ink, bad vellum, difficult text."

"This parchment is hairy."

"Thank God, it will soon be dark."

Taking his seat, Thomas dipped the tip of his pen in the ink and tested it on a scrap of parchment. The iron-gall ink he used was made from a mixture of tannin, obtained from nutgalls, and iron sulphate. Pale in the inkwell, it darkened on the page. He moved the pen with a confident hand, satisfied with the black trail it made. It was so much better than the ground soot and gum arabic mixture used by the scribes who had penned the Vulgate.

He glanced out the window. The trees stood silhouetted against a hazy bluish-white horizon. A few minutes more and it would be light enough to begin translating.

Taking a piece of parchment, he spread it over his desk and began smoothing it with pounce, first the hair side, then the flesh side.

Parchment! That's right! He would need to purchase the parchment for Lord Harborough's Bible. That would entail a trip to a parchment maker, possibly at Winchester or Canterbury. The thought thrilled him. He'd heard so many grisly stories about them. The morbid side of him wanted to see for himself. From what he'd heard, making parchment was not a desirable occupation. For one thing, parchment factories smelled like slaughterhouses. For this reason, they were built outside of—and downwind from—monasteries and towns.

After the skin had been stripped from the animal—sheep, calf, or goat—it was soaked in a bath of lime and water for three to ten days to de-hair it. Then, excess fat and flesh were scraped off. The pelts were washed and returned to a cleaner lime bath for a few more days.

The wet, rubbery pelt was then stretched onto a wooden rectangular frame with ropes fixed to wooden pegs that could be tightened slowly. While the skin was taut, it was scraped with a crescent-shaped knife. A paste of ashes, lime, and water was rubbed on it to remove excessive oils.

The pelt air-dried after scraping. Finally, egg whites, varnish, size—bits and pieces of skin and scrapings that were boiled into a gelatin—or linseed oil were applied, depending on the desired finish.

Thomas was particularly interested in seeing what some of the finer finishes looked and felt like. Lord Harborough would undoubtedly want the best parchment if the Bible was to be a present for the King.

Early morning light blinked through the window and struck the parchment in front of him just as the scribe who shared Thomas's desk arrived for work. Thomas knew little about the man other than he was older, had gray hair, and was thin with twig-like wrists. He usually arrived late and left early. One other thing, and this, in Thomas's mind, was the most telling detail of all. The man's work was replete with proofreader's dots—a set of three dots underlying every mistake made on the man's parchment. Thomas estimated that the man spent more time scraping and correcting mistakes than he did in actual copying.

The man's work and behavior were odd, given the fact that he labored on an unlawful translation for which he could be arrested and tried. It just didn't make sense to Thomas that a man could be so careless and yet take such a great risk.

With his awl and ruler, Thomas began to prepare the parchment to receive the text. He did so by pricking it at desired intervals with the awl held against the ruler. Then, with a dry metal stylus, using the prickings as a guide, he scored the parchment horizontally. Next he would add vertical lines to mark off complete blocks in which he would print the columns of text.

His scoring prompted another thought regarding Lord Harborough's Bible. Layout and design! Someone would have to design the codex. Also, an illuminator would have to be chosen. Thomas could barely sit still. This project would be unlike anything else done in this scriptorium. The Bibles produced here were simple ones, intended for preaching Lollards. Functionality took precedence over design. No concern was given to decorations and pictures. Lord Harborough's Bible would be different.

Colored inks. Drawings. Oversized capital letters. Extravagant. Gold? Thomas held his breath at the thought. Would Lord Harborough want gold-pressed decorations? Thomas had never borne the responsibility for such procedures before. The thought alone created a level of uncertainty within him that quickened his pulse. These were things he would discuss with Dr. Wycliffe.

With his parchment scored, Thomas was ready to begin the actual translation work. He flipped the pages of the Vulgate to the text Dr. Wycliffe had assigned him. He squinted at the text, then squinted even harder. The fuzzy black patch that obscured his vision was never more prominent than when he was translating. He refused to be put off by it.

To read, he scanned past the word and then read the words with his trailing vision. It was a continuing and increasingly difficult problem, but one that he inevitably forgot once he lost himself in the text.

Dr. Wycliffe had taught him to read through an entire passage first before starting to translate, so that translation decisions could be made in light of the context of the entire passage.

PSALMVS CXXI

Levavi oculos meos in montes, unde veniet auxilium meum. Auxilium meum a Domino, qui fecit caelum et terram.

"Oh, my."

The words escaped Thomas's lips like a moan, as if he had just seen a towering cathedral spire for the first time or received a surprise gift of great value. This was Thomas's initial response to the passage. It grew from there. The feeling the words generated within him began to build until he felt he would explode if he didn't shout.

Then he remembered where he was and managed to hold his excitement in check. He glanced around. At every desk men were bent over their own parchments in studied silence. Save for the occasional clearing of a throat or scraping of a stool against the floor, there was no sound at all. Thomas's shout died of strangulation.

He continued reading:

Non det in commotionem pedem tuum, neque dormitet qui custodit te. Ecce non dormitabit neque dormiet qui custodit Israel. Dominus custodit te, Dominus protectio tua super manum dexteram tuam. Per diem sol non uret te neque luna per noctem. Dominus custodit te ab omni malo; custodiat animam tuam Dominus. Dominus custodiat introitum tuum et exitum tuum ex hoc nunc et usque in saeculum.

From ecstasy to awe, Thomas was overcome. What a glorious passage! What a crime to keep words such as these locked away in the hidden code of an ancient language. These words demanded to be shouted from the rooftops of every city and village and hamlet. Oh, what a difference these words would make to the struggling peasants of Fearnleah who labored day after day knee-deep in poverty and squalor and death!

He had just gotten started, yet already Thomas couldn't wait to get home to tell Felice and Howel about this song, this message, this promise from God.

With trembling hand he loaded his pen with ink. At the top of the first column he printed:

Psalm 121

He read the first sentence in Latin again, studying each word, analyzing the sentence structure, searching for the best way to express the thought in English. He wasn't striving for a strict, literal, word-for-word translation; Dr. Wycliffe's translation had already accomplished that. Thomas's task was to find the words and phrasing that would best communicate the intent and spirit of the text while still being true to the letter.

He translated the first sentence on the parchment, then sat back and read it to himself silently. As he did so, his spirit quickened within him.

Next to him, the expressionless scribe with the twig-like wrists scratched boringly at one of the many mistakes that marked his parchment.

The meager form slumped in the high-backed wooden chair, his frail frame no challenge for the sturdy piece of furniture. Four men his size could sit in the chair before it would utter its first groan.

꒦ ꒦

A HEAVY MANTLE OF black cloth was draped over Dr. Wycliffe's shoulders and arms as he studied Thomas's translation. His hair was thin on top and long, his mustache and beard full, though they did little to conceal sharp, bold features. Intelligent eyes honed in on each word as he silently read the English text.

It had taken Thomas all day to translate the psalm. Now, he sat in the rector's study awaiting Wycliffe's evaluation of his effort.

Without looking up from the translation, the aged man said, "In this first sentence, you have translated, 'I lift up mine eyes . . .' What is the root verb in Latin?"

"*Lavare*," Thomas answered.

"And the conjugation?"

Thomas referred to the Vulgate that he held open in his lap. "Um . . . *levavi*. First person, singular."

"The tense?"

Thomas looked up. "Perfect tense."

He was greeted by a knowing smile. "Perfect tense," Wycliffe repeated. "The voice of experience. The testimony of a man who has done something and learned a valuable lesson!"

The rector closed tired eyes and leaned a weary head against the back of the chair. He began quoting the Psalm from memory. So familiar was he with the psalm one would have thought he'd written it himself.

"*Levavi oculos meos in montes, unde veniet auxilium meum . . .* I have lifted up mine eyes unto the hills, from whence cometh my help? My help cometh from the LORD, which made heaven and earth. He will not suffer thy foot to be moved: he that keepeth thee will not slumber. Behold, he that keepeth Israel shall neither slumber nor sleep. The LORD is thy keeper: the LORD is thy shade upon thy right hand. The sun shall not smite thee by day, nor the moon by night. The LORD shall preserve thee from all evil: he shall preserve thy soul. The LORD shall preserve thy going out and thy coming in from this time forth, and even for evermore." The old man inhaled deeply. "'From this time forth, and even for evermore.'"

The study fell silent. His breathing shallow, the rector's eyes remained closed. His face glowed with a satisfied spiritual glow.

In the history of the world, there have been but a handful of men so spiritual they lived on a higher plane than other men. They saw things more clearly. The desires and cares of this world held no attraction for them. In their presence, powerful men were powerless; wealthy men were paupers. The world was not worthy of them.

Such a man was Dr. Wycliffe.

Thomas couldn't remember a time when he'd left Wycliffe's study without having learned something, without having been brought up short by his own petty ambitions, and yet without somehow feeling ennobled and strengthened by the visit.

"The one hundred and twenty-first psalm is a song of ascents," Wycliffe said, his eyes still closed. As he spoke, it was evident he was describing a scene that was vivid in his own mind. "It was a song sung by a weary and life-worn pilgrim as he climbed the heights upon which the city of Jerusalem was built. He is beset by enemies from without and the weight of personal concerns from within. As he trudges up that long, winding road he sings, 'I have lifted up mine eyes unto the hills.'

"Will he find safety and relief behind the walled city? Will the city leaders have the answers to his problems? Can the standing army that guards the walls protect him from his enemies? Will he find within that city set upon a hill the help he so desperately seeks?"

A smile spread across thin lips as Wycliffe shook his aged head from side to side. "No. The answers lie not in the hills of Jerusalem but in the One who fashioned the hills with His hands. 'From whence cometh my help? My help cometh from the LORD.'"

Wycliffe opened his eyes. He stared earnestly at Thomas. "Perfect tense. This is the lesson the aged pilgrim learned from experience. Men who had promised him protection had failed him. Walls that had protected him in the past no longer seemed high enough or strong enough to withstand the attacks of his enemies. Now, as he looks at the hills, he realizes how foolish he has been not to have recognized this truth years ago. So he sings this song to remind himself, lest he forget."

Was this aged warrior still speaking of the psalmist? Or was he now referring to himself?

"Thomas, this was no random translating exercise. I chose this passage of Scripture for you because there are things I must tell you before it is too late—things it is important that you understand."

Thomas closed the Vulgate and laid it aside. He leaned forward. Apprehension filled his belly.

"I fear my days are short," the aged scholar began. "My enemies encircle me and my health fails me."

Wycliffe had had at least three episodes with ill health over the last few years of which Thomas was aware, one of them severe enough to convince his enemies that the Oxford don was at death's door. Each of the four ecclesiastical orders of the Church, Thomas had been told, had sent delegates to Wycliffe's bedside. "You have death on your lips," they reportedly said. "Be touched by your faults and retract in our presence all that you have said to our injury."

Calmly, Wycliffe let them have their say. Then, with a servant assisting him, he raised up on his pillow, fixed his eyes on the delegates, and said, "I shall not die but live and again declare the evil deeds of the Church." Whereupon, the delegates rushed from the room. True to his prediction, Wycliffe recovered.

Since then, however, Wycliffe had been struck twice more with a debilitating blow that each time left him weaker.

Reading the concern on Thomas's face, Wycliffe said, "But it is not my health that concerns me. It is my enemies. Even now, despite my advanced age and ill health, they have designs to kill me."

"Surely not!" Thomas cried. "Is not Parliament still on your side? And local nobles, have they not sworn to protect you from your enemies in Rome? I know for a fact that Lord Harborough is still for you."

Wycliffe waved aside Thomas's defense. "I do not fear death," he said. "My life is in God's hands. I fear for you, my dear young friend."

"Me?"

Wycliffe nodded solemnly. "When I die, my enemies will become your enemies. They will do everything in their power to stop our efforts to publish the Bible in English. Are you aware that the Pope has summoned me to Rome to answer for my actions?"

Thomas felt a sudden, deep chill. "No, I wasn't aware."

"Many feel that if I were to go, I'd never return."

"Surely, the Pope wouldn't harm you!"

"Life in the papal states these days is a boiling cauldron," Wycliffe said. "With the papacy divided between Rome and Avignon, the ecclesiastical climate on the continent is a whirlpool of conspiracy, suspicion, and rancor; impassioned cardinals jostle for power and some, God forgive them, for personal gain. In such a climate, no one is safe. But it is my health that prevents me from going."

Thomas nodded, overwhelmed by the talk of Pope and Parliament, politics and power. To think, he was sitting in the same room with the man who was at the center of this storm.

"One good thing came of the invitation," Wycliffe said. "The summons gave me an opportunity to address the Pope. And you had better believe I took advantage of it!"

Thomas grinned at the aged rector's feistiness.

"I informed the Pope that I am always glad to explain my faith to anyone, and above all to the Bishop of Rome, for I take it for granted that if it be orthodox he will confirm it. If it be erroneous he will correct it. I told him that I assume, too, that the Chief Vicar of Christ Upon Earth, the Bishop of Rome, is of all mortal men most bound to the law of Christ's Gospel. Also, that Christ, during his life upon earth, was of all men the poorest, casting from him all worldly authority. From that I deduced as a simple counsel of my own that the Pope should surrender all temporal authority to the civil power and advise his clergy to do the same."

"Has the Pope responded?"

Wycliffe's countenance grew heavy. "Not directly. But I have learned that the bishops of England are organizing to move against me. It is they who are spreading the rumors—in an attempt to turn the nobles against me—that these popular uprisings are fueled by the English Bible."

Bishop Pole came immediately to Thomas's mind. Not that Thomas doubted Wycliffe's word, but he found it difficult to imagine the amiable, food-loving, chant-singing bishop being anyone's enemy.

"Thomas, listen to me."

Thomas leaned closer.

"Beware the bishops."

He nodded, though he didn't fully understand.

"Beware the bishops, Thomas!"

Thomas nodded harder.

"When the three bulls came from Rome calling me to account for my teachings, it was the bishops alone who acted by summoning me before the primate at Lambeth. Thomas, take heed. When

I am gone they will seek other targets for their venomous arrows. I fear one of those targets may be you."

Thomas bowed his head in thought. He'd not given much thought to being someone's target. He didn't relish the idea.

"I hear you have gained the attention of Bishop William Pole," Wycliffe said.

Thomas's head snapped up. "I have made his acquaintance. We have a relationship of sorts."

"A relationship?"

"A friendship."

"And upon what is your friendship based?"

"A mutual love of things. Chants mostly."

"Has he spoken to you about your translation work?"

"In a manner of speaking, I suppose."

A quizzical expression formed on Wycliffe's face. Clarification was required.

"I have been practicing at home using strips of cloth in place of parchment. Bishop Pole happened to see some of them. He thought they were demeaning to God's Word."

"Cloth strips?" Wycliffe thought about this for a moment. If he shared the bishop's view, he didn't say. "That's all he has said of the matter? He hasn't quizzed you about your work here? He hasn't threatened you about its illegalities?"

"No."

Wycliffe turned his head aside in thought. When he turned back to Thomas, he changed the subject.

"Do you know why I chose you for this project, Thomas?"

"Lord Harborough said you needed another copyist."

Wycliffe sat up in his chair. The aged rector reached forward and touched him on the hand. "You are not just another copyist, Thomas. God has given you a wonderful mind. A gift for languages. Normally, I would recommend a young man with your abilities enroll at Oxford."

Again, the promise of Oxford. Thomas felt a pang of longing to attend the university.

"But you discouraged me from attending Oxford," Thomas said.

Wycliffe nodded. "And for good reason. I fear the academics would have ruined you. You see, Thomas, I believe that God has a much higher purpose for you than merely copying texts. You have two qualities that uniquely equip you for the project that has become so dear to me these last few years."

"Translating the Bible into English."

"Precisely. Your gift for languages gives you insight into the Latin text. And your upbringing, unspoiled by academicians, has given you an ear for common English. My boy, you have within you the ability to refine my translation so that it might touch the hearts of our countrymen like nothing has ever touched them before."

Thomas realized suddenly that Lord Harborough must have heard Dr. Wycliffe say something similar about him—and that helped explain what the noble had said in his manor on the night before Christ's Mass. It also explained why Wycliffe had assigned him translation exercises while all the other copyists attended to their regular duties.

The earnestness of Dr. Wycliffe's demeanor struck Thomas dumb. He was both humbled and excited at the task which was laid before him. But who was he to improve on the work of such a great scholar?

While Thomas's mind spun wildly at the implications of what he was hearing, Wycliffe leaned back into his chair and assumed a professorial posture.

"Thomas, Christ and his apostles taught the people in the language best known to them. It is certain that the truth of the Christian faith becomes more evident the more the faith itself is known. Therefore, the doctrine should be not only in Latin but also in the common tongue, and as the faith of the Church is contained in the Scriptures, believers should have the Scriptures in a language familiar to the people, and to this end indeed did the Holy Spirit endow them with the knowledge of all tongues. If it is heresy to read the Bible, then the Holy Ghost himself is condemned who gave tongues to the apostles of Christ to speak the Word of God in all languages that were ordained of God under heaven. If Christ was so merciful as to send the Holy Ghost to the heathen men to make them partakers of his blessed word, why should it be taken from us in this land of Christian men? If you deny Christ's words as heresy, then you make Christ a heretic. If you condemn the Word of God in any language as heresy, then you condemn God for a heretic who spoke the Word, for He and His Word are all one. And if His Word is the life of the world how may any anti-Christ take it away from us, and allow the people to die for hunger in heresy?"

For the first time Thomas felt the full weight of the task ahead of him. He'd been so caught up with himself as a peasant boy rising above his position that he hadn't considered the importance of the task itself—especially if he failed. For the first time, he began to doubt himself.

"Are you sure this isn't a task better suited to a university scholar?" he asked.

Wycliffe smiled. "An unlearned man with God's grace does more for the Church than many graduates. It has been my observation that scholastic studies breed rather than destroy heresies. So don't let your lack of academic study discourage you. Discover what knowledge helps you most to a virtuous life and labor hard to grasp it! Thomas, Christ's church does not need learned graduates promoted to fat benefices, but simple men following Christ and his doctrine."

The elderly scholar slumped back. The massive chair caught him and cradled him. He looked tired. So very tired.

"I'll do my best," Thomas promised him.

An unsteady index finger rose in warning. "Like the psalmist," Wycliffe said, "at times I have placed my faith in men of power and wealth to assist and strengthen me during times of travail, only to be deserted by them. Foolishly, I looked to the hills. Thomas, trust the words of the psalmist. Put not your trust in kings or nobles or clergy. Put your trust in God alone. 'From whence cometh my help? My help cometh from the LORD, which made heaven and earth. He will not suffer thy foot to be moved: he that keepeth thee will not slumber.' That's all for today, my son. Come again tomorrow."

His mind afloat with lofty thoughts as he walked the halls of the Lutterworth church, Thomas was nearly back to the scriptorium before he realized that he'd forgotten to discuss Lord Harborough's Bible with Dr. Wycliffe.

"AFTER THE WORSHIP SERVICE, I'll introduce you to him," Thomas whispered to Felice who was sitting next to him.

It was the Sunday following Christ's Mass. Thomas had persuaded Felice and Howel to take the half-day journey to Lutterworth to hear Dr. Wycliffe preach.

Having spent most of the week in Lutterworth, Thomas had not yet settled matters with Felice. The two of them had not been alone long enough to do so. However, he was beginning to wonder if he would need to say anything at all. In the brief times they were together, while she hadn't been exactly warm to him, she hadn't been hostile either. In fact, if there was any change at all worth noting in the household, it was between father and daughter. Howel and Felice seemed closer and more loving to each other than ever before. Thomas attributed this to the holidays. They were probably compensating for the absence of Ives and his family.

"We shouldn't bother the rector," Felice whispered back to him. "I'm sure he's too busy for us."

"It's no bother!" Thomas insisted. "He'll want to meet you."

Felice cut the discussion short by pressing her forefinger to her lips then motioning to the front. The service was about to begin.

The aged rector required assistance to step up to the pulpit. The ornately carved lectern wrapped around him on both sides, giving his trembling hands something with which to support himself.

The sanctuary that had moments before rustled with the restless movement of its worshipers stilled as the people situated themselves for the sermon. Thomas glanced at Felice and Howel. Both of them looked expectantly at the venerable old scholar. Although they had often heard Thomas speak of him—and although everyone in England knew who he was—this would be their first time to hear him preach. Thomas was confident that they wouldn't be disappointed.

"Whosoever thou art that desireth to love God," Wycliffe began, his voice steadier than his frame, which was clad in a black robe, "if thou wilt neither be deceived nor deceive, if thou wilt be saved and not fail, if thou wilt stand and not fall, study to have this name *Jesus* constantly in mind."

Thomas glanced at Felice and Howel. Already, they were caught up in the message. He smiled.

"This name, *Jesus,* truly held in mind, rooteth up vices, planteth virtues, bringeth charity or love to men, giveth men a taste of heavenly things, removeth discord, produceth peace, giveth everlasting rest, and doeth away with fleshly desires. All earthly desires, all earthly things, it turneth into heaviness. It filleth those that love it with spiritual joy. The righteous deserveth to be blessed, for he hath truly loved this name, *Jesus.* He is called righteous, because he seeks earnestly to love *Jesus.* What can go wrong for him who unceasingly yearns to love *Jesus?* He loveth and he desireth to love, for thus we know the love of God to stand; for the more we love, the more we yearn to love."

Thomas felt something tap his arm. Looking down he saw a huge hairy hand. He followed it across Felice's midsection to Howel.

"Would it be possible to meet Dr. Wycliffe following the service?" he asked.

Thomas grinned. He nodded and couldn't help but glance at Felice who was pretending not to pay attention to the two men conversing across her.

"Good," Howel said. He sat back in the pew and folded his arms. Thomas pictured the two men meeting; one physically frail, the other a giant; one a simple ploughman, the other an Oxford scholar. Even so, he was confident that the two men would greet each other like old friends.

"O thou good name!" Wycliffe thundered from the pulpit. "O thou sweet name! O glorious name! O healthful name! O name to be desired! Wicked spirits may not abide thee, when they behold Jesus, either in mind, or hear him named in mouth. I sought to love Jesus, and ever the more I grew complete in his love, so much the sweeter his name savored to me. Therefore, blessed be the name of *Jesus* for ever and ever, so be it. Amen."

Following the sermon, preparations were made to dispense the Lord's Supper. The aged rector turned to face the congregation. Assistants stood beside him at each elbow.

He raised both arms and opened his mouth to speak. Nothing came out. His mouth twitched. So did his hands. The aged saint slumped, then fell into the arms of one of his assistants.

Thomas was stunned, as was the rest of the congregation. Silently, they stared in horror as Dr. Wycliffe was assisted to a chair, which was then used to carry him out a side door to the rectory. Men and women alike stood by helplessly and watched. Several began to pray aloud. Many wept.

Felice took Thomas's arm. She said nothing. She didn't have to.

❧ ☙

ALONG WITH THE LUTTERWORTH congregation, the three of them remained in the church for the remainder of the afternoon, awaiting the infrequent reports regarding Dr. Wycliffe's condition: He was resting. He was unable to speak. His eyes opened, but only for a short time. Church officials asked everyone to pray.

By late afternoon, Howel suggested they return home before it got dark.

For two days the reports from Lutterworth weren't good. Wycliffe lay motionless, unresponsive to touch or sound. But he was breathing. And Thomas knew that as long as there was breath there was hope. After all, people had given him up for dead already once before and he had rallied.

Everywhere, people prayed. Thomas prayed more in those two days than he ever had in his life. Every time he closed his eyes, he saw Dr. Wycliffe sitting across from him in the rector's study, leaning forward in his chair, his eyes charged with concern.

"Thomas, listen to me. Beware the bishops. Beware the bishops, Thomas! I have lifted up mine eyes unto the hills ..."

❧ ☙

ON DECEMBER THIRTY-FIRST, as Thomas was hunched over his desk in the scriptorium, putting the finishing touches on his translation of the one hundred and twenty-first psalm, he received the news. Wycliffe had died.

SEVEN 🕊

*S*TRANGE. THE WHOLE WORLD felt different. A single mortal had passed from the face of the earth, and nothing was the same. It never would be again. How could the demise of one man alter life to such a degree?

For a day or so after Wycliffe's death, Thomas passed off the hollow feeling in his chest as just that—a feeling. But then a week passed, and a month, and then another month and his awareness of how much things had changed was stronger than ever.

An omen?

Thomas shrugged aside the thought. Omens were superstitions. He didn't believe in superstitions. Yet the feeling persisted.

Life at the scriptorium changed. Thomas had expected as much. Rumors abounded. One rumor held that their funding was being withdrawn, that the nobles who had supported Wycliffe in life were growing fearful now that he was dead. Another rumor held that the English bishops would soon raid the scriptorium and arrest everyone, to test Parliament and the nobles. Would they protect Wycliffe's men now that Wycliffe himself was gone?

Many copyists didn't show up for work in the days following the rector's death. It soon became clear that they were never coming back. The man with twig-like wrists was among them. Their vacant seats contributed to Thomas's cavernous sense of loss.

Nor was he alone in that feeling, as he could see, each time they glanced up, in the hollow eyes of those copyists who remained. With nerve-wracking frequency, empty gazes scanned the room. At the slightest sound, everyone jumped.

The tension was contagious. Someone would cough or scoot his stool, and Thomas's heart would seize within him. It was impossible to get any work done.

Thinking he might be able to accomplish more at home, Thomas tried working at the desk Howel had made him. It was no different. He couldn't concentrate there either. Time and again he would find himself just sitting, his pen poised over a half-drawn letter, the ink on both the parchment and his pen dry. If he wasn't listless, he was looking over his shoulder at every sound that came down the road, panic rising within him, certain that someone was coming to get him.

To calm himself, he began taking walks in the woods that grew increasingly longer as the days went by. There, alone, he found peace. The emerging greenery of an early spring calmed him. He found that he could stand contentedly for over an hour doing nothing more than watching the dappled sunlight play across freshly furled leaves.

Thinking he'd found the perfect sanctuary, he began to spend his nights in the woods, alone with his thoughts and God's nature. On the first night, Howel came looking for him. Thomas explained as best he could how peaceful he felt in the woods. Whether Howel understood or not, Thomas couldn't tell; the ploughman simply nodded and returned to the house, leaving him on his own.

After several days, Thomas felt strong enough to return to his duties. It was time. The moment he stepped from beneath the arched branches, however, demons of doubt and fear swooped down on him. Their attacks were vicious, unrelenting. Nothing he did could fend them off. He told himself that his fears were imaginary, but the heart-pounding jitters he felt were real. He tried praying but found himself so distracted he was unable to form words or thoughts.

So he fled back into the woods. Safely under the outstretched arms of the trees, he could breathe again, think again; his heart beat normally again. Maybe he wasn't ready after all. He began to wonder if he would ever be ready to return to normal life.

Late that afternoon, as he sat with his back against a tree at the edge of the forest—on the edge of the boundary that separated sanity from chaos—he saw Felice walking toward him.

The year was young, barely three months old. And like most infants it went to sleep early. If this had been a summer day, it would not yet be half over. Yet now the sun reclined lazily on the western horizon. Yellow-orange highlights gleamed in Felice's hair. Her slim figure stood in silhouette, casting a shadow that reached him long before she did.

"You're still mourning," she said.

Thomas didn't reply. It was easier to let her think he was still mourning than to tell her of the attacks, the anxieties, the fears.

At the moment, his thoughts were far from grief. From the moment he'd spotted her, his mind had become preoccupied with how beautiful she looked as she walked toward him. She was gorgeous. Beyond gorgeous. His eyes, which had spent so many hours staring at branches and bushes and leaves, hungered for a human shape. And without a doubt she satisfied his craving. He felt like— and he chuckled at the thought—Bishop Pole might feel while devouring a Golden Steamed Custard. His puckish grin didn't go unnoticed.

"What's so amusing?" Felice asked.

Without answering, he stood and enveloped her in his arms. Oh, she felt good. He buried his face in her hair and nuzzled her neck.

"Thomas! What if someone sees us?"

She protested and squirmed, but made no serious attempt to escape.

"You must be feeling better," she giggled.

He was. She made him feel better. He rocked her gently, side to side, not wanting to let her go. It was a moment unlike any he'd ever felt before. With the safety and peace of the forest and Felice in his arms, life was perfect.

The sky was majestic—deep blue overhead blending to bright orange on the horizon. It was as though they were in Eden—just the two of them beneath an arched canopy of tree limbs with the first stars twinkling overhead. The chill in the air served only to make the warmth of her body against his that much more pleasurable. Their hearts beat side by side; their arms and bodies entwined; they breathed in unison. He closed his eyes and felt the heat of his own breath reflected back against her face.

In life, a person is granted one or two perfect moments. For Thomas, this was one of them. And he wanted it never to end.

"Tell me you love me," Felice whispered.

"You know I love you."

"I need to hear you say it."

"I love you."

"Again."

"I love you."

"In Latin."

Thomas laughed.

"Please."

"*Te amo*," he said.

Felice sighed. "Do you know any other languages?"

"How about this one?"

He pressed his lips against hers and lingered there. Her shoulders slumped in surrender.

"You need to teach me that language," she said.

"It will take years to perfect."

"Years?"

"A lifetime."

"Promise?"

"I promise."

He sat with his back against the tree. She sat between his legs with her back against his chest, his arms encircling her. The last glow of the brilliant orange horizon gave way to pale blue. Stars spangled the sky overhead. Sparks from hearth fires buzzed over the huts and cottages of the village like fireflies. Darkness hid them from the wandering eyes of any travelers who might happen by.

"Come home tonight, Thomas."

"I'm not sure I can."

"What's stopping you?"

Thomas let his gaze drift off into the distance. He didn't want to think about it, let alone talk about it. All he wanted was to hold Felice in his arms.

"We're concerned about you, Thomas."

Thomas drew a long, ragged breath.

"Whatever it is . . . surely we can face it together."

Thomas sniffed. He started to say something, but emotion choked back his words.

Felice laid her head back against his chest and stared up at him. Her eyes were soft. Moist.

"It's something Dr. Wycliffe told me," he said. "He said that when he died, his enemies might very well come after me. I'm afraid, Felice. Afraid of what they might do to me. More than that, what they might do to you."

She listened to his confession in silence, then nestled closer against him, her cheek against his chest. He held her tight, grateful that she didn't dismiss his fear lightly.

Felice stirred. She reached for something in her belt. "Maybe this will help," she said.

She held up a scrap of cloth with crude letters printed on it. Thomas rested his chin on her shoulder and squinted at it in vain. The lack of light together with the growing dark spots in his eyes made reading impossible for him.

"I can't make it out."

Holding it eye-level, she read it for him. "'My flesh and my heart faileth: but God is the strength of my heart, and my portion for ever.'"

"You can read that?" Thomas cried in astonishment. "When did you learn to read?"

"Did you think we'd stopped practicing what you taught us?" she said.

"We?"

"Father and me."

"Howel is reading too?"

"You're missing the point!" Felice cried. "Do I have to read it to you again?"

His mind was still whirling from the surprise that Felice could read. But at her insistence, he turned his attention to the Scripture passage. "It's from the seventy-third psalm," he said. "The first verses of the psalm say: 'Truly God is good to Israel, even to such as are of a clean heart. But as for me, my feet were almost gone; my steps had well nigh slipped. For I was envious at the foolish, when I saw the prosperity of the wicked.'"

"Sounds like someone I know," Felice said softly.

"Hmmm," Thomas replied. "Now tell me about you and Howel reading."

It was apparent that Felice was not happy with his response to the Scripture, but she allowed herself to be diverted anyway. "Father tries hard," she said. "He can make out most letters, but he just can't seem to grasp the idea that when letters are put next to each other they form words." She laughed. "He attempts to fool me by picking up a piece of cloth and pretending to read it. His act is quite convincing."

"Act? I'm not following."

"He's able to repeat exactly what's written on the cloth."

Thomas's brow furrowed. "So then, he's reading it."

Felice laughed again. "He's a charlatan! It took me a while to figure it out, but I finally caught him. Do you know what he does? He learns the verse by heart. Then, when he's handed a cloth he recognizes which verse it is by the first letter. Once he has that, he rattles off the verse as though he's reading it."

"And the verses that begin with the same letter?"

"That's how I caught him. So now, he looks at the first and last letters in the verse."

Thomas chuckled. "How can a man who is so clever be so dull when it comes to learning how to read?"

"Lord knows, he tries," Felice said.

They fell into silence for a time. Thomas thought of how much he admired the steady, open-minded, kindhearted ploughman, even if he was a little slow.

"Do you believe it?" Felice asked.

"Hm? Believe what?"

"What's written on the cloth," she said, steering the conversation back to the Scripture.

"I suppose so. Why wouldn't I?"

Thomas leaned back against the tree. Felice reclined her head against his chest.

"What are you trying to say?" Thomas asked her.

"It's just that . . . no, it's not for me to say."

"Go on," Thomas insisted. "Say what's on your mind."

Despite his insistence, a few moments of silence passed before she said, "It's just that if you really believed that God was the strength of your heart and your portion forever, the rest of the verse would no longer matter."

"It's not that simple," he said.

"Oh? It seems to me either you believe something or you don't."

Thomas sighed. He placed his cheek against hers. "I want to believe it," he said.

"Thomas, I've known since we were children," Felice said, "that God was watching over you. I believe He has great things planned for you."

A long moment passed. All of a sudden the choice between staying in the forest that night or returning to the house with Felice became much less difficult to make.

Thomas kissed her on the cheek. "Let's go home," he said.

❦

THE SIGHT OF FLICKERING lights in the distance thrust an icy stab into the warmth of Thomas's feelings as he and Felice walked arm-in-arm toward home. Torches, two dozen or more of them, formed a ragged line in the distance, rising and falling to the rhythm of loping horses. The sound of hooves gradually grew louder.

The torch-bearing riders reached Howel's cottage at the same time as Felice and Thomas. The noise of the approaching riders brought Howel to the door. His shoulders nearly filled the doorway, blocking the interior light and creating an imposing silhouette as the horsemen reached the house.

"Good. You're all here. Now I only have to say this once."

The speaker was the lead rider, Bailiff Gar Bromley. Beside him, to Thomas's surprise, rode a subdued Lord Harborough. Behind them were a good number of men on horseback carrying a threatening array of weapons.

"Let it be known," Bromley began, looking straight at Thomas as he spoke, "that from this day forward the presence of illegal Bible translations or similar writings of Scripture within this jurisdiction will no longer be tolerated. Anyone caught with an illegal Bible or Scripture verses in his or her possession will be burned at the stake as an example to others who would choose to flout the laws of the land and the Church."

Thomas stared questioningly at Lord Harborough. Had Lord Harborough had a change of heart? Was he being pressured by the other nobles? And what of the Bible he had commissioned? But from the grim line of Lord Harborough's mouth, it didn't appear that there would be any ready answers tonight. From atop his steed, he looked down at Thomas with dull, emotionless eyes, his silence indicating his consent to Bromley's words.

The bailiff noticed the silent communication between Thomas and his lordship. It prompted a smirk.

"Thomas Torr," he said, "your work at the scriptorium at Lutterworth has come to an end. Your parchments and writing tools there have been confiscated and destroyed. Should you attempt to return there, you will be arrested and imprisoned."

"Oh, Thomas!" Felice gasped.

Thomas said nothing. His only reply was a hardened glare.

"Nor should you make any attempt to contact any of Wycliffe's traveling preachers," Bromley continued. "All Lollards have been declared outlaws. They are being rounded up and imprisoned with all due speed. If you are found to be in association with them in any way, you too will forfeit your freedom and possibly your life."

Thomas's head was spinning. He thought of Dr. Wycliffe. *My enemies will become your enemies.* And what of the remaining clerks at the scriptorium. Had they too been threatened?

Bromley turned to the men behind him. Pointing at Thomas's workplace on the side of the house, he said, "Search the desk."

Howel stepped from the doorway to intercept them.

Bromley drew his sword. "Stand, ploughman! It would be a shame for you to die over a handful of words you can't even read."

Howel pulled up as two men ransacked the desk.

"Nothing here other than writing implements and these," one of them reported. He held up a fistful of blank strips of cloth.

"Burn it all!" Bromley ordered.

The man holding the cloth strips stood motionless, puzzled. "Destroy these?" he asked, holding up the cloth strips, obviously unaware of their purpose.

"I said burn it all!" Bromley roared so loudly it startled his horse.

Before Howel had time to flinch the second man had ripped the desk from its place. Pens and ink and papers and strips of cloth scattered everywhere. Within moments the desk was reduced to a flaming heap of rubble.

"Search the house," Bromley shouted. "Bring me anything with writing on it!"

Howel stepped back into the doorway. His fists were clenched. The message was clear. Anyone entering his house would have to go through him. The two men approaching the house hesitated.

"If he doesn't move, strike him down!" Bromley shouted.

One man drew a sword. The other wielded a torch like a club. Howel didn't move.

"Wait!" Felice cried. "There are cloth strips inside with writing on them. I'll get them."

Before Bromley could answer, she ran past the armed men to the doorway. She said nothing to her father, pleading passage with only her eyes. Howel stepped aside. Within moments she'd returned with two handfuls of cloth strips. Some had writing on them; some were unmarked. She handed them to Bromley.

The bailiff refused them, instead motioning for her to toss them atop the burning desk. She did.

"Are those all of them?"

"Yes," Felice answered.

Bromley gazed down at her. Inexplicably, like the passing of a storm, his anger subsided. "Very well," he said softly.

At that moment, Thomas saw something in Bromley's eyes he'd never seen before. Tenderness. It frightened him. What did it mean to have a serpent look tenderly at the one you love?

"We've done what we came to do, Bailiff," Lord Harborough said. There was a note of unmistakable sadness in his voice. He deliberately avoided eye contact with Thomas as he turned his horse to leave.

Bromley reined his horse around, but not before issuing one last warning glare in Thomas's direction. The bailiff and his armed men rode after Lord Harborough in the direction from which they had come.

Howel was seething. He strode a short distance after them, glaring at their backs, his fists clenched. He wanted to hit something. Anything. Instead, he kicked the burning desk sending sparks and firebrands scattering.

Without a word, he walked into the darkness. This was Howel's way of diffusing his anger: he would chop wood or hammer something or go for a walk.

"Wait!" Thomas said. Howel stopped and looked back. Then, to Felice, Thomas said, "Do you realize what you just did?"

Felice looked back at him fearfully.

"No, it's a good thing!" he assured her.

"What did I do?"

"Come. I'll show you."

Thomas led Felice and Howel inside the house. While they stood by the hearth, he went to his bed and pulled out a canvas pouch from beneath it. In their presence, he opened the pouch. He held up a bound Bible and several loose leaves of printed text.

"It's one of Dr. Wycliffe's English translations," he said. "The unbound pages are my translations. I brought them home with me."

Felice raised her hands to her face.

Thomas grinned, seeing that she now understood. "Had you not done what you did, Bromley's men would have searched the house and found them. They would have destroyed these."

"I didn't know!" Felice cried.

Howel placed a thick arm around his daughter's shoulders. "God knew," he said.

◄§ §►

"THE BOY CAME TO me," Bishop Pole said, entering the room unannounced. "The day after your visit."

"As expected," Bromley replied. He didn't get up from his chair in front of the fireplace, nor did he turn around. "What else could he do? We gave him nowhere else to turn."

"He has one of the English translations."

"What?" Bromley bolted from his chair. "Where did he get it?"

"I don't know. But it's not a concern. It works well into our plan."

Bromley was not mollified. He stared at the fire, visibly disturbed by the news of the Bible.

The bishop gazed on the bailiff with loathing. Theirs was an unholy alliance that grieved him the longer he remained associated with the sinister man. Pole consoled himself by reasoning that it was a means to an end. God willing, he would not have to suffer the indignity of the association much longer.

"It must have been in the house," Bromley mused. He whirled about suddenly. "Either that, or possibly the forest."

"What?"

"Wycliffe's translation!" Bromley shouted. "Pay attention, man! For once in your life take your mind off your stomach long enough to conduct business!"

Pole hadn't noticed until the bailiff mentioned it, but it was approaching meal time. And there was a delightful aroma coming from beyond the door, but of what? Roast venison? Or was it pork?

"Pole!" Bromley shouted.

"*Bishop* Pole," the bishop insisted.

Bromley ignored him: "We'll pay our Little Wycliffe another visit, seize the translation and the boy and have done with it!"

"No!"

Bromley was going too far. Although it took all the courage the bishop had just to muster the protest, he was not going to let the bailiff's haste ruin his plans.

In response, the bailiff stood with his hands on his hips. Dark eyebrows arched over black, menacing eyes. Behind him lay dozens of dead peasants on the enormous tapestry.

"What did you say?"

"We're sticking to the original plan," the bishop insisted, surprised at how calm his voice sounded. "I'm taking Thomas with me to Rome. I've already spoken with him about it and he has agreed to go."

"That was *your* plan."

"It was our plan."

"Things have changed."

"No they haven't! Everything is going according to schedule."

Bromley grinned, apparently amused by the bishop's fortitude.

"I don't think you have the nerve to complete the plan," Bromley said.

"I'll do my part."

The bailiff walked slowly toward him and said, "Like you did with Lord Harborough? If I remember correctly, you told me you'd take care of him. But it was I who forced him to abandon his bastard son."

Pole's eyes widened with surprise. Bromley knew about Lord Harborough's indiscretion?

Bromley chuckled. "Yes, I know about that. How do you think I've controlled our righteous Lord Harborough for all these years? He's a man of conscience and deep conviction. I have found that to be profitable from time to time."

Blackmail. That explained much.

"However, in this particular instance, more was needed. My faithful old dog just wouldn't hunt this time."

"What did you say to him?"

"To Lord Harborough? Oh, nothing directly! It's the message I conveyed to the other lords and certain members of Parliament that did the trick. It seems that they're quite concerned about the recent popular uprisings. I merely suggested that now the good Dr. Wycliffe has passed on, his death might become a rallying point of sorts for greater rebellions."

The bishop's years of observing political maneuvering in the papal states was coming into play. He not only understood what was said but what was implied as well. "So you led them to believe that Lord Harborough would be less than enthusiastic in his attempts to quell any uprisings based on his relationship with Dr. Wycliffe, thereby forcing him to do something dramatic to separate himself from things associated with Wycliffe."

Bromley spread wide his arms. "You have a keen political eye, my dear bishop. And it seems our good Lord Harborough isn't quite ready to stand alone against the combined lords and Parliament on the side of a dead heretic, a bastard boy, and a vulgar translation." Bromley chuckled. "The man is not entirely dense."

Bishop Pole rubbed the palms of his hands against one another in thought. He despised the man standing in front of him. Yet Bromley's actions were serving his purpose. Now, in his report to the Pope, he could state that England was standing united against the heresy of Wycliffe.

So why did he feel he was in league with the devil?

"I'm taking Thomas to Rome," he said firmly.

"And the translation?"

"We'll take it as well."

"For what purpose?"

Bromley folded his hands on his paunch in a casual manner. With this posture and a firm voice, he intended to assure Bailiff Bromley that he had everything under control.

"For the purpose of converting Thomas Torr to the side of the Church. Upon his return, he will denounce not only Dr. Wycliffe's translation but the good doctor himself. The boy's voice will do much to quiet the widespread discontent and turn the populace back to the Church—without bloodshed." He said it again for emphasis. "Without bloodshed."

"And you're confident you can accomplish this?"

"I have already penned letters to several cardinals. Thomas will be granted the audience he craves. The cardinals and I will then demonstrate to him the error of this rogue translation, after which we will commission him to take a message back to England as a spokesman for the Holy Church."

"And you're assured the cardinals will be able to convince him?"

Bishop Pole nodded confidently. "They are scholars; he is but a boy."

"And if they fail?"

"They will not fail."

This answer did not satisfy Bromley. He stepped within inches of the bishop.

"I do not share your confidence," he said. Then, almost in a whisper, "I want your assurance that, should the boy not convert, neither he nor the translation will ever make its way back to England."

The bishop closed his eyes and spoke slowly, as though addressing an obtuse child. "I assure you, the cardinals of Rome will—"

"Neither the boy, nor the translation returns!" Bromley thundered.

"My dear bailiff—"

But Bromley wasn't listening. He stomped toward the door, the pounding of his feet echoing against the rafters.

"I should have done this my way from the beginning," he said.

"Bailiff Bromley, come back!"

Bromley gave no indication he heard Pole calling to him.

Pole shouted all the louder: "Bailiff Gar Bromley, if you value your immortal soul, stand where you are!"

At the doorway, the bailiff paused. "I'll ask you one more time," he said. "Give me your word as a man of God and a servant of the Church that if you fail to convert Thomas Torr, he will never set foot in England again."

The bishop felt a gnawing pain in his stomach. He had played a dangerous card. Was he now willing to go through with it?

Threat of censure and excommunication had always been an effective weapon against secular rulers, even kings when necessary. Usually, all a cleric had to do was make the threat and the leader would capitulate. But Bailiff Bromley showed no sign of fear or of backing down.

His threat, Pole now discovered, had one serious limitation: what does a cleric do when the person so threatened fears neither man nor God?

No matter. The bishop had faith in his plan. He would make Thomas see the light.

"You have my word," said the bishop.

"Thomas will not return to England?"

"I gave you my word."

"Even if it means his death?"

What was it with men like Bromley? Why must they always reduce everything to fear and death?

"Yes," the bishop said quietly.

"Good!" Bromley cried. Instantly, he was a different person. Slapping his stomach he said, "Let's eat. I'm famished."

Bishop Pole shuffled sullenly to the dining room. He had lost his appetite.

EIGHT &

HER KNEES PRESSED INTO the soil, Felice arched her back and stretched. The spring sun did wonders to thaw winter muscles. She had spent the morning checking her perennial plants—green onions, hyssop, and sage—and now began preparing the ground for her spring vegetable crop.

Where was Thomas now? It had been three days since he left. Was he aboard the ship yet? Was he sailing off the coast of France? Never having traveled farther than Coventry, it was difficult for her to judge time and distances for a journey the magnitude of Thomas's.

Standing, she stretched out the kinks in her knees, chilled by the ground. With Thomas gone and Howel in the fields, she was alone. On one hand, it was a good feeling. Having been cooped up with two men all winter, she welcomed the solitude. On the other hand, every time she thought of Thomas being so far away, her heart ached.

A hole in the corner of the fence caught her eye. Something had chewed its way through the wattle. She made a mental note to gather a few limbs and twigs to repair it. She looked up and sighed. If only her relationship with Thomas could be repaired as easily.

The day Thomas left for Rome, Felice had refused to wish him a safe journey. Now, she wished she hadn't been so stubborn.

No! No, she didn't! She took back her wish. Why should she feel guilty when she knew she was right?

The argument had started when Thomas told her he was going to Rome. As soon as the words were out of his mouth, a black nauseating wave of impending doom had swept over her, and she had known that Thomas's journey would end in disaster.

At first, she had denied even having the feeling. But that only seemed to feed it. Then, thinking that if she put the feeling into words she might realize how silly it sounded, she told Thomas.

"Nothing bad is going to happen to me!" Thomas insisted.

"You can't say that for certain!" Felice argued. "Look what happened to Ives—and he was here in England! A storm could capsize your ship or dash it against a rocky coast. You could become sick with fever. What if something happened to you in Rome? You don't even know the language. How could you get help?"

"You're being overly dramatic," Thomas replied dryly. "Yes, there's risk, but it's a risk worth taking. Besides, you said it your-self—I don't have to leave England for something bad to happen, it could happen to me right here, before I leave!"

"Thomas, I'm begging you. Please don't go."

"Felice, I can't let this opportunity pass. It's the only chance I have of making things right—for me, for England, for the English version of the Bible, for us."

"Don't include me on that list," Felice said bitterly. "You're doing this for *you*. If you were concerned about *us,* you'd stay here."

"How can you say that?" Thomas cried. "My entire life's work is at risk. If I can get the cardinals in Rome to realize the value of an English translation, I can rescue my work. If not, I might as well join your father in the fields because I'm not trained to do anything else."

"Better a ploughman than dead."

"Now you're just being ridiculous."

"Ridiculous? It's ridiculous for me to warn you not to throw your life away?"

"It's not as though I'm traveling alone. I'm going with Bishop Pole. I'm in good hands."

That only brought up another sore point. "One thing is certain. You spend more time in his hands than you do with me."

Thomas paused, hurt. "Now what prompted that?"

"It's the kind of comment a desperate woman makes when she's trying to save the life of the man she loves!"

"No, I'll tell you what kind of comment it is," Thomas said. "It's the ranting of a woman who, for no good reason, wants me to turn my back on the biggest chance of my life simply because she has a bellyache!"

"Ranting?"

"Would you prefer bleating? Because that's what it sounds like to me. You're not making any sense at all."

Those had been the last words they'd spoken to each other.

Between then and the time Thomas left, with each passing day, the feeling inside her grew stronger. More than ever, she was convinced that if Thomas took this journey she would never see him again. By the time he was to leave, she felt as though she was standing beside his grave. Good wishes would be like tossing handfuls of dirt onto the body.

She refused to wish him Godspeed.

Thomas took offense and departed in anger.

Was she wrong to be so stubborn over a feeling? No! Thomas may not have understood her feelings, but he at least should have respected them.

One other thought troubled her, though. Was she afraid that Thomas would not return, or was she afraid that he would not return to *her*? There was always the possibility that he would fall in love with Rome, with the cardinals—and they with him, as Bishop Pole apparently had. Men were strange that way. Was that her real fear? Not that he would die, but that he would find something there he loved more than her?

No . . . no, that wasn't the source of her unease. Thomas was in danger. She could sense it. Feel it. It was so real to her that she had not been able to think or do her work or eat for days. She felt like she was decaying from within.

Standing ankle deep in the freshly turned soil of her garden, Felice lifted her face heavenward. "Oh God, when You made men, why didn't You give them at least a measure of good sense?"

"Maybe God compensated for that by creating women."

Felice whirled around, her heart nearly leaping from her chest. "Kendall! I didn't hear you approach!"

Kendall leaned casually on the fence. "Forgive me if I startled you," he said. "It was not my intention."

As always, he was dressed in bright finery. While his tunic was a quiet yellow silk, his breeches were a loud orange.

Felice hastily smoothed the wrinkles of her own tan smock and attempted to brush the dirt from her knees. To her embarrassment, she could do nothing to hide two wet spots above each knee. She looked up and caught Kendall staring at them.

"What brings you this way?" she asked, turning her back to him under the pretense of continuing her work. As she did, she smoothed the backside of her dress, feeling for wet spots and trying to remember if she'd sat down anytime this morning.

"Actually, I came to speak with Thomas."

"Thomas?" She studied his face to see if he was jesting. There was no sign of levity. "I thought you knew," she said. "Thomas left three days ago."

Kendall reacted with surprise. "But I thought . . . well, I must have heard incorrectly." He was clearly disturbed by this news.

Forgetting her soiled knees, Felice approached him. The nauseous black feeling was stirring inside her again.

"Kendall, is something wrong?"

"I'm not sure. Possibly." He looked aside as he tried to make sense of what he knew.

Reaching over the fence that separated them, Felice grabbed his arm. "Kendall! Tell me what you know!" The level of panic in her own voice frightened her.

"Lord Harborough came to the manor today."

"He came to your manor?"

Kendall nodded, pleased that she understood the implication. Lords don't go calling, they summon.

"What did he want?"

Shrugging somewhat sheepishly, Kendall said, "Mind you, I wasn't exactly invited to join the conversation."

"But you heard something, didn't you?"

"Thomas's name," Kendall said.

"What about Thomas?"

"Lord Harborough was asking for assurances from my father that he was safe."

The very request implied that Thomas was in danger. Felice had been right all along! Why hadn't she insisted that Thomas stay home? Her legs grew weak.

"What did your father say?" she cried.

Kendall shook his head. "I don't know."

"You don't know?" She screamed the words.

"I'm sorry!" Kendall cried. "But that's all I was able to hear. I was hoping to catch Thomas before he left and warn him."

Felice shook her head as she ran worried fingers across the top branches of the wattle fence. "He left with Bishop Pole," she said. "They're on their way to Rome."

Kendall banged the fence in disgust. "I knew there was a reason father was sending me on all those meaningless errands!"

"But why would your father want to keep you from ..." A white haze passed over Felice's eyes. She felt faint. Her knees gave way. Somehow she managed to catch herself against the fence. Kendall caught her too. Doing his best to hold her up he managed to climb over the fence. Tenderly, he lowered her to a sitting position on the ground.

"What's wrong? Should I get you something?" he asked.

Felice raised a hand. "Thank you, no. I'm fine. Really. I don't know what came over me."

She tried to stand up.

Kendall held her down. "Just stay still for a little while," he said.

She didn't argue. The attempt to stand probably would have been short-lived anyway; her knees were still weak. Kendall sat beside her. In the dirt. With no regard for his clothing.

"Thank you, Kendall," she said. "You're a good friend."

He smiled, started to say something, then swallowed his words.

"What?" Felice asked.

Kendall shook his head.

"Tell me."

He was hesitant. "I was just wondering something."

"Wondering what?"

"I probably shouldn't say this to you."

Her curiosity was piqued. "Tell me," she said.

"I was wondering if you'll ever realize how much I care for you."

Felice felt her face flush. She glanced away and looked for words that were not there.

"I knew I shouldn't have told you," Kendall said.

"No ... Kendall ... I'm glad you did. It's just that—"

"Thomas."

She turned her head and looked him in the eyes.

"Yes. Thomas."

Kendall's shoulders rose and fell with a sigh. He reached down and picked up a pebble and proceeded to brush all the dirt from it as though it was something that needed doing.

"I like Thomas," he said. "I really do. That's what makes this so difficult for me. Thomas deserves someone like you. You deserve someone like Thomas."

Felice's vision blurred with tears. The instability of her emotions surprised and concerned her. "What a sweet thing to say."

Kendall chuckled. "Well, maybe not so sweet. I guess I'm just growing accustomed to the facts of life. The years Thomas lived at our manor—they were the happiest and saddest years of my life."

Holding the pebble between his thumb and forefinger, Kendall examined it. Seeing no more dirt to remove, he flicked it aside and picked up another pebble to clean. Felice was content to wait until he was ready to continue.

"When Lord Harborough arranged for Thomas to live with us, we became friends quickly enough. Of course, you probably know, but the idea was for us to take lessons together. I wasn't exactly interested in studies, and Lord Harborough, for reasons I've never known, wanted Thomas educated. Probably saw his potential or something, because it didn't take long to discover who the real student was."

"He told father he wanted Thomas to be more than a ploughman," Felice said.

Kendall took that in, then continued, "I didn't even mind that Thomas was smarter than me. I was just glad to have someone to talk to and horse around with. And when the tutor began spending more time with him than he did with me, I saw it as a blessing. If Thomas was answering the questions, it meant I didn't have to."

Felice chuckled.

"Unfortunately, my father didn't see it that way. He simply would not abide an illegitimate boy showing up the bailiff's son, even if Lord Harborough was the boy's guardian. So he made life a living hell for both of us. And . . . well, I'm sure you know the story from there better than me."

"Thomas returned to us."

Kendall nodded and flicked another clean pebble into the garden. "I've missed him," Kendall said.

"Why didn't you ever come to see him?"

"Father forbade it. Then, when I did see him at the market or along the road, we'd grown so far apart we had nothing in common."

"Yet your father allows you to visit now."

Kendall grinned a wide grin. "To see you, not him. Ironic, isn't it?"

"Has your father told you why the sudden change of heart? I mean, our fathers have been enemies since before I was born."

Shaking his head, Kendall replied, "I fear my father is up to no good. And if I were wise, I'd stay clear of you. But unfortunately, my desires are greater than my wisdom. I'm sorry."

"Please don't apologize."

Kendall abruptly stood. He offered her his hand. "Do you think you've recovered sufficiently?"

Felice took his hand and he helped her up. But once she was on her feet, he continued holding her hand. Her eyes met his and saw in them a depth of compassion and emotion.

"God forbid that anything should happen between you and Thomas," he said. "But if, for whatever reason, you should find that Thomas is not the one for you, do you think there is any hope for me?"

Again the tears filled her eyes and she wasn't sure why. Lowering her gaze, she stared at her hand cradled in his and didn't know what to say.

❧ ❧

AT FIRST GLANCE, ROME was disappointing. All Thomas saw was bright sunlight against monotonous houses. He could make out little trace of the fabled seven hills. Unlike England, which was all too familiar with gray, there were no halftones in Rome. Everything either glared with light or cowered in the darkest shade.

Then, the more they wandered the streets, the grander the scene became as the sun eased itself toward the horizon. The faces of buildings turned golden; shadows ripened into velvet purple hues.

The streets faded into a mystical mist and the Colosseum blushed soft rose, then dimmed in the dusk.

With one hand shading his eyes as he gazed up at the crumbling arched outer shell of the famous home of the gladiators, the bishop said, *"Par tibi, Roma, nihil, cum sis prope tota ruina; Quam magni fueris integra, fracta doces."* Thomas followed the bishop's gaze and mentally translated: "Rome, without compare, though all but shattered; Your very ruins tell of greatness once enjoyed."

For a peasant boy who knew only fields, pastures, dirt roads, and an occasional manor or cathedral, Rome turned out to be an architectural treasure trove. Everywhere he looked there were statues, arches, columns, gardens, fountains, mosaics, memorials, and domes—each one grander than the last, each one rooted in a past he'd heard about but never seen until now.

Deposited by their ship the day before in the Tiber estuary, Thomas and the bishop had spent the night on the coast. It was there the bishop began his commentary on the countryside. He told Thomas how Pope Urban V had landed on that very spot seventeen years earlier when, ignoring the advice of the Curia and the King of France, he decided it was time to return the Holy See to Rome. Urban rode into the city on a white mule to an uproarious welcome.

Unfortunately, his plan was short-lived. When the papal presence failed to calm Rome's rival factions and news from France became increasingly threatening, he was forced to return to Avignon. This too was an unpopular decision.

A familiar prophecy declared that if the Pope abandoned the site where Saint Peter had been martyred, he would be punished. And sure enough, two months after his return to France he was dead. It was left to his successor, Gregory XI, to terminate the Avignon exile once and for all.

His was a courageous act undertaken despite the fact that most of the cardinals, the King of France, powerful members of French society, and his own relatives opposed him. But it had been the right decision. The Holy See was once again in Rome.

The bishop had continued with the history lesson, but a road-weary Thomas fell asleep. The last thing he remembered hearing was that Ostia, where they had landed, had once served as ancient Rome's naval base.

It was on Thomas's second day in Italy that they crossed the Tiber River and entered Rome. The sky was incredibly blue. There was a slight breeze. It was warm with the promise of increasing afternoon heat. A Mediterranean day, just as he'd imagined it would be.

The bishop and Thomas abandoned their carriage at the outskirts of the city with instructions to the driver to deliver their baggage to Saint Peter's. According to the bishop, the best way to see Rome was to walk her streets and drink in the ancient atmosphere that lay several layers deep at every turn.

He was right.

After only an hour, Thomas's neck ached from turning it this way and that as they wandered the narrow passageways where dwellings were stacked upon dwellings in man-made canyons. The thought that he was walking the same streets once traveled by ancient Romans and early Christians turned his skin to gooseflesh. What must it have been like for the early believers to slip through the shadows of these buildings on their way to secret meetings in the catacombs where they worshiped a Christ who had been outlawed by the government? What must it have been like to turn a corner and see and hear the Apostle Paul preaching? Or to follow behind the Apostle Peter and listen to him tell stories about his life with Jesus in Palestine?

After recrossing the Tiber River and walking a short distance, the bishop stopped and spread wide his arms. "And so we've saved the best for last," he said. "Vaticanus and Saint Peter's Basilica."

They stood in a courtyard facing a grand structure with a pillared narthex stretching before them, the entryway to a church built by the emperor Constantine more than one thousand years earlier. The structure that loomed high over the covered patio had a peaked roof crowned with a cross, the face of which was adorned with statues of apostles and saints. Lower roofs jutted from both sides like angel's wings.

Thomas stared with openmouthed wonder not only at the building, but also at the bustle of cardinals, priests, clerics, and others who had business at the Holy See. In his lifetime he had seen a priest and a bishop in the same building with maybe a friar or two for good measure. But here, everywhere he looked there were holy men of God.

Beside him, Bishop Pole beamed as he enjoyed Thomas's initial reaction to the Vatican.

"Impressive, is it not?" the bishop asked.

"Beyond words! I can hardly believe I'm here!"

"Come," said the bishop. "It gets better."

He led Thomas to the south side of the basilica, waving his hand over the landscape in general. "This is where the Emperor Caligula began building his famous circus, which Nero completed. You're standing on part of the track where the chariot races were run. The spectator stands were here." A broad sweep of his hand indicated the basilica's south wall. "The median of the track ran parallel to the wall, right about here." He pointed to a large obelisk and said, "This stood in the middle of the center median. It is the only thing which remains of the circus.

"When Rome burned in A.D. 64, Nero blamed what was then an obscure sect who called themselves Christians. He arrested thousands of us. Some he threw to wild beasts. Others, according to Tacitus, he tarred with pitch and mounted on posts where they were set afire to serve as lamps when daylight failed. It was on this spot where we now stand that, in agony because of their faith, they lit the night."

A pang of grief lodged in Thomas's chest as he imagined the scene of their sacrifice. Ordinary men and women, just like him and Felice, gave their lives rather than betray their faith.

"And here," the bishop said in hushed tones, "here is the most sacred spot of all."

He led Thomas a short distance away to a curved, open canopy supported by four serpentine pillars. Within the shelter was a three-niched monument.

"On this spot," he said, his voice choking, "the Apostle Peter was martyred. Crucified, head down. *Juxta obeliscum*—next to the obelisk."

From early morning and with each passing hour, Thomas's emotions had welled up within him as he and the bishop journeyed from one historical site to another. He had taken to heart the layer upon layer of memories of past lives and events and tragedy and sacrifice, of common men and women and of uncommon apostles and saints. It took his every effort to contain the rising tide of awe that threatened to burst the weakening dam of his resolve. He had come here, after all, not to submit but to contend and persuade.

Now, standing beside the shrine that marked the site of the Apostle Peter's death, he gazed upon the obelisk, aware that this was one of the last things the apostle saw before he died. It was on this very spot that the eyes that had once fixed themselves upon Jesus closed forever.

It was here that the ears that once had listened to Christ's Sermon on the Mount heard only jeers and the hammering of soldiers as they prepared the instrument of his death.

It was here that the mouth that had eaten the bread and drunk the wine with Jesus on the night before he died tasted his own blood, gritty with Roman dust as soldiers crucified him head down.

And it was here that the lungs that had once breathed the words, "Thou art the Christ, the son of the living God," collapsed and breathed their last.

And what of the Christians in the circus stands who secretly witnessed his death, knowing that in all probability they would soon join their brothers and sisters in the Lord as the flames of Nero's vengeance engulfed them?

Thomas sank to his knees. Whether it was from weariness or emotion, he didn't know. All he knew was that he didn't feel worthy to stand on the same ground as those Roman Christians who had gone before him.

❧ ❧

THAT NIGHT, THOMAS LAY with his hands behind his head on his cot and stared at the dancing shadows created by the solitary candle that lit his cell. The sensations of the day were still fresh in his mind. And though sleep occasionally tugged at his eyelids, his mind was a whirlwind of activity.

He couldn't get over the fact that he was in Rome. At Saint Peter's. Tomorrow morning he would address the College of Cardinals. If all went well with them, he would gain an audience with Pope Urban VI himself. Wycliffe's Bible lay in the canvas sack a few feet away on the floor. The spirit of his mentor seemed to hover over him, chatting amiably with the spirit of the Apostle Peter. Both of them were holy men of God. In a way, both were responsible for his presence here. He felt humbled. Frightened.

It was one thing to think about changing the world from the relative safety of Dr. Wycliffe's scriptorium in Lutterworth. Here, he didn't feel as confident. He was on unfamiliar ground, a boy without scholastic education about to address a room full of church scholars on the merits of the English Bible.

Thomas, beware the bishops.

Wycliffe's warning. He wondered: Did the warning apply to cardinals too?

No, this was different. Wycliffe had always been summoned before English bishops who had already made up their minds regarding his translation; Thomas had been invited by one of their own. He had an advocate. Bishop Pole had paved the way for him. That was the difference—and a significant one. "Of that I'm sure," Thomas mumbled.

His mind drifted to home and Felice. What was she doing? He wished she were here with him now. She would love Rome as much as he did.

Hmmm. An idle thought crossed his mind. Shaking his head, he dismissed it. Then again, it was a lovely image. Dare he even think it? He indulged himself.

What if the cardinals were so taken by his work that they invited him to oversee its production here in the Vatican? What better place to launch a new translation of Scripture? And he and Felice could marry and live in Rome. He laughed aloud, the idea was so farfetched. Still, it was a lovely idea.

He remembered the bitter way he and Felice parted. It brought another chuckle, not because he found it humorous, but because they had both acted so childishly. She, for her unwarranted fears; he, for overreacting as he did. Her concern had been for his safety. He could see that now.

How relieved Felice would be if she could only see how wrong she had been. The ocean voyage had proven to be fascinating and uneventful. He grunted. Except for the first two days, that is. The choppy seas of the English channel had played havoc with his insides. For the first forty-eight hours, the only scenery Thomas saw was the watery surface as he leaned over the edge of the rail and heaved.

The third day was better. The bishop helped him take his mind off the unsettled feeling by singing chants to him. By the fourth day he and the bishop were singing together, both with full voice. From that day on, everything about the voyage was an adventure. The white-capped waves. The thrill of seeing distant shores. The wind and sea and sun and tangy salt air that made his exposed skin tingle. Thomas was looking forward to the trip home.

In the courtyard, a cock crowed.

Thomas rose, unsure of the hour. No matter. One thing was certain. He wasn't going to get any sleep tonight.

Pulling his copy of Wycliffe's translation from his carrying sack, he laid it on the edge of the bed and knelt beside it. For several moments he stared at it, gently caressing its cover with the flat of his hand.

Then he bowed his head over it and prayed. He prayed for the wisdom to convince the cardinals of the virtue of the English version of the Bible. He prayed that he might complete the work that Wycliffe had started. And, remembering all the things he'd seen that day, he vowed to live a life worthy of the memory of those who had gone before him.

◈◈

BISHOP POLE PREPARED HIMSELF for bed, pleased that his plan was progressing so nicely. The gauge he used to judge the progress of his plan was Thomas's visible reactions to Rome. He saw himself in Thomas, as though the boy was acting out the bishop's exact feelings the first day he toured the city.

They had much in common, he and the boy. Intelligence. Love of music and worship. And an appreciation of spiritual things, though the boy's priorities were misguided in this area. But that would soon be remedied.

He thought of Jesus' parable of the prodigal son, the story in which a son demands his inheritance, squanders it, comes to himself, and returns home to his father amidst much rejoicing.

The bishop pulled a nightshirt over his head.

The thing that made him think of the story was that he had always been annoyed with the father in the parable for acting so passively. Young men are often led astray, as was the case with Thomas. The boy simply did not have the education to recognize error and confront it. And, unlike the father of the story, a truly spiritual man would not sit idly by waiting for the boy to "come to himself."

The trip to England. Standing up to Gar Bromley. Bringing Thomas to Rome. Arranging for a friendly confrontation designed to redeem the boy. These were the marks of a spiritual father.

Climbing beneath the bedcovers and extinguishing the candle on the bed stand, Bishop Pole settled in for a welcomed night's rest.

A lone thought disturbed him. He'd expected a visit from Cardinal Melozzo soon after their arrival. A briefing with his confidant before the meeting tomorrow would have been preferable, but it was not essential. Cardinal Melozzo was a man who could be trusted. Pole could rest assured that everything would be in place, otherwise the cardinal would have gotten word to him.

The bishop grinned in the dark. A feeling of excitement pulsed through him. Tomorrow would be a special day for him and the Church. The Church would reclaim one of her own, one of her brightest. He could see himself standing beside Thomas—encouraging, teaching, persuading, beaming upon seeing the first light of realization shine in Thomas's eyes.

He wondered what the cardinals and bishops would think if they knew that Thomas Torr was his son.

❧ ❧

"MOVE YOUR THUMB AND I'll read it."

"Read as much as you see."

"How do you expect me to read the first word if you're covering it?"

"Only the first letter. There's enough for you to make out the word."

Howel sat back in a huff. "Why are you trying to make this difficult for me?"

Felice looked her father in the eyes, but not without a smirk. His anger was diversionary. She was onto him and he knew it. "I'm making it difficult because you've been cheating!"

"I learn differently, that's all," Howel said. He got up from his seat beside her on the bench and poked the fire alive.

Felice had an idea. She shuffled through the scraps of cloth on her lap. The same day Bromley confiscated her last bundle of cloth scripture, she had begun replacing them. Some from memory, others with Thomas's help. By the time he left for Rome, their supply was replenished. And the extra writing practice had proved beneficial to Felice. She could print as quickly and clearly as Thomas, though her range of words was limited compared to his.

"I'll give you another chance," she said. "Read this." She held out a white piece of cloth to him.

Howel looked at it suspiciously. "Are you going to cover up any of the words?"

"You can hold it yourself. I won't even touch it."

Squinty eyes indicated he still didn't trust her, but he couldn't figure out what she was up to, so he took the cloth from her.

He stared hard at the cloth. His lips moved silently. He even closed his eyes for a moment before saying, "Sing unto the Lord!" With triumphant smile, he handed the cloth back to her. "I'm right, aren't I?"

Felice smiled. "Very good. Now try this one." She handed him a brown strip of cloth. "I wrote this one this afternoon."

He cocked his head. It was trick. He could smell it. But the twinkle in his eye told her that he refused to be outfoxed. He took the cloth and studied it.

A few moments and lip movements later, he said, "I knew it! It's a trick!"

"What makes you say that?"

"They're the same words! 'Sing unto the Lord.'"

He handed it back to her, pleased that he'd seen through her ruse.

"That's not what it says."

Howel shook his head wisely. "It won't work, Felice. I know what you're up to."

"And what's that?"

"You think that now I'll say, 'Oh? It's not?' and you'll say," he mimicked her voice, "'See! You don't know for sure! I fooled you. They are the same words!' Well, it's not going to work."

Felice laughed at her father's imitation of her voice. "You have it all figured out, don't you?"

"You can't fool an old fox."

"An old fox who pretends he can read but can't."

"The proof of the pudding is in the reading!"

"Exactly!" She held up the white and brown strips of cloth. "These do not say the same thing. But you wouldn't know that, because you memorize the verse, then recognize it by its first and last letters."

Howel folded his arms, waiting for her to prove her accusation. She could tell he suspected he'd been caught, but he wasn't going to make it easy for her.

"Look here," she said, holding up the white cloth so he could see it. She read: "'Sing unto the Lord.'"

"Exactly the way I read it."

Felice smiled at his persistence. After all, he tried so hard. Maybe reading was beyond him; maybe it would always be. But she knew one thing: as long as he was allowed to *pretend* he could read, he would never learn.

"However," she said, exchanging the white cloth for the brown one, "This one reads: 'Sing unto God.' I began printing it this morning and had to stop when the cow got loose. The entire verse says, 'Sing unto God, ye kingdoms of the earth; O sing praises unto the Lord.'"

Howel stared hard at both cloth strips. She knew what he was looking at.

"Both verses begin with the letter S. And both end with the letter d. But, see?" She pointed to each word separately. "This verse has four words. And this one on the brown strip has only three."

Howel sank to the bench as though someone had let the air out of him. "It's a sad day when a father can no longer fool his daughter," he said. "There was a time when you believed anything I said without question."

Felice smiled warmly at the recollection of her father walking her by the hand through the woods, teaching her about nature or telling her stories about departed family members or lessons learned through the failure or mistakes of a member of the village. For most of her life, he had been her teacher.

She took his arm and rested her cheek against his massive shoulder. "As much as I would like you to be able to read," she said, "I think I'm more proud of the fact that you are able to remember the verses by heart."

Howel grinned a satisfied grin. "Not bad for an old horse, eh?" He got up, stretched, and announced he was going to bed.

Alone, Felice cleared away the cloth strips, checked the fire in the hearth, and latched the door. With a single candle lighting her steps, she made her way across the rushes to her sleeping area. Behind the partition that separated her bed from the rest of the house, she dressed for bed.

She thought of Thomas and prayed that wherever he was and whatever he was doing, he was happy. As usual, whenever she thought of him, the thought came to her that she might never see him again.

And each time, the thought was a little more familiar, a little less painful.

NINE ❧

THOMAS SAT ALONE ON a hard bench in a long corridor of Saint
Peter's, clutching Dr. Wycliffe's Bible with his own translated
pages wedged inside the cover. He was weary from waiting.

The wait had begun in his cell well before sunrise, as he'd sat on
the edge of his cot holding the Bible against his chest in much the
same manner as he did now. Bishop Pole had told him to be ready
early, and he was. A shaft of light appeared through a small window
high above his head. It projected an elongated square of light against
the opposite wall. Thomas tracked the square as it traveled down
the wall, becoming more square-like with each inch until it matched
the size and shape of the opening exactly. Then it stretched itself
again as it neared the floor. The patch of sunlight was equally
divided between the floor and the wall by the time Bishop Pole
came for him.

Thomas moved on stiff legs as he accompanied the bishop up
one corridor and down another. The bishop's pace was brisk. After
several turns, Thomas had lost all sense of where he was in location
to anything familiar.

The bishop lectured as he walked, leaning close to Thomas's ear
and always speaking in a hushed tone. "The Church's business is
eternal," he said. "At times it may seem like an eternity before any
progress is made." He chuckled at his own play on words. "But I
assure you, everything is as it should be."

Thomas said, "I thought we were to be the first order of business this morning."

The bishop smiled a patronizing smile. "We are. It is not uncommon for a previous day's business to spill over into the next day. Why? Do you have urgent business elsewhere in Rome?" Again the bishop chuckled at his own wit.

But he had a point. What was Thomas's hurry? So when the bishop deposited him on the bench in the corridor, Thomas at first occupied himself by envisioning what it would be like to address the College of Cardinals. He prepared well-constructed arguments he could call upon when needed.

That, though, had been hours ago. His wits had long since become dull and sleepy; one-by-one, his clever arguments had been kicked into a dark closet of remembrances, some of them doubtless lost forever.

Since the bishop had left him, the long Vatican corridor had echoed only twice with the sound of footsteps. Neither time had they belonged to the bishop. The light that streamed through the windows was turning sunset golden. It cast window shadows that crept up the wall on the far side of the corridor.

A numbness crept over Thomas from lack of movement and food. He was exhausted from mentally preparing himself all day. He sat slumped over. Wycliffe's Bible lay beside him on the bench.

The clicking of footsteps aroused him. Bishop Pole! Thomas jumped to his feet. He grabbed the Bible and tried to rouse his mental faculties, though his head felt like it was stuffed with cotton and his eyes felt as rumpled as his clothes. When his faculties failed to stir, he began to panic. This was no way for a man to meet his destiny.

"A thousand apologies, Thomas," the bishop said. "But the cardinals have adjourned for the day."

Thomas stared at the bishop with vacant eyes. He was searching through the dense fog in his head for some kind of response. He found two feelings: disappointment that the much anticipated day had come and gone without the much anticipated audience, and relief, since he was no longer in any condition to do justice to Dr. Wycliffe's Bible.

"I have been assured that we will be heard first thing tomorrow morning," the bishop said.

"We've come this far," Thomas said with a sigh. "What's one more day?"

"That's the spirit," said the bishop, his own words lacking emotion. Was he too experiencing disappointment?

"Is anything wrong?" Thomas asked.

The bishop was slow to answer. When he did, he said, "Not wrong, just odd. I have yet to make contact with a good friend of ours, Cardinal Melozzo. I'm sure it's nothing to worry over. Cardinals are busy men these days, as today's aborted schedule can attest."

Thomas nodded, but he was not convinced. Something was troubling the bishop—something more than a missed meeting with a friend.

Thomas's second day in the Vatican was identical to the first. He sat and waited. In the same corridor. On the same bench. With the same results. Late in the day, Bishop Pole again appeared with apologies. If there was any difference at all between the two days, it was that on the second day the bishop seemed even more worried.

On the third day Thomas began to feel like a piece of furniture. The two clerics that passed him—both of them twice each day and on identical schedules—no longer acknowledged his presence. He had become no more noticeable than a plant or a Vatican vase.

Thomas slept through most of the fourth day, the weariness of doing nothing day after day having taken its toll. By the fifth day, he doubted the cardinals would ever find time for him. He began thinking what it would be like to return to England without having completed his mission. He didn't tell the bishop his doubts. He couldn't bring himself to add to the bishop's burden, for each day he seemed more harried and apologetic. To make matters worse, the bishop had yet to meet with Cardinal Melozzo. For the fifth time, Thomas accepted the bishop's promise that they would address the cardinals the first thing the next morning.

Thomas didn't know how long he'd been asleep, but it couldn't have been long. His cot was barely warm. Bishop Pole hovered over him. Light from the open cell door highlighted the man's round facial features.

"Thomas! Get up! They'll see us now!"

Moments later Thomas was running after the bishop, trying to smooth and arrange his wrinkled clothes without dropping the

Wycliffe Bible. Exaggerated blinking did little to clear his head of slumber or his eyes of grit.

The maze of corridors through which they passed were familiar to him by now; still, the long hallways looked strangely disconcerting in the dark as they seemed to stretch into nothingness. The labored grunts and huffs and puffs of the overweight bishop, the hurried rustle of his robes, and the echo of their footsteps brought a chill to Thomas's flesh.

A single question formed repeatedly in his head: Why were the cardinals meeting this late at night?

They reached a doorway flanked by two beefy guards with lances. Before a word was exchanged, the guards pulled open large wooden double doors.

The bishop waited at the doorway for Thomas, muttering under his breath. It wasn't until Thomas was beside him that he could make out what the bishop was saying. The man's eyes were wide and glazed over with distracted thought. He was saying, "This isn't right. This isn't right."

Days of speculation about what it would be like to address the College of Cardinals were shattered the moment Thomas got his first glance inside the room.

It was cavernous. The span of the arched ceiling resembled the heavens themselves. The surprise was what lay beneath this great expanse.

There was no grand assembly awaiting them. There was not even a small assembly. Two lone cardinals sat hunched and whispering at the far end of the room, looking like rabbits sharing a cabbage leaf in the corner of a vast field.

At the sound of the doors closing, the two cardinals looked up. Straightening themselves in their high-backed padded chairs, they watched in placid silence as the bishop and Thomas approached them, a long walk across that immense room.

The cardinals' robes, black as midnight and trimmed in red, stretched down to and partly covered their shoes. Beside them, a lively flame jumped and leaped hungrily in a fireplace, casting a flickering light on their stony features.

Thomas swallowed his nervousness. Where were all the other cardinals? He glanced at Bishop Pole, who seemed as puzzled as he.

Adorning the walls were tapestries and paintings on panels, depicting scenes from the Bible and Church history. An inverted Peter on a cross. Mary seated on a throne holding the baby Jesus, both of them crowned with golden, disk-like halos. In one center panel was a much larger picture of an adult Jesus seated on heaven's throne. His right hand was raised in blessing. A circular tapestry featured a multitiered depiction of the last judgment. People were portrayed inhabiting various levels of heaven and hell. Maybe it was just nerves, but it seemed to Thomas that everywhere he looked, the eyes in some painting were staring at him.

Thomas and Bishop Pole reached the far end of the room. Neither cardinal spoke. Their stares alternated between Thomas and the Wycliffe Bible he held in his hand.

Bishop Pole greeted the two cardinals, then said: "Thomas, allow me to introduce Cardinal Barberini."

The elder of the two cardinals had a thick face and thick hands. The man's broad nose, wide lips, and piercing black eyes looked as though they'd been chiseled from rock. Large black eyebrows were fixed in a judgmental expression.

"Your Eminence," Thomas said.

The cardinal offered no response.

"And this," Bishop Pole said, his voice beginning to quaver, "is Cardinal Guignard."

The second of the two cardinals was pale and thin with high cheekbones. A large mole high atop his left cheek drew attention to itself. The man's eyelids drooped in seeming indifference, but the orbs that lurked beneath them, like crouched black leopards, gave evidence that the man was very much alert.

"Your Eminence," Thomas said.

Like the first, neither did this cardinal respond to Thomas's greeting.

Before continuing with the introductions, Bishop Pole glanced nervously over his shoulder. Whoever he was looking for was not to be found. This troubled him.

"Y-y-your Eminence," he said, returning his attention to the cardinals, "allow me to introduce from England a young man it has been my privilege to—"

"Is this the scoundrel who persists in perpetuating the error of the heretic Wycliffe?" Cardinal Barberini interrupted.

"Begging your pardon, your Eminence," Bishop Pole said, again glancing in the direction of the door, "before we begin may I inquire as to the whereabouts of Cardinal Melozzo? I fear there has been some sort of scheduling error. It is he who was supposed to have arranged for Thomas's presentation to the College of—"

"Cardinal Melozzo has been reassigned to other matters," Cardinal Barberini said.

"As for the College of Cardinals," added Cardinal Guignard, "I'm surprised at you, my dear bishop, that you would harbor such a naïve impression that all one has to do to gain an audience with such an holy body is show up on the Vatican doorstep."

"Your Eminence," said the bishop, "it was never my intention to disparage such an holy assembly." Great drops of perspiration streamed down his temples. "But considering the magnitude of this matter, I thought it wise—"

Cardinal Barberini interrupted again, "Let us get on to the matter at hand. It has fallen upon us to examine the boy, to determine if he is indeed a heretic, and if he is, to fix his punishment."

Bishop Pole was nearly beside himself. "But your Eminence—"

"Do you doubt our qualifications for the task?" Cardinal Guignard interrupted this time.

"No, your Eminence. Forgive me if I gave any indication that I was questioning your qualifications," the bishop cried. "It's just that ... well, if I might have a moment to speak to Cardinal Melozzo ..."

Cardinal Guignard said, "We have already told you, Cardinal Melozzo is unavailable."

With a stubby finger, Cardinal Barberini pointed to the book Thomas was carrying. "Is that the heretic's translation?"

Thomas looked to Bishop Pole for direction. The bishop's eyes were fixed on the book, terror-stricken.

Thomas had an idea.

He opened the book. "With all respect, your Eminence," he said, "have you read or heard any of it?"

Cardinal Barberini bristled. "One does not have to dabble in heresy to recognize its evil. The very existence of that translation is a threat to everything that is holy."

"Is God or His Church threatened by His own Word? How can that be?" Thomas inquired.

Cardinal Guignard erupted. "Impertinence! It is we who will determine what is and what is not God's Word!"

"Your Eminence, please, allow me," Bishop Pole offered. Having regained some of his composure, he turned to face Thomas. To Thomas's surprise, the bishop moved closer to the cardinals into a position that clearly established that it was three against one.

"Thomas, believe me when I say this isn't the way I'd intended this encounter to unfold. But you must understand the position of the Church! You see, Christ gave his Gospel to the clergy with the charge that they dispense it to the laity and more infirm persons. The harm of Dr. Wycliffe's translation is that it has taken the Gospel from the Latin and put it into an unholy language and, by so doing, has tossed it to the ignorant masses without offering them any enlightened guidance or interpretation. Surely you can see how harmful this can be! In essence, he has thrown the Gospel pearl before swine that they might trod this priceless gem underfoot. What has been treasured and protected for centuries by the clergy has been turned into sport for the laity. Think, Thomas! Do you really believe God intended that the fate of His most holy Word should rest in the hands of an ignorant ploughman like Howel?"

Thomas was stunned, not so much by what the bishop said but by the realization that this had been his plan all along.

Cardinal Barberini stood. Pointing a condemning finger at the book, he snarled, "That which you hold in your hands is pestilential and the most wretched product of damnable memory. It was penned by the hand of John Wycliffe, a child of the old devil, and himself a child or pupil of the Antichrist who, while he lived, walked in the vanity of his own mind and crowned his wickedness by translating the Scriptures into English."

Taken aback by the intensity of the attack on Dr. Wycliffe and the English translation, it took Thomas a moment to gather himself. "With all due respect, your Eminence," he said, "have you read it? It's beautiful! As for the common people, you should see the effect of Scripture on them. I've seen these words bring tears to a ploughman's eyes and comfort to his dying brother. Listen to just one psalm . . ."

He flipped the pages toward the middle of the book, then remembered his own translation.

The bishop attempted to intervene. He stretched a restraining hand toward him. "Thomas . . . ," he said.

Thomas backed away from him while pulling his translation from between the pages of the Bible. He had to act quickly knowing they would not let him go unchecked for long. Smoothing the page atop the Bible with a single hand, he took a hurried breath. He couldn't help but glance up at the cardinals. Once he had, he wished he hadn't. Two faces carved in stone glared at him. His heart sank. He forged ahead anyway.

He looked down at the first word. He couldn't see it! All he could see was a black inkspot-like dot covering the first two words. He blinked, but it did no good. He knew it wouldn't; it was a reflexive reaction.

Not a problem, he told himself. It's only the anxiety of the moment. Reading around the black dot had become a way of life. There were just certain inconvenient moments, such as this one, when his affliction seemed more monumental than it actually was.

He moved his line of vision to the right, further down the sentence. As expected, the black dot shifted to the right, covering the words "mine eyes unto." He could now, however, see the first of the sentence, "I have lifted up" in the peripheral portion of his vision.

In this way, he read, "'I have lifted up mine eyes unto the hills, from whence cometh my help? My help cometh from the LORD, which made heaven and earth. He will not suffer thy foot to be moved: he that keepeth thee will not slumber. Behold, he that keepeth Israel shall neither slumber nor sleep. The LORD is thy keeper: the LORD is thy shade upon thy right hand. The sun shall not smite thee by day, nor the moon by night. The LORD shall preserve thee from all evil: he shall preserve thy soul. The LORD shall preserve thy going out and thy coming in from this time forth, and even for evermore.'"

He looked up, hoping that the Word of God had melted the stony expressions of the cardinals. It had not. Their faces were unchanged.

"The page you read from is not part of Wycliffe's translation," Cardinal Barberini observed.

"No, your Eminence, it is not. It is my translation."

Cardinal Barberini mused a moment, then said softly, "May I see it?" He held out his hand.

Thomas stared at the outstretched hand suspiciously. His instincts reacted as though it was the bared teeth of a lion. Nevertheless, Thomas decided to take a chance. He handed the page to Cardinal Barberini.

The cardinal took the page, then sat back in his chair and studied it. Cardinal Guignard looked over the elder man's arm and studied it too.

When he had finished, Cardinal Barberini handed the page to Cardinal Guignard who sat back in his seat and continued to examine it. Barberini said, "And may I see Dr. Wycliffe's translation?"

Thomas's instincts screamed with alarm. It was one thing to relinquish a single page of his own work, but to hand over a complete Wycliffe translation? But then, he'd come this far. And hadn't he challenged the cardinals to read the translation for themselves?

He looked to Bishop Pole for some kind of signal one way or the other. But the bishop was intrigued himself by the interest the cardinals were showing in Thomas's translation.

Thomas took a deep breath and handed the translation to Cardinal Barberini. Stubby fingers received it, then proceeded to turn page after page as he examined the English text. As before, Cardinal Guignard leaned over the senior cardinal's arm.

After a few moments of reading, Cardinal Barberini's substantial eyebrows raised. Apparently, something had piqued his interest. Grabbing large sections of pages he proceeded toward the back of the book, the New Testament. Handfuls of pages gave way to the flipping of single pages, which eventually slowed until the cardinal found the passage for which he was looking. Upon finding it, the eyebrows lowered in concentration as he read.

Thomas's challenge was working! The text itself would convince them. He knew it would! He glanced at Bishop Pole who was also following the cardinals' actions with interest. Thomas congratulated himself. His instincts had been proved true. The best way to win over Bible scholars is to let the translation defend itself.

The next thing he heard was the sound of parchment being crumpled and ripped. Thomas couldn't believe it! Pages of Wycliffe's translation were balled up in Cardinal Barberini's fist. He tossed them into the fire with disdain as though by touching them his fingers were soiled.

"No!" Thomas ran to the hearth. Dropping to his knees he reached into the fire to retrieve the pages. Flames chewed them hungrily and he managed to pull out only a few scraps, but he paid a price with burned fingers.

More ripping. Pages flew past his head into the waiting flames.

"Stop!" Thomas cried.

Double handfuls sailed past him now as both cardinals tore apart the book. Bishop Pole inched backward, his jaw dropped in disbelief.

Thomas couldn't keep up with the destroyers. There were two of them and only one of him. Lunging at Cardinal Barberini, he grabbed what remained of the book and tried to wrestle it free. The old man's strength surprised him. Thomas's fingers screamed with pain from the burns.

Cardinal Guignard came to Barberini's aid. He managed to secure an edge of the book.

But Thomas had youth on his side. The grips of the two cardinals were slipping, if he could just ignore his own pain long enough.

In unison they bellowed for the guards.

Just as Thomas was about to wrest the book free, large, powerful guard hands grabbed him from behind and yanked him away. At first there were two, then four guards on top of him. Thomas was overpowered. Helpless.

"Hold him!" a red-faced Cardinal Barberini shouted. "I want him to witness this."

With deliberate slowness, the cardinal took the tattered remains of the Wycliffe translation and ripped page after page from it and fed the fire. Cardinal Guignard tossed Thomas's single page into the flames.

Bishop Pole gazed at Thomas sympathetically. "It is harsh medicine, my son," he said, "but someday, you will understand that it has to be this way. If allowed to be distributed unchecked, the Bible would cause chaos to erupt around the world. You mean well, Thomas, but think of what would happen if heathen were allowed to get their hands on it."

Thomas heard the bishop's words, but he wasn't listening. His eyes were fixed on the last of Wycliffe's translation as it was fed to the flames.

It was his stubborn pride and arrogance that had led to this moment. He never should have come to Rome. He never should have brought the Bible translation with him. He never should have trusted Bishop Pole and told him about it in the first place! Wycliffe had warned him. Felice had warned him. But he wouldn't listen. As a result, one of Dr. Wycliffe's priceless translations—the last, for all Thomas knew—was destroyed.

And it was all his fault.

TEN ஜ

HEY WERE DOOMED. BISHOP Pole had surmised as much the moment he saw Barberini and Guignard sitting side by side in the hall.

The two cardinals were the bitterest of enemies. Cardinal Barberini was the most powerful of the Italian cardinals, while Cardinal Guignard was the spokesmen for the French cardinals. If these two men were working in concert, it could only mean that they found in Thomas a cause greater than their mutual abhorrence.

Bishop Pole's plan had hinged on their division. Knowing he could never hope to gain the sympathy of the French cardinals for a plan that would benefit England, his strategy had been to enlist the support of the Italians and use their majority in the congress to his advantage. Before Thomas's arrival, Cardinal Melozzo had promised Pole a united Italian coalition. But Bishop Pole had known, the instant he saw Barberini and Guignard sitting next to each other, that Melozzo had failed utterly.

At that point, Pole had seen but one chance to save himself and Thomas: get the boy to forsake the errant translation for the greater good of the Church. When Thomas had seemed to gain the advantage by courteously but courageously challenging the cardinals to examine his own translation for themselves, he couldn't have been prouder of the boy. And for a moment, like a star shooting across the black expanse of night, hope had sparkled. Though Pole had known that the cardinals would never, *never* endorse the English version, he had prayed that they would see in the translation the boy's potential.

Then came the ripping.

The fire.

The struggle.

The guards.

A heavily perspiring Cardinal Barberini stood triumphantly over the burning pages as the last of the heretic version was consumed. Beside him stood the placid Frenchman. Their feigned interest in the English translation had been merely prurient, or perhaps a means to an end. They had used Thomas's eagerness and naïveté against him to get their hands on the book.

"Consumed by fire," Cardinal Barberini muttered threateningly. "Such is the end of all things that dare to stand against the Holy Church of God."

The bishop watched Thomas. The boy could not take his eyes from the fire. His face showed not fear, but horror and sadness. Burned fingers dangled helplessly at his side.

To the guards Cardinal Guignard instructed, "Take the boy away. Secure him for the night. We will question him tomorrow, after which we will set his punishment."

Cardinal Barberini kicked back into the fire a burning page of text that had fallen onto the hearth. "I would advise you, young man, to spend this night in prayer," he said. "For your answers tomorrow will most certainly determine your eternal destiny."

The guards escorted Thomas to the door. He resisted not at all.

"Your Eminence—" Bishop Pole interjected.

Cardinal Guignard's upraised hand and scorching gaze cut him off. "Hold your tongue, bishop. You will be granted permission to explain yourself once the boy is gone."

"But I wish to speak on his behalf."

Glowering at him, Cardinal Barberini warned, "You had best concern yourself with the fate of your own soul."

The sound of scuffling at the doorway drew their attention. The bishop swung around in time to see one guard fly backwards and skid across the floor on the seat of his pants. Guards' arms waved in all directions, like an octopus attempting to hold onto a squirming fish. None of them managed to gain a grip. Thomas slipped away. Running footsteps echoed down the hallway. "Halt!" the guards yelled, as all four of them took up the chase.

Bishop Pole turned to the cardinals. "The boy is not a heretic, merely a misguided youth. Given the proper guidance, I believe he can be useful to the work of the Holy Church in England."

Cardinal Guignard said, "The boy is no longer your concern."

Cardinal Barberini added, "Your task, bishop, will be to explain to us why we should not bring charges against you. Did you or did you not allow the continued propagation of this heresy, knowing that the Holy Church has issued several bulls outlawing this rogue translation?"

Bishop Pole felt the full weight of the accusing eyes of the two most powerful cardinals in the Vatican focused upon him. Clearly, more than his position in Rome was in jeopardy. If he failed to disassociate himself from this heresy, his entire career could be forfeited.

"Your Eminence, my goal was one of redemption, not sedition. Sometimes a little slack in the line is needed to land the fish. I saw in the boy an intellect that would be useful to the Holy Church."

Cardinal Guignard harumphed. "This is your way of guiding that intellect? By encouraging the boy to bring the damnable writings of John Wycliffe into the very halls of the Holy See?"

"And by attempting to pit cardinal against cardinal?" Barberini thundered. "You would turn men of God against each other in order to mollycoddle an English peasant boy into obeying the laws of God?"

The irony of the accusation was not lost on the bishop. He had formulated his plan only after carefully observing the successful political maneuverings of both these men. The bishop was wise enough, however, to know that counter accusations would only make things worse. He was overmatched and he knew it. His only recourse was contrition. He hung his head. "Your Eminence, let me assure you—"

A guard stumbled into the doorway. He gasped for breath. "Your Eminence," he cried, "the boy has escaped."

Bishop Pole saw his chance and jumped on it. "Your Eminence," he cried, "let me find the boy. I'll bring him to you."

Cardinal Barberini gazed upon him skeptically.

The bishop pleaded, "Allow me to find this heretic and deliver him into your hands. Then you may do with him as you will. I beg of you. Grant me this task. It is my only chance to redeem myself in your eyes."

Pole hated the words that were literally jumping from his mouth. But he was fighting for his life.

The two cardinals exchanged glances. Two gods conferring on the fate of a lesser being.

Cardinal Barberini said, "Go. Return without him and you will suffer his fate."

≈§§≈

HAD THE LEAD GUARD not stumbled and, by doing so, tripped up the trailing guards, they would have caught Thomas. He escaped by blind luck—literally "blind," given his poor eyesight and the poorly lit corridors—yet somehow Thomas managed to find his way outside. Then he ran until he felt his lungs would burst.

He stood with his back pressed against the stone cold obelisk. His heart was hammering, his legs and arms quivering, his mind racing.

Nothing made sense to him.

He had been tricked. Of that he was sure. And they had destroyed Dr. Wycliffe's Bible. Fed it to the flames. It was an image that would haunt him until he died.

And what part had Bishop Pole played in all this? Had he been in on it from the beginning? No. The bishop had seemed just as surprised as Thomas had been. Still, the bishop *must* have known beforehand that the true purpose of the audience was to condemn the translation. And what about all those hours they'd spent together? Singing chants. Talking about the things of God. The promises that had been made. Was all of it a lie? A lure?

Beware the bishops.

Thomas slumped back against the stone. His head ached. He didn't know what to think. Who to trust. What to do. Where to go. He knew no one in Rome except the bishop. He couldn't speak the language. He had no money. No food. And should he manage to survive the night, come morning the guards would be questioning the local citizens asking if they'd seen an Englishman wandering the streets. It would be best if he avoided all human contact.

The urge within him to keep moving was strong. But which direction? He dare not go back. Not yet, at least. He had to think. Sort things through. He needed time.

Putting his head back against the stone, he moaned. Think. *Think!* But the only thought that came to him was that he was glad Felice and Howel couldn't see him now. He felt so stupid. He knew he couldn't face them. At the moment, he couldn't imagine that he would ever be able to face them again.

Behind him guards shouted, coordinating their search. In front of him the landscape stretched into infinite darkness.

Pushing off, Thomas bolted across the open ground that had once been stained with Christian martyrs' blood. He ran, not knowing where he was going. He ran until he no longer heard voices behind him, until his legs buckled beneath him, and then again, and again. He ran because he wanted to put as much distance between himself and Saint Peter's as he possibly could while it was still dark.

He ran. And as he ran, an idea came to him.

❧ ❧

BISHOP POLE SHADED HIS eyes against the blazing noonday sun and the estuary that mirrored its light with a thousand sparkling points.

"An Englishman. No more than a boy," he said, trying not to react to the offensive odor emanating from the sailor to whom he was speaking. The man probably hadn't bathed since his ship left port. And if the sailor's ripeness was any indication, they had come a great distance.

Fortunately for the bishop, a sweet breeze swept in off the water and spared him for the rest of their conversation.

"An Englishman, y'say?" asked the sailor.

"A lad. Not very tall. Wiry. Squints a lot."

The sailor shook his head. "Best ask the cap'n."

"I've already spoken to your captain. He hasn't seen the boy. I thought you might have."

The sailor scratched a grizzled chin. "If the cap'n ain't seen 'im, I ain't seen 'im. What'd he do, this lad? Get drunk on your holy wine?"

The sailor guffawed loudly, highly amused by his own humor. His cackling laughter grated on the bishop's tender nerves. He wanted to throttle the cretin—if not to emphasize the seriousness of the matter, then simply to give his growing anxiety an outlet.

He peered down the coastline. Several hundred feet away, a couple of guards were questioning the crew of the last boat in a long line of craft. The two sailors with whom they spoke were both shaking their heads.

The bishop swallowed a curse. Producing a handkerchief, he patted dry his perspiring brow. It was warm along the coast. Even warmer inland. He set his eyes toward Ostia. If Thomas hadn't attempted to catch a ship to England from here, he might try there. It was a remote possibility, but one that couldn't be overlooked.

He signaled to the guards with a wave of his hand. As he walked toward his waiting coach the dust was stirred by his steps. It settled on his damp skin. He hated the gritty feeling of summer travel. Normally, on days like this, he refrained from travel in favor of the cool shade of the Vatican gardens. He could afford no such luxury today. In fact, if he failed to find the boy, he would doubtless never enjoy such luxury again.

Patting dry his brow, which had already beaded up again with perspiration, he trudged toward the coach. The bishop wondered how much of the perspiration was from the heat and how much from fear.

⤳ ৡৈ ⤳

THOMAS LAY CRUMPLED AND shivering at the base of subterranean stone steps. The dank air penetrated his clothing and chilled his flesh. Although it was midday, he lay in the dark, the only available light being that which stole past the edge of the rock that concealed the entrance to the catacombs.

A trickle of sewage water tumbled down the tufa steps like a series of miniature waterfalls before collecting in a pool near his feet and continuing its journey into the dark recesses of the tomb.

It was the sewage water that had led him to the concealed entrance. The bishop had told him about the catacombs during their tour of the city the day they arrived. He remembered the bishop telling him that the catacombs had once served not only as burial places, but also as hiding places for the early Christians.

The bishop also said that during the third century, churches above ground were destroyed by imperial order. Some of the churches relocated their worship services into the large catacomb chambers. Later, as their hiding places were discovered and at times violated, Christians destroyed the old entrances and made secret ones.

It was the memory of this information that had prompted Thomas's idea the night he fled from the Vatican. He knew that his chances of finding one of the secret entrances would be remote, but it was the best hiding place he could think of. No, it was the *only* hiding place he could think of. Throughout the night he had searched open fields and cliffsides without success.

When the night began to wane and sunrise colored the sky, Thomas had been on the verge of abandoning his plan—until he'd spotted the stream of sewage. What caught his attention was the fact that as it emptied out of a side street it came to an abrupt end under a bush. No pool formed, neither was there an outlet.

Not exactly a sign from God, but Thomas's hopes were raised.

As the first rays of morning burst over the ancient city, touching domes with flashes of gold, Thomas pulled back the branches of the bush, revealing the edge of a large flat stone. With burned, swollen fingers, he attempted to move the stone. The effort was excruciating as the rock tore into tender flesh. Worse, the stone didn't move. His effort did nothing more than crack the dirt around the stone's edges. He wasn't in yet, but his suspicions were confirmed. Breaking off a branch from the bush he dug around the edges before trying again.

He looked for something to use as a lever. But the only things long enough were the branches from the bush, and they weren't nearly strong enough. He had no choice but to use his hands.

The rattle of cartwheels echoed down the side street. An early morning vendor announced his wares in a language Thomas couldn't understand. But the sound of the voice was enough to alarm him. He couldn't let himself be seen! Especially disappearing into a hole in the ground.

Quickly Thomas pulled his tunic over his head. He draped it over the edge of the rock in an effort to spare his throbbing fingers.

His second attempt fared better. He managed to move the stone slightly, enough to reveal a narrow opening. He tried again. With a loud grunt, he shoved the rock far enough to one side that he was able to see steps leading into the ground.

The rattle of cartwheels was growing louder. One more attempt provided a sufficient opening. Thomas scrambled down the steps into the darkness, then waited, his heart pounding, his fingers throbbing. When he thought he'd given the vendor enough time to move on, he cautiously poked his head out the hole.

The side street was deserted. He glanced in every direction and saw no one. With his branch, Thomas brushed the ground to remove all traces of his footprints. He arranged the limbs of the bush to cover the opening again. Then, climbing back inside, he pressed his shoulder against the stone and moved it back into place. The stone moved with surprising ease. But then, from the steps he was able to use his upper body and legs.

He descended the steps. With no torch to light his way, he thought it best not to wander far from the opening. He would wait until night, then sneak into the city and scrounge for food and some kind of light.

Curled in a ball, he attempted to keep warm and rest. Cold and darkness were his only covering. Occasionally, a gust of summer air would waft down the steps and brush away the chill, his only indication of how hot it was on the surface. The rocks against which he leaned had not been touched by the sun for hundreds of years—and felt like it.

The steady trickle of sewage water didn't help. Nor did its odor, which combined with a heavy, musty, mossy smell to make the air nearly unbreathable.

Thomas tried not to think about the discomforts. He refused to let the dankness of his surroundings seep into his soul. He tried to think of things that would make him laugh.

An amusing thought struck him. Ironic, really. It concerned his predicament and surroundings. Whereas early Christians had once hidden in this very place, only later to become the Church, he was now hiding here from the very Church they had created.

He chuckled and shivered. The deep sound of his voice echoed against the walls, indicating that he was in a large chamber. The thought made him colder still.

After a time, his legs ached horribly at the knees. But in order to stretch them he would have to get up, and he didn't want to surrender the warmth he'd managed to create with his legs against his chest. Reaching down, he stretched his tunic over his feet to warm them. He felt a tattered piece of cloth along the edge of the tunic. It had probably been torn during his fight with the guards.

Thomas ripped off the dangling piece of cloth and tossed it aside. Closing his eyes, he thought of England. And Fearnleah. And Felice.

Thomas spent the last hours of twilight on the entrance steps staring through the cracks at the sky, thinking the day would never end. He was cold, but he was even more cautious. Undue haste now would mean his capture, so he deliberately waited twice as long as he thought necessary before removing the rock and stepping out into the dark summer night.

The air was so fresh and warm it made him giddy. For nearly an hour he did nothing more than stand and breathe and stretch, glad for the opportunity. Before wandering into the city, he collected dry brush, limbs, and twigs, and tossed them down the steps into the catacomb. He'd had enough of the dark and the cold.

In the city, he clung to shadows. He managed to find a cart of spoiled fruit and stale, moldy bread atop a trash heap. Eating around the spoiled portions, he was able to find enough food to satisfy his hunger for the time being.

He also found some discarded timbers that could be used as torches. Now came the difficult part. How could he light the torch and take it back to the catacombs without being seen? After much thought, he decided that there *was* no way—he would just have to take a chance.

He found an unattended street lamp. For several minutes he watched and waited. No one came by. Still he was hesitant. Several more minutes and still no one. Moving quickly, but not so quickly as to draw attention to himself, he left the shadow, approached the lamp, and lit his torch. All around him darkness fled. He was a walking beacon to anyone with eyes. He moved quickly toward the catacombs.

Later, Thomas concluded that God must have been watching over him, for he managed to retreat outside the city without encountering a soul. Soon, he was safe inside the catacombs again with the entrance sealed. The torch light provided him with a good look at his surroundings.

Thomas stood in the midst of a large chamber with an arched ceiling. On every side recesses had been cut into the walls, one above another. It was here, presumably, that the bodies of Christians had been laid to rest.

The walls were heavily decorated with mosaics and frescoes depicting a variety of biblical themes—Christ holding a gospel; the Good Shepherd cradling a little lamb in his arms; Abraham offering his son Isaac on the altar; an anchor; Daniel in the lions' den; Jonah and the whale; fish and loaves of bread.

He remembered that the bishop had told him the catacombs usually consisted of several levels, up to four or five. Concerned that a passerby might catch a glimpse of light protruding around the edges of the entrance stone, Thomas decided it would be better to move down one more level. He searched for and found another stairway.

Descending the narrow steps, he entered a chamber similar to the first one, with frescoes and mosaics. Not the most pleasant of surroundings, but he felt safe. He would stay out of sight during the day and forage the city at night until he could figure a way to get back to England. The only thing left for him to do was to build a fire.

Returning to the first level, he gathered up an armload of the wood that he'd tossed down. As he bent down to pick up some of the smaller twigs for kindling, something caught his eye. A strip of cloth. It was the piece he'd ripped from his tunic.

Odd. It wasn't the same color as his tunic. And it looked like it had writing on it!

The wood clattered to the stone floor as Thomas dropped to his knees to examine the cloth. He recognized it the moment he picked it up. Felice! It was her handwriting. She must have sewn it into the hem of his tunic for him to find.

His hands trembling with emotion, he read what she had written: *My flesh and my heart faileth: but God is the strength of my heart, and my portion for ever.*

Thomas gripped the cloth to his chest and closed his eyes. His throat clenched; his heart stopped beating. Tears came. He couldn't stop them.

"Felice," he whispered.

He could see her. Feel her presence. Yet she was so far away. So very far away.

Never had he loved her more than now. Never had he yearned for her as much as he did at this moment. The feeling was so strong, he thought his insides would rupture from the intensity of his longing.

What a fool he had been. A proud, stubborn, arrogant fool. Now he was paying the price for his pride. And what a steep price it was! He might never see his Felice again. He might never again enfold her in his arms, lose himself in her eyes, her laughter, her wit.

Even if he succeeded in returning to England, he would be an outlaw. He couldn't return home as if nothing had happened. And how could he return to her knowing his very presence would endanger her? All because he wouldn't listen. He was always so cocksure. He always knew what was best. What a fool he had been to think he could breeze into Rome and do what even Dr. Wycliffe had not been able to do.

It sounded so ridiculous to him now. If he hadn't been in such despair, he would have laughed.

Against everyone's warnings he'd taken a chance. He'd gambled with their lives.

And lost.

Lost everything.

His freedom. His home. Felice.

Thomas gripped the cloth so tightly his fingers burned and his hand trembled. His sobs echoed against the painted walls of the catacombs.

❧ ❧

ON HIS THIRD NIGHT in hiding, Thomas heard the sound. He was lying on the steps beside the trickling river of waste, peeking through the cracks, waiting for the sky to darken, as he had each night before. But this time, he heard a sound from the surface side of the stone.

There it was again!

He cocked his head. Whistling. It sounded like someone was whistling! And it was getting closer.

He backed down two steps and held his breath, expecting at any moment the entrance stone to fly away and leave him staring up into the faces of Vatican guards.

But the stone didn't move. The whistling stopped.

Thomas strained to hear something. Anything. The clearing of a throat. The shuffle of feet. The rustle of the bush. Anything.

He heard nothing.

Had it been his imagination? No, he knew what he'd heard . . . at least, he thought so. But the longer the silence, the less sure he became.

No, he couldn't have imagined it, could he? For it was more than just whistling. It was a tune. A tune he recognized.

Slowly, with cat-like moves, he crept back up the two steps so that his ear was nearly touching the underside of the entrance stone. He strained to hear beyond the stone. But all he could hear was his heart thumping in his throat—so loudly that, even if the whistling started up again, he thought for sure the thumping would drown it out.

He tried to calm himself. He closed his eyes to concentrate on listening.

And he waited.

The only sound he heard was that of his own breathing against the rock and the trickling of the sewer water.

Suddenly, his heart seized again.

The sewer water!

It had guided him to the entrance. Was it guiding someone else too? Was someone, at this very moment, standing on the other side of the entrance stone, face bunched up in thought, following the water's path to the bush and wondering why there was no pool or outlet? Had the trickle of sewer water become a large finger pointing to his hiding place?

He was trapped. Where could he run? In his exploration of the second level, he found what looked like an opening leading to another level, but it proved to be nothing more than a shaft that went straight down. How far, he didn't know.

He needed a hiding place.

Another sound from beyond the rock. Not whistling this time. But humming. The same recognizable tune. This time words were occasionally tossed in.

Thomas knew this song!

Sancte deus,
Sancte fortis,
Sancte misericors salvator,
Amarea morti ne tradas nos.

He strained from different angles to see through the crack, to get a glimpse of the person or persons above. But his vision was restricted to a thin, ragged portion of sky. Dare he move the stone?

No. Too risky.

The voice became louder. More words this time. So familiar.

A figure passed in front of the ragged opening. Thomas flinched. He wanted to descend the steps into the darkness to conceal himself. But he also wanted to see who was making that music. His curiosity won. Thomas pressed his forehead against the rock, his eye right up to the opening.

Nothing! He could see nothing but sky and the edge of the bush. He backed away. But just as he did, the singing continued! This time, however, the volume was diminishing. Whoever was out there was moving away from him. All Thomas had to do was wait and whoever was out there would soon be gone.

He couldn't do that. His curiosity was too great. There was something about the voice and the song that lured him. He had to venture a look.

Moving up one step, Thomas put his shoulder to the stone. As quietly as he could, he raised it just enough to enlarge the crack for him to poke his head out. His first effort wasn't enough.

Pushing against the rock a second time he managed to shift it even further. This time there was ample space. Cautiously, he raised himself until his eyes cleared the rim of the catacomb opening.

He saw the back of a single traveler moving away from him. Bulky. Wearing a black robe. A cleric.

Could it be?

Thomas glanced all around to see if there was anyone else nearby. There wasn't. The man was alone. He climbed out of the hole and followed the cleric a short distance. The man continued singing:

Sancte deus,
Sancte fortis. . .

From a distance, Thomas followed him down several streets, thinking that at any moment the cleric would meet up with someone. He didn't. He seemed to be alone.

Thomas was cautious. The risk was formidable. It could be a trap. But the longer he followed the cleric, the more convinced he was that the cleric was alone. He had to risk it. What other choices did he have? He was in an unknown country. He couldn't speak the language. And he was a wanted man. If it was a trap, at least he would know where he stood.

It was decided. But he wasn't so foolish as not to take precautions. They had wandered far from the catacomb entrance. His hiding place was still a secret. Should it be a trap, Thomas could simply make another run for it.

It wasn't much of a plan, but it was all he had. He closed the distance between himself and the humming cleric.

"Bishop Pole?"

The cleric gave a start. His hand flew to his heart. He whirled around.

"Thomas!" he cried.

"What are you doing out here?" Thomas asked.

"Searching for you, my boy. Searching for you."

❧ ❦

BISHOP POLE GAZED WITH wonder at the frescoes on the catacomb walls. It had been a tight fit for him navigating down the narrow stairways, but with a little maneuvering he had managed to make it to the second-level chamber.

"I had a hunch you might come to the hollows," he said.

"The hollows?"

"The catacombs. Derived from the Latin, *ad catacumbas*, meaning 'at the hollows.'"

Thomas smiled warily and nodded. He'd known that, once he'd decided to reveal himself to the bishop, there would come a moment of truth when he would have to decide whether to trust the man. When the bishop had urged him to return to the Vatican, Thomas had countered with the catacombs—and this only after he was completely confident that the bishop was indeed alone. The catacombs would give Thomas time to evaluate the bishop's motives more fully.

"Singing the chant was a brilliant idea," Thomas said.

The bishop grinned. "I thought so," he said. "It was something the two of us shared."

"Had it not been for the song I never would have given a passerby a second thought."

"Then it served its purpose well."

For several moments they sat in silence, gazing at the small fire. A thin pillar of smoke rose from it to the ceiling and gathered there, billowing like a thundercloud.

"I hope you'll reconsider and return to the Vatican with me," the bishop said.

Thomas thought about this a moment. "How can I be sure it's safe?" he asked.

The bishop expressed surprise. "Thomas, you wound me! Do you think for one moment I would lead you to harm?"

Not intentionally, Thomas thought. He said, "You abandoned me to the cardinals."

The bishop's face reddened. "Things did not turn out as I planned," he said. "That was an unfortunate encounter."

"The truth is, the English translation never had a chance. You sought to destroy it all along."

"That's not true!" the bishop cried. "At any time I could have seen that the translation was destroyed. I could have had Bromley destroy it in Fearnleah."

"Why didn't you?"

"Let me answer your question with one of my own: Why did you tell me of its existence? I am a representative of the Church whose position on such translations is clearly hostile."

Thomas thought a moment, then said, "The day you returned to Fearnleah, you persuaded Bailiff Bromley not to arrest me. And then, even though you knew that I was working with Dr. Wycliffe, you befriended me. And when Lord

Harborough weakened and Bromley shut down the scriptorium, I needed someone to turn to. I figured our friendship was greater than our differences."

"And so it is!" the bishop cried.

"Still, you never intended to champion the English translation with me."

"It's a blasphemous work, Thomas! My hope was that the cardinals and I could convince you of this. Come back with me. Sit down with true biblical scholars. Let them open your eyes to the truth! You have always wanted to attend Oxford, true? Thomas, this is even better!"

Thomas stared at the fire noncommittally. But he had to admit to himself that the offer to study with Vatican scholars was appealing enough to confuse him even more.

The bishop leaned forward and spoke in a reassuring tone: "Believe me when I say that no one wants to harm you, Thomas. Granted, the cardinals' zeal can be heated at times. But you must remember that the administration of the Church of God has been granted to them as a sacred trust. One day they will stand before the judgment seat of the Almighty and give an account of their stewardship. So if they are zealous, they are zealous for the Church of God. As am I, Thomas, as am I."

Thomas said nothing. Neither did he look at the bishop, concentrating instead on stirring the fire. He could feel the bishop's reassurances working on him like a balm. Thomas wanted to believe him. But the more he thought about it the more he wanted simply to walk out of this place, to leave the strife behind, to board a ship and go home where he could lose himself in Felice's arms and forget he had ever journeyed to Italy.

Whatever had made him think he could change the world all by himself? Who was he to challenge—or consort for that matter—with Vatican scholars who had studied the Scriptures for more years than he had lived? Who did he think he was to come here and challenge Church leaders? He was nothing. Nobody. A peasant without a scholastic degree. Mostly likely the bastard son of an English nobleman and a servant girl. Let them have their Church and their Bible. All he wanted was to go home.

"Come back with me, Thomas. All is not lost. We can make amends. I am confident that, given time, the cardinals will see in you the potential that I see."

His head lowered, Thomas said softly, "I want to go home to England."

The bishop rubbed his eyes wearily and stood. He arched his back to stretch out the aches.

"Do you ever wonder about the people who lie in these *loculi?*" he asked.

"*Loculi?*"

"The early Christians called them *loculi*—sleeping places, the recesses in the walls. Who were these people? What was life like in their day? What were their hopes? Their dreams? Whom did they love? Hate? How did they die? Did they have any regrets?"

Thomas stood. He too stretched and stared at the walls.

"For example, look over here," the bishop said, pointing to writing scratched in the wall. "*Cuius dies inluxit* . . . 'the day in which she entered into light.'" He turned toward Thomas. "Have you thought about death, Thomas? Have you ever wondered what it would be like to die? What was it like for this woman the day she entered into the light? What is it like for her now to live in that light?"

In truth, Thomas had not given much thought to death. It was a common enough occurrence, he supposed. But he had been too engrossed with his studies to give much thought to dying. At the moment, however, it seemed a natural enough subject, standing here surrounded by the dead. Yet it wasn't the corpses that made Thomas feel uneasy, it was the peculiar tone in the bishop's voice when he talked about death.

"Here is another one," the bishop said, pointing to words someone had scratched into the walls. He read the words aloud: "'O holy Souls, remember Marcianus, Successus, Severus and all our brethren.'" The bishop's eyes had a catlike quality when he swung around. "Who were these men? Close friends? Or are they listed together because they were martyred on the same day? And what of the admonition itself? Is there anyone alive today who knows their story, possibly passed down from generation to generation? Fascinating stuff, Thomas! Fascinating! It's almost as though we are standing on the threshold that separates this world from the next."

For the next hour or so the bishop encompassed the room in this way, reading the writing scratched in the walls, analyzing the primitive frescoes, and wondering aloud about the people who labored in this chamber in hopes of preserving the memory of those who lay in the recesses.

Thomas mostly listened. Though the topic was eerie, he was reminded of the many hours the two of them had spent studying chants. Once again, it was teacher and student.

When the room's teaching material was exhausted, the bishop returned to the fire. His eyes sparkled when he looked at Thomas as they had during the afternoon of Christ's Mass. "Think of the fun we can have learning together, Thomas! What can I do to persuade you to return with me to the Vatican?"

They were once again sitting opposite each other in front of the fire. Bishop Pole's shadow loomed against the far side of the catacomb wall exaggerating his every movement.

Again, the bishop had managed to revive Thomas's love of learning, but it was no match for his yearning to return home. He said, "I want to thank you for all that you have done for me. But come morning I'll go to the estuary and negotiate passage back to England."

He said this to test the bishop. The cleric's answer would not only confirm Thomas's status with the cardinals at the Vatican but also the bishop's true position.

For several moments, Bishop Pole stared at the wall behind Thomas. The random movement of unfocused eyes suggested he was searching for the words to express a thought that was difficult for him.

"What I'm going to tell you," the bishop said haltingly, "no one else knows save God alone."

He spoke with a muted tone as though he feared the dead themselves might be listening. Nervously, he settled and resettled himself, clasping and unclasping his hands. His gaze shifted to the fire, but his eyes saw the past.

"On the night Lord Harborough brought Callie—your mother—to the parish church, he confessed to me that he had had his way with her. It had been a random act of passion. The lord was quite shaken by it all. To his unmitigated horror, he had sacrificed

194

a lifetime of cherished beliefs for a moment of fleshly pleasure. Fearing a recurrence of this heinous sin, he sought shelter for your mother outside the manor, for her sake as well as his."

The bishop fell silent.

Thomas waited for more, but none seemed to be forthcoming. This was hardly the news he'd expected. Was the bishop now waiting for some kind of response from him? With a voice barely more than a whisper, he said, "You have confirmed what I have suspected for years."

The bishop lifted his head. "You know?"

Thomas nodded. "I've more or less assumed it—what with the village rumors together with the guardianship Lord Harborough has always extended to me."

The bishop nodded. There was more, as Thomas had suspected. He could see it in the bishop's eyes. It was a look that went beyond hesitation and reluctance. Was it fear?

"I've wanted to tell you . . ." He stopped, choked back emotion, then began again. "I've wanted to tell you this since the day I returned to England and saw you standing in front of that cottage. I was astonished at how much you'd grown and how learned you'd become in spite of a lack of formal training."

Again the bishop's gaze fell onto the fire. It seemed to fuel his resolve.

"I remember well that night when Lord Harborough delivered your mother. I remember feeling disgust for the man. Here was a nobleman, a man of power and stature, a man of upbringing, heretofore an exemplary model of Christianity, and for him to have allowed himself to succumb to such base desires . . ."

The bishop's voice trailed off. He was reliving the emotions of that night. Thomas could see the disgust in his eyes.

When he next spoke his voice was softer. "Then . . . he brought the girl in. She emerged from the darkness . . . and the light of the candles seemed to grace her countenance, her hair, her eyes. Never, never before had I beheld a woman of such natural beauty, one so attractive . . . alluring . . . and without any effort on her part. It was simply who she was . . . and . . ." He began to weep. "God forgive me. In that moment, I understood Lord Harborough's weakness. I knew his temptation—I knew it, because I shared it. Me, a man who had never once battled with lust. A man so in love with the Church he had never been tempted by a woman! But in that instant, a battle was waged—and lost—within my soul. For I knew I must have her. I must have her!"

Thomas's heart quickened. Was the bishop saying what he thought he was saying?

"You must believe me, Thomas," the bishop pleaded, "that I fought it for days. I busied myself with manual labor. I took long rides to the farthest reaches of the parish just to put distance between us. And I prayed. Oh, how I prayed! As God is my witness, Thomas, I prayed for strength to resist this temptation."

Earnest tears glistened in the bishop's eyes. He shook his head helplessly from side to side.

"My prayers, my resolve, my righteous intentions . . . all for nought! Nothing . . . *nothing* was able to quench the fire that raged within me! And so, one rainy summer evening . . ."

His tears flowed freely now and he did nothing to stop them. With uplifted head, he looked Thomas in the eyes as he made his confession.

"I stole into your mother's room . . . and forced myself upon her."

Emotionally exhausted, the bishop's chin dropped to his chest. He wiped his cheeks with the palms of his hands.

Thomas stared at him, struck senseless by the bishop's confession. It was as though he'd never seen the man before this moment. Completely numb, bereft of all thought and feeling, Thomas stared at him. Like a marble statue with blank eyes, he stared.

With raspy voice the bishop continued. "I never meant to hurt her! Thomas, please believe that! I know how foolish it sounds, but I never meant to hurt her."

The bishop looked to Thomas for some indication of absolution. There was none forthcoming.

"Sometime later that night," he continued, "she ran away. I went after her, knowing she had no family, no place to go. I found her huddled beside a stone fence, seeking shelter from the rain. She was drenched and shivering. Somehow I managed to convince her to return to the church with me, promising profusely that what had happened would never happen again." The bishop sighed heavily. "And by the grace of God I made good my word. Then, after several weeks, it became clear that Callie was with child."

Thoughts and feelings and words whirled within Thomas's head, round and round and round like a top.

"Thomas! Please listen to me!" the bishop pleaded. "Do you believe that good can come from evil? Because if you do, you can understand how I felt the day I saw you standing outside that cottage at Fearnleah! O Thomas, don't you see? Right then I knew . . . I *knew* that God had taken my sin and turned it into something wonderful! It was you, Thomas! You!"

Using the wall for support, Thomas struggled to his feet. His head felt like it was splitting. "You're telling me . . ." The words were there, he just found it incredibly difficult to speak them. "You're telling me that *you're* my father?"

The bishop paused, weighing his words. "Of course, it's possible Lord Harborough is really your father, but how else would you explain the fact that you and I are so much alike? We're of the same height and build. And then there's your gift for languages, and love of music, and history, and theology! It all adds up, Thomas!"

"So that's why you've been—"

"Protecting you? Mentoring you? Treating you like . . ."

Thomas completed the sentence. "A son."

"I remember the day you were born, Thomas! I watched over you from a distance."

"You were there when I was born?"

The bishop smiled warmly. "The image of your mother cradling you as a newborn infant in her arms—"

"You were *there?* But my mother fled the church. I was born at the base of an abandoned tower."

"That's right, Thomas. And as God is my witness, I don't know why your mother ran away just as she was giving birth. I've asked myself a hundred times—"

"You were there when I was born?"

"Yes, I was. I saw your mother leave. I followed her."

"You followed her?"

"I watched her give birth from a distance."

"And you did nothing to help?"

"Thomas, what do priests know of birthing babies? My presence served no useful purpose other than to behold the miracle! Besides, your mother was remarkable, it was as though she'd given birth dozens of times before. And should she have needed help—"

"You left her there."

The bishop flushed. In his exuberance, he'd said too much.

"Thomas, believe me, your mother was doing just fine when—"

"She died at the base of that tower."

"There was no hint of any trouble—"

"She died with a stick in her hand."

"Who told you that?"

"Howel. He said my mother had a stick in her hand when he found her."

"I didn't know that."

"What was the stick for, bishop? Howel thought she was defending me from animals. Maybe she was defending herself from you."

A blow to the face would not have caused Bishop Pole to recoil any more than from this accusation. "How can you—"

"At *best* you abandoned her and me!" Thomas shouted. "You left us there to die."

"Thomas, I had duties. I could not stay there."

"What sort of man abandons a woman and a newborn infant?"

"Thomas, try to understand—"

"Had you not left her, my mother might not have died!"

"You can't say that for certain, Thomas!" the bishop shouted defensively.

"What can we say for certain?" Thomas said. "One, you raped a young woman who was brought to you for protection. Two, she ran away to give birth and died in the process. You were there. You could have helped, but you didn't."

"My sin has haunted me all these years—"

"Now let's fill in the blanks," Thomas interrupted. "What kind of thoughts do you suppose would go through a man's mind at such moments? Maybe he would think that since Lord Harborough had already violated the poor thing, he could do so with impunity. After all, if she were to become pregnant, she would never know for certain the identity of the father. And when she does become pregnant, maybe the priest goes to her to try to convince her that she would be better off claiming that the lord of the manor is the father rather than a poor parish priest. Maybe, in her confusion and shame, the young woman runs away, not wanting to accuse anyone. She gives birth. Then, something goes wrong and she dies. And maybe, just maybe, the priest who is watching all of this is secretly grateful, because the only person who knows his sin is now dead."

"Then why am I telling this to you now?" the bishop cried. "If my chief concern is secrecy, why tell you? Why tell anyone?"

Thomas's head hurt so badly it was painful to think, to talk, even to look at anything.

"No one else knows," the bishop pressed. "Why do I take the risk? One word from you and my career is finished! Why risk that, Thomas, if I didn't truly care? Why? *Why?*"

Thomas ducked his head, placing his hands over his ears. "I don't know!" he shouted.

He slumped against a wall and slid to the floor.

The bishop came to him and knelt beside him. With soothing words, he said, "Thomas, regardless of past events, I love you as a father loves a son. Doesn't that count for something?"

The bishop's words bounced off Thomas and fell to the floor. At the moment, Thomas was no longer thinking, no longer feeling. A singular thought was lodged in his brain; all other rhetoric, logic, and discussion served as so much packing material around it.

"Tomorrow I sail for England," he whimpered.

"Thomas, I know this is difficult for you to understand. Give it time. Come back with me to—"

"I'm going home to England!" Thomas insisted.

At first there was only silence. A minute passed, two, then three. Finally, in a resigned tone the bishop said, "I'll go with you to the estuary."

Thomas shook his head.

The bishop persisted. "There is a ship sailing for England with the tide. I know the captain and I can get you passage. Maybe when you get home, you can reflect on what you've heard tonight and find it in your heart to forgive a foolish man."

Thomas didn't move. Nor did he acknowledge that he'd heard the bishop. Confusion and exhaustion were his covers, cloaking him until his eyes fluttered closed and merciful slumber stole him away from the chaos of the waking world.

Bishop Pole sat at a distance and watched the boy sleep fitfully. His heart was heavy within him.

It went without saying that he'd hoped for a different reaction. In anticipating the boy's response, he had expected some initial confusion, some anger. His mistake was in allowing his enthusiasm to override his control of the facts. He shouldn't have admitted to being present at the boy's birth. That mistake had cost him his son—which, in turn, complicated his present predicament.

Oh, what to do, what to do?

He couldn't allow Thomas to return to England. Bailiff Bromley would have both their heads. And it seemed increasingly unlikely that Thomas would willingly return with him to the Vatican. Even if he did, what reception would he get? In all likelihood, the cardinals would design a punishment that would serve as a warning to anyone else who would dare translate the Bible into a foreign language. The bishop knew that he'd stretched his assurances to Thomas beyond what he could reasonably expect, but not beyond what he hoped for. And the boy couldn't have a more passionate advocate.

The bishop moaned. He was running out of alternatives.

And what of his own predicament? Returning to the Vatican without the boy would be political suicide. Cardinal Barberini would ship him off to some mountainous monastery where he'd spend his days in ignominious obscurity.

Suddenly the bishop's surroundings seemed ironically appropriate, for his grand plan to restore England to the Church's good graces was as good as dead.

He stared at the sleeping form of his son.

Time. That was all he really needed. Given time, he was confident under his tutelage Thomas would come to love the Church as he did—to love her like a mistress; to put her needs above his own desires; to protect her at the cost of his own life; to realize that no sacrifice on her behalf was too great.

The fire began producing more smoke than light, filling the chamber with a gray haze, stinging his eyes. Leaning forward, the bishop stirred the fire until it was bright again. Satisfied, he tossed the stirring stick on the top of the blaze.

Rubbing his eyes, he glanced around the room, forcing them to focus on the fresco paintings on the walls—Jesus holding a lamb in his arms; an open tomb with an angel hovering above it; Abraham and his son Isaac . . .

The bishop's gaze froze in place.

An image became a thought; the thought became an idea; the idea became a plan.

Could it be?

The plan sickened him, but he could not dispel it from his mind. He could think of no other option that satisfied all concerned. He told himself he couldn't do it. He told himself he must do it. Hadn't he just reminded himself that no sacrifice was too great for the advancement of the Church?

Didn't all great spiritual endeavors come at a price? Wasn't it the writer of the book of Hebrews who wrote that some were tortured and refused to be released that they might gain a better resurrection? And others faced jeers and floggings. Still others were chained and put in prison. They were stoned. Sawed in two. Put to death by the sword. They went about in sheepskins and goatskins, destitute, persecuted, and mistreated.

Was the bishop's plan any greater price than they had paid? They had moved ahead by faith. So must he. In obedience to God. For the good of the Church.

And it all made sense! England could still be saved. He would continue in his position at the Vatican. And most importantly, the Church would not suffer loss.

Still, he didn't know if he could go through with it. Surely, there must be another way! He could let Thomas return to England. No, there were Bromley and the cardinals to consider. He could slip out quietly now and inform the guards of Thomas's presence. The cardinals would have their vengeance—but Thomas would never forgive him, and the months he'd spent in England would be a loss.

There was no other way!

The bishop rested his head in his hands and rocked back and forth. He didn't want to do this. But he had no other choice. He wept and prayed for strength.

Lifting his head, he gazed at the fresco on the wall, the solution to his problem and the source of his agony. How ironic that the artwork of an anonymous believer who'd lived hundreds of years ago would offer the perfect solution to his dilemma.

Pole was mesmerized, emboldened by the simple crude brushstrokes. He saw an altar. And Abraham, a father who loved his son dearly. And Isaac, the son. Bound. Lying atop the altar. Abraham's dagger was raised over the boy. The sacrifice that God required.

The bishop knew exactly how Abraham must have felt.

Do you trust God? Will you willingly offer your son as a sacrifice?

Abraham had said yes.

Bishop Pole, rocking back and forth in the silence of the catacombs, whispered, "Yes. Yes, Lord, I am willing."

⁓ֆ ֆ⁓

Sancte deus,
Sancte fortis,
Sancte misericors salvator,
Amarea morti ne tradas nos.

Thomas hung suspended between the realms of slumber and waking. The chant pounded in his head. To which realm did it belong? The words sounded distant, as though they were coming from a far country. An unseen traveler perhaps. No, not just someone. Thomas recognized the voice. It belonged to Bishop Pole.

A dream? Possibly. Maybe not. His mind grabbed for a piece of wakefulness. Pushing himself away from the realm of dreams he reached for reality, where he managed to gain a foothold.

But now that he was almost there, he wasn't sure he wanted to remain. His head was splitting. His burnt fingers throbbed horribly. He was curled into a ball. His back ached, as did his hips. And he was shivering. With the growing realization of his physical condition, he moved closer to the waking world.

His eyes were still shut, but he was more awake than asleep. The words were clearer now. He identified them as coming from the waking realm.

Holy God,
Holy strong one,
Holy and merciful savior,
Do not betray us to bitter death.

The chanting stopped. For a time there was no sound at all except the crackle of the fire. Thomas began to lose his foothold in the waking world. Slumber was not done with him. She tugged at him, pulling him back into the darkness. He was content to let her do so. In the brief moments he'd been more awake than asleep, he'd remembered where he was and how much he hurt. Even worse, he'd remembered the events just before he drifted off.

Bishop Pole's confession.

His own confusion. Revulsion.

His outlaw status.

His distance from Felice.

Reality was too painful. Better to sleep, to succumb to the darkness. To escape. Forget. To lose himself in nothingness.

He began to slip into the dark reaches of his mind when the words began again. Not a chant. Different. Spoken. Solemn. Low.

Lord, as Abraham offered. . .

The dark tug pulled him away so he failed to hear the completion of the sentence. Then, like the ebb and flow of the tide, he was back.

Even so I . . . my son . . . now I understand . . . born for this purpose . . .

Bishop Pole's voice. Praying over him. Without opening his eyes Thomas winced. Prayer was not going to make him change his mind.

Take him now, Lord . . . thy kingdom . . . in the spirit with which Abraham offered . . .

Take him . . . to England. Thomas was going nowhere if not to England. In the morning. No matter who tries to stop . . .

. . . my offering to you . . . my son, fruit of my . . .

Take him . . . take him? Abraham offered . . . my offering?

Like a bolt of lighting, an image flashed in Thomas's mind. Abraham. Isaac. An altar. A dagger.

His eyes shot open. A menacing shadow stretched upward against the catacomb wall, higher and higher. At its apex, a shank, a point. A knife!

Thomas rolled. The blade aimed at his heart slammed into his shoulder, slicing the flesh, glancing off the bone; he could hear his scream echoing in the far reaches of the catacomb, and knew he had to move again, for another blow was coming. This time his eye caught a glimpse of the blade, sparkling in the firelight, spotted with his blood, raised high, quivering, now coming down. He rolled again and heard a clank, metal against stone—Pole had missed, and the miss had thrown him off balance, for the portly man lay sprawled across Thomas's legs, but he was scrambling to get up, to right himself, to attack again. Thomas rolled; he tried to push himself up; he was helpless on the floor, must get to his feet, must defend himself, but when he pushed with his injured arm it crumpled under him like a brittle twig. He crashed against the stone, his shoulder taking the brunt of his weight; white light flashed before his eyes, followed by blackness, though his eyes were still open. He was losing consciousness. *No, no, black out and you're dead; must move, keep moving!* The blade came down again—Thomas reversed the direction of his roll, but Pole had anticipated his move, overcompensated, missed.

How quickly his attacker was up again, raising the knife, ready to strike, to kill, cajoling Thomas to his death: "Don't struggle, Isaac didn't struggle, I'm sending you to the Father!" Thomas didn't want to go—not yet, anyway. His eyes darted this way and that, looking for either weapon or escape. Run to the first level, move the stone—no, it was too heavy, Pole was too quick, he'd be stabbed in the back as he tried. There must be another—Thomas spied the black shaft, the unfinished stairway or cistern. Pole was on his knees, lunging at him; Thomas rolled out of reach; another lunge, another roll, and this time he kept rolling, over and over, toward the shaft, not knowing how deep it was. It didn't matter. He was losing blood and consciousness; unless he escaped, he would die—the knife would find its mark. He rolled with all his might, Pole yelling something, crawling after him, lunging—then the floor disappeared; Thomas was falling, tumbling, hitting the sides of the stone cavity. Time and gravity were suspended. He was falling, but at least he was out of Pole's reach; at least he was safe.

Everything went black.

❧ ☙

BISHOP POLE STARED DOWN the shaft.

"Thomas?"

No response.

"Thomas? Can you hear me?"

Again, no response.

With a frustrated sigh, he slumped to a sitting position.

"Oh, Thomas, must you always do things the hard way?"

He rose and plucked a burning brand from the fire, then held it over the shaft and looked down. His hand was trembling. The light gave out before finding bottom.

"Thomas! If you can hear me, make a sound."

He strained to hear something, but heard nothing. With a tired groan he sat next to the shaft, waiting, listening. If Thomas was alive, it was only a matter of time before he would make a sound.

The bishop stayed beside the shaft in the second level of the catacombs well past the time he estimated that the sun would rise. Then, he made his way noisily up the steps to the first level, then into the daylight.

It was a ruse. He believed Thomas was playing possum, so he spent the day watching the hidden entrance, waiting for the stone to move and for Thomas to poke his head out. But the stone didn't move. Thomas never appeared.

As evening descended, the bishop tossed a fresh supply of firewood down the steps. He spent the night beside the shaft, listening as before. Listening for a grunt. Or a moan. Any sound that might indicate that Thomas was alive.

Come morning, when he'd heard nothing, he concluded that Thomas was dead. As he gathered himself to leave, he noticed a piece of cloth on the floor. Picking it up, he found that it had writing on it. Scripture. In English. He took the cloth with him and left the catacombs.

ELEVEN ∞

FELICE PILED THE STRIPS of cloth, inkwell, and quill pen atop the board she used as a lap desk and placed them inside the bottom drawer of a chest of drawers. She always put them away before retiring to bed because Bailiff Bromley had made it his practice to stop by at irregular intervals. He made only a cursory search, but why was one needed at all? Thomas wasn't there. Felice had concluded that the bailiff did it for no other reason than to anger her father—which it did. Still, it paid to be cautious. Last night, however, a headache struck with such force she could barely find her way to bed. The writing materials had been left out.

As she bent over to slide the drawer closed, blood rushed to her head. She winced, still feeling the effects of the headache. She stuffed the pile of cloth strips down to get the drawer to close. Without Thomas around to read to them, most of the cloth strips bore duplicate passages, but she continued to print them because she feared she'd lose her ability to print letters if she didn't practice.

Straightening herself, the blood drained from her head. White pain passed before her eyes. She had to place a hand on top of the chest of drawers to steady herself. As the wave of pain subsided, it was replaced by a steady throb.

She hated days like this. She knew she shouldn't complain. Rarely was she ill. And she'd heard stories of pain and suffering from other women that made her cringe at the remembrance. Maybe getting away from the musty, smoky odors of indoors would help.

She reached for her cloak. Would she need it? Spring had arrived, but its effects were inconsistent. Swinging open the door, she was greeted by pleasant warm air. Fresh, with the scent of tender grass. Leaving her cloak behind, she grabbed the sack of chicken feed and closed the door behind her.

She strolled leisurely, tossing the seed as the chickens came running. The sun was warm; the view sparkling clear. This was the second such spring since Thomas had left.

She had heard not a word from him or about him. If she dwelt on his absence, her heart would ache. If she didn't dwell on it—and this was what frightened her—she hardly missed him. The number of days on which she completed her daily chores without once thinking about him was increasing. Was this God's way of preparing her for a missive from Rome from Thomas—telling her that he had been offered a position there and that he was not returning?

There had been a time when thoughts like that would cast a gloom over the rest of her day. Now, she felt only a slight pang. Of course, she would be devastated by such news—but she also knew now that life without Thomas was possible.

Just then she noticed a hole at the base of her garden fence. Rabbits! Again! No matter what she tried, she couldn't keep them out of her garden!

With a frustrated sigh, she tossed the sack of feed aside and walked to the edge of the forest to gather twigs with which to repair the fence for probably the twelfth time this year already.

She had barely a handful of twigs when she noticed an approaching rider. The height of the pluming dust behind the horse indicated that the rider was riding hard. She watched unafraid. Danger came in twos or threes or more. Besides, she had a suspicion as to the rider's identity.

As the rider got closer, her suspicions were confirmed. It was Kendall. Not a week had gone by since Thomas's departure for Rome that Kendall had not visited her. In fact, his visits were so frequent that the town tongues had stopped wagging about them and had moved on to fresher bits of gossip.

Felice found herself smiling. Already the day was improving, though the speed with which he rode and the hour caused her some concern. He normally didn't visit this early.

Kendall's regular appearances and his gentlemanly manner and kindness had won over even her father. To her utter surprise, Howel had even invited Kendall to dinner one Sunday afternoon. The two men found common ground in that they both respected Thomas, cared for Felice, and despised Kendall's father. Felice took pleasure in the company of both men. Sunday dinner had become a regular event for the three of them.

Still riding hard, Kendall was close enough now she could see his face. It was clouded with bad news. Her heart lurched. Father? Had something happened to father in the field?

Felice dropped the twigs and ran to meet him. "Kendall, what is it? Is it father?"

Horse's hooves muted her questions as Kendall reined the steed to a halt. He was off the horse while the dust was still rising.

Kendall's eyes met hers. He started to say something, but nothing came out. Tears glistened in his eyes. They looked foreign there. She had never seen Kendall when he was not fully in control of his emotions. It frightened her.

Felice grabbed him by the arm. "Kendall, is it father? Is father hurt?"

Kendall shook his head. Whatever the news, he was having trouble getting it out.

"Kendall! Tell me!" Felice cried, nearly beside herself. In her mind she could see her father lying hurt in the field.

Finally, Kendall managed to spit out a couple of words. "Bishop Pole . . ."

The two words stung her. Not because of the person they represented, but because of the person associated with him. Thomas! Kendall had news of Thomas!

Gaining a measure of control, enough to speak, Kendall managed to say, ". . . returned. Bishop Pole has returned."

There was more. Such news would not create this kind of emotion. Felice wanted to hear it, but then again, she didn't want to hear. She feared the worst.

She cried, "And Thomas? Is Thomas with him?"

A fresh wave of emotion swept over Kendall. He was concerned for her. He knew the news was going to hurt her.

"Kendall, tell me!" Felice was frantic now.

"He's dead," Kendall cried. "Thomas is dead."

There it was. The news. Out in the open. It hit her like a wave crashing against rocky shoals.

Thomas dead? No, it couldn't be. Similar news had reached the village before, only to be found to be false. A mistaken identity. Another person with the same name. These kinds of mistakes were common.

"How do you know? Who told you?"

Kendall looked at her sadly. She could see it in his eyes. He wished his source was not credible. For her sake he wished it. "Bishop Pole," he said.

"You overheard him?"

Kendall shook his head. "I was standing next to my father when the bishop told him the news."

Then it was true! If it was any other source there might be an element of doubt. But not the bishop. The bishop would know.

Thomas . . . my Thomas . . . dead?

The last sliver of hope that the report was somehow false dissipated. Death had visited the village once again. And this time he'd taken her Thomas. How many other houses had he visited? What had made her think he would never darken her door again?

She remembered the last time she saw Thomas. Her fears had come true. There was no consolation in being right. Just the opposite. She had told him he would die. Predicted it. Had her prediction caused his death? She hated herself. What a horrible thing to say to a person. To tell them they're going to die. That they'd never return. She had planted the seed in his mind! And it had borne fruit. Her Thomas was dead!

Felice buried her head in Kendall's chest and sobbed convulsively. She could feel Kendall's cheek pressed hard against her hair. His chest heaved, for he was sobbing too.

Sitting in the middle of the road, Felice lost herself in his embrace.

❧ ☙

A WOODEN PLATFORM HAD been erected in front of the parish church for the town meeting. The location was as good as any other, considering that there was no central location in the sprawling village. For two days prior to the meeting, criers circulated among the villagers summoning the people to gather on this day. The penalty for failing to attend, fixed by Bailiff Bromley, was a tax equivalent to a year's wages.

Felice stood next to her father at the crowd's edge. His strong arm was wrapped securely around her shoulders. It provided security for her still-weak knees.

Three days had passed since she'd heard of Thomas's death. Yet she still found herself subject to sudden fits of weeping, often prompted by nothing at all. Her father too had wept when first he heard the news. It was the first time she'd ever seen her father cry, an image she would never forget. Like her, he had not yet recovered emotionally from the news. Each day he woke up somber and went to bed sullen.

Twin figures mounted the platform steps. Both men were dressed in black. Together, they represented authority in heaven and on earth. Bishop Pole and Bailiff Bromley. The absence of Lord Harborough went unexplained.

Felice spied Kendall standing at the foot of the platform steps. They exchanged nods. Although he had wanted to stand with her, his father had insisted he take a position near the platform in keeping with his role as son and heir-apparent to the bailiff's position.

The bailiff spoke first. Marching boldly to the front of the platform, he assumed an authoritative stance with his feet spread wide.

He shouted, "Bishop Pole, recently returned from Rome, wishes to address you on the subject of heresy. After which I will inform you of the law as it pertains to heretics."

Howel leaned toward his daughter. He said, "Ought to be an inspiring afternoon."

Hiding a grin, Felice shushed him. It was the first sign she'd seen that her father was getting over his grief.

Bromley stepped back to give the bishop center stage. Bishop Pole assumed the center position unhurriedly, in keeping with the image of a holy man. He carried a large piece of paper in his right hand.

"I begin on a sad note," he said. "Although I'm sure most of you have already heard, today we mourn the loss of one of our own. One of the brightest, most promising young men it has been my good fortune to know. I speak of Thomas Torr who departed with me on a journey to the Vatican, but who, for reasons God alone can fathom, died needlessly before he could complete the journey home.

"Thomas was killed when he lost his balance and fell down a deep shaft while we were exploring the catacombs of Rome. I wish I could convey to you the excitement of this young man in that historical city. We had gone to the catacombs because Thomas wanted to worship at the final resting place of the early Christian martyrs. Then, in a careless moment, he stumbled and fell to his death. I grieve with you. For I had come to love this young man as though he was my own son."

The bishop's voice broke with emotion. It took him several moments to recover. Felice and many of the other villagers shared his emotion, all except Bromley who wore an expression of disdain, an indication he felt the bishop was wasting time.

Collecting himself, the bishop began again. "At least Thomas did not die in vain, for his work in Rome has left a spiritual legacy that will shape England for generations to come."

It was a bold statement, one that was not wasted on this small village gathering. Even Felice set aside her grief in anticipation of what the bishop was to say next. The thought that one of their own had accomplished an historical landmark for England was exciting news.

"Again, mere words fail me. For I wish I could convey to you the scene of our bright young scholar engaged in theological debate with the most brilliant minds at the Vatican. And how, when these godly men demonstrated to him the error of Dr. Wycliffe's heretical translation of the Bible, Thomas not only was able to grasp such high and lofty concepts, but was able to embrace them as his very own."

Felice flinched. Could this be true? It didn't seem possible. Thomas concluding that Dr. Wycliffe's Bible was heretical?

"I cannot tell you how many cardinals approached me singing the praises of Thomas Torr. They were impressed beyond measure. And no more so than when he, as a symbolic gesture of his commitment to the Church and the Holy Bible, personally placed Dr. Wycliffe's translation in the fire and stood there until it was nothing more than ashes, lest a portion fall out and find its way into the hands of some unsuspecting reader and so corrupt his mind and lead him down a path to hell."

This was too much for Felice to believe. Thomas would never burn Dr. Wycliffe's translation! But how was she to know? Could the cardinals have changed Thomas's mind? She supposed that was possible.

Felice looked around her. No one else seemed to have a problem with what they heard. In fact, there was a glow about them. A glow of pride that one of their own was consulting with cardinals at the Vatican! Everyone, except Howel. He too seemed troubled by what he heard. His brow was furrowed and his head moved slowly side to side.

Bishop Pole lifted the paper he'd carried onto the platform. "This is Thomas's statement, signed by him and witnessed by two of the most powerful cardinals of the Vatican." Bishop Pole read the statement aloud. It condemned the Wycliffe Bible as the work of an unrepentant heretic. Furthermore, it condemned all who read it or distributed it. Finally, it affirmed that the Holy Word of God had been entrusted to the Church for safekeeping and that any dissemination of the Bible without the approval of the Church was a sin against God and His Holy Church.

Holding high the paper, the bishop pointed to the bottom portion. He said, "Signed by Thomas Torr!"

The villagers erupted with cheers.

Their jubilation did nothing to erase Felice's doubts.

"Our original plan was for Thomas and me jointly to present this to the King of England. Due to Thomas's unfortunate demise, I am forced to do it alone. But be assured, King Richard will most certainly hear not only this statement, but also of the heroic faith and deeds of Thomas Torr of Fearnleah! And may God be merciful to us all."

Sustained shouts and cheers rippled like waves across the crowd.

Felice could feel her father's breath next to her ear. He said, "That doesn't sound like our Thomas."

"No, it doesn't," she agreed.

Bromley was once again center platform. "In response to what you have just heard, let it be known that I will redouble my efforts to track down and punish all who print and distribute the heresy of Dr. Wycliffe. Any information you might have regarding this renegade Scripture and those who promote it will be rewarded. As long as I am bailiff of this region, Fearnleah will remain loyal to both King and Church. Those who would attack either of these with their seditious acts or writings will be hunted down, captured, and put to death."

The villagers went wild. Never before had Felice seen the town in such a mood, not even during the Christ's Mass celebration or carnival days.

Again, her father leaned close to her to speak. "I wonder where Lord Harborough is? You would think he would be here for such an occasion."

Before Felice could respond, a sudden hush fell over the townspeople closest to them. Looking up, she saw why. Bishop Pole had left the platform. He was walking toward them.

Standing before them, the bishop took Felice by the hand. "My sincere condolences over Thomas's death," he said. "I'm sure you already know this, but he loved you very much. Yes, he confided in me. There were several times in Rome when he turned to me and said, 'My only regret is that Felice is not here to see this,' or 'I wish Felice could hear this.' He so much wanted you to understand the transformation that took place in his thinking."

Felice didn't know what to say. For some reason the bishop's words did not ring true. But she had nothing upon which to base her doubts. For the moment, she chose a cordial route.

"Thank you, your Excellency," she said. She used the moment to search the bishop's eyes. She saw only concern and sympathy in them.

"Thomas's death is an unthinkable loss for us all," said the bishop. "However, I am consoled by the fact that he lived long enough to complete his quest for the truth and guide others to follow him through this printed statement."

"May I see it?" Felice asked.

The bishop gazed at her with a puzzled expression. "You can read?"

"Just seeing and touching the document will allow me to feel close to Thomas one last time."

The bishop smiled condescendingly. He produced the document. While she rested her palm on the surface of the document, her gaze went straight to Thomas's signature, an action not lost on the bishop.

"Thank you for your kindness," she said to him.

"Oh! I almost forgot!" cried the bishop. "I have something else for you."

Reaching beneath his robe he brought out a strip of cloth, the sight of which took Felice's breath away. She gasped.

"I thought you would recognize it," the bishop smiled. He scanned the crowd around him, then leaned closer to her. "I wouldn't want Bailiff Bromley to see me giving this to you," he said magnanimously. "He wouldn't understand. But between us, we can appreciate this ragged tie to Thomas's past, in the days of his error. If nothing else, it's something for you to keep from his own hand."

The bishop held the cloth strip next to Thomas's signature on the paper document.

"Unmistakably from his hand, wouldn't you say?"

Felice compared the signature with the cloth strip. There were clear similarities in style between the two pieces of writing.

She accepted the cloth strip and discreetly tucked it away. "You are most kind," she said.

Bishop Pole extended his condolences one last time before leaving. Howel placed his arm around his daughter. "Let's go home," he said.

They were barely out of earshot from the other villagers when Felice whispered, "Something is wrong. Terribly wrong."

Howel looked at his daughter. Apparently the expression on her face distressed him enough to stop him in his tracks.

"Are you all right?" he asked.

"I don't know," she said. She was trembling.

"What is it? Tell me?"

She pulled out the cloth strip. "This is what's wrong."

"What about it?"

"You saw how it matched up with Thomas's signature?"

"Are you saying the two did not come from the same hand?"

"No, that's just the problem. It was obvious they were meant to look as though they came from the same hand."

"I don't understand," Howel said.

Felice held up the cloth strip. "Thomas did not print the words on this. I did."

❦

THE MEMORIES OF THE shaft haunted him.

Thomas lay in a torn hammock in a cramped compartment beneath the deck of a merchant galley. Bilge water sloshed beneath him. Its odor, while still disagreeable, no longer turned his stomach. The ship lay off the coast of France. They had just taken on supplies and would set sail with the tide in the morning.

He tried to get some sleep, but every time he closed his eyes, images of the shaft came to mind. His face pressed against the cold wet stone at the bottom of the pit. Slick with moss, wet, acrid; the bulk of his weight above him, pressing down on a bloody, knife-pierced arm, now shattered, or at least broken from taking the brunt of the fall; scrapes and cuts and bruises covered his arms and legs and face from bouncing against the walls as he tumbled down the shaft; lying there in the same position in which he'd landed, unable to move—knowing that if he did, the bishop would hear him and attempt to finish the job or send guards to do it or seal off the entrance to the catacombs and let nature take its course.

For days he'd lain there, as still as possible, afraid that the slightest movement, breath, cough, sneeze, moan would give him away; afraid that the bishop would pretend to leave, but then return—as he once had. So Thomas lay as still as death in the dark, dank, cold of the catacomb shaft, slipping in and out of consciousness, sucking on the bitter moss to quench his parched throat, not knowing if it was day or night, or how long he'd been down there; listening to the bishop's voice as it echoed down the shaft, first calling to him, then day after day torturing him by humming or singing the same song over and over and over as light from the fire flickered against the opening high above.

Sancte deus,
Sancte fortis,
Sancte misericors salvator,
Amarea morti ne tradas nos.

Then finally, nothing. No sound. No light. Still, he waited. One day? Two? Three? A week? Or merely hours? He had no way of knowing. No variance of light and dark; no pattern to his periods of consciousness and unconsciousness.

He waited until he feared he'd waited too long, was too weak to do anything to save himself.

His first movement was rewarded with pain so strong he nearly blacked out. How long it took him merely to right himself, he didn't know; but eventually his feet were where his head had been. Exhausted from the effort, he slumped to a sitting position, his knees against his chin.

While resting for his next effort, he took inventory of his injuries. His right arm was useless. He couldn't raise it from the shoulder; he couldn't flex his elbow; he couldn't feel, let alone move his fingers. But let it brush against the side of the shaft, and you would think someone had pummeled it with a blazing torch.

As for his other wounds, he had a large gash on his forehead and a multitude of bloody abrasions, which were irritated by matching ragged edges of ripped clothing. Some of the wounds and cloth edges were plastered together with dried blood.

In preparation for the climb out, he slept.

At first, getting out of the shaft seemed hopeless. He worked himself to his feet and must have groped the sides of the shaft a hundred times looking for something to grab, some place in which to wedge his foot. But there were no such places. So he attempted to make them. Using his good hand, he dug with his fingernails, and then with his shoes, attempting to gouge footholds in the side of the shaft. Though the rock was relatively soft as rocks go, his fingers were softer. His shoes managed to make progress, but it was slow going. He would work until he was exhausted, then he'd slump to the bottom of the shaft. Weary from effort and pain, he'd sleep.

A possible solution came to him one time upon awaking. He'd attempted to stretch by pushing his feet against the side of the shaft while pressing his back against the opposite side. In doing so, he lifted his backside off the ground.

That's when it came to him. Maybe he could walk out.

With his back pressed against the shaft, Thomas planted his feet on the opposite side. Wiggling first his feet, then his back up the side of the shaft he made upward progress. Soon, however, his legs would begin to tremble and his shoulders and neck would cramp. Reversing his course, he lowered himself to the bottom. Better this than falling.

He tried to think of another way out. But there was no other way. So he rested. Conserved his strength. Prayed. Steeled himself for one grand effort. The risk was great. Should he get halfway or further and should his strength give out, he would tumble to the bottom again. This time, in all likelihood, to his death.

The time came for him to try. He was as strong as he was going to be, given his injuries. No amount of waiting was going to make him any more ready.

Planting his feet against one side of the shaft, he pressed his shoulders against the other side and scooted himself up.

With no light above him, there was no way for him to know how far he'd climbed or how much farther he had to climb. After a time, his legs began to weaken and shake. His shoulders and neck cramped.

He continued on. It was too late to think of turning back.

Soon his legs were shaking uncontrollably. His shoulders and head ached so badly he couldn't think. Blind with pain, he inched his way up the shaft. He wasn't going to make it. His strength was gone. He would plummet to his death.

Then, miraculously, the crown of his head fell backward. There was no rock for it to hit! He was at the opening! His neck rested against the edge while his shoulders bore the weight! It was the most glorious feeling he'd ever felt.

Cautiously, for failure now would mean certain death, he worked his shoulders to the edge and with one final shove, he pushed himself over the edge, feet scrambling, his good hand pushing against the side, the floor, anything it touched.

There was a moment of teetering, when it could have gone either way. Then, his foot hit the edge. He pushed. And was over. Safe on the floor of the catacomb.

For how long, he didn't know, he lay there. Gasping for air. His muscles cramping. Shivering in the dark. But none of that mattered. He was out of the shaft!

When he'd recovered a measure of strength, he groped his way in the dark until he found the stairway to the first level, then the stairway to the secret entrance.

Just as he was ready to push aside the covering rock, he feared that Pole might have ordered the entryway sealed or guarded. There was only one way to find out. A shove with his good shoulder moved the rock. It hadn't been sealed. He cautiously poked his head out. He breathed easily for the first time in who knew how long. There was no guard. No one was in sight! Thomas exited the catacombs and once again felt the sun against his skin.

He continued from there under the assumption that Pole thought him dead. He had no reason to believe otherwise. And it was by sheer providence that on his way to the Tiber estuary, a short distance outside Rome, he stumbled upon a boarding house once heavily frequented by Crusaders on their holy pilgrimages to Jerusalem, now the haunt of merchant seamen.

Faint with hunger and weary to the bone, he entered the one-room structure intent on trading work for food or, if necessary, begging outright, unconcerned that language would be a barrier. Starvation was a universal language.

To his good fortune it was there he met Captain Wilford who frequented the establishment regularly, not so much for food but for physical comfort. Over his many years the captain and Elberta, the owner of the boarding house, had developed an unusual trading and personal relationship that they renewed every time the captain was in harbor.

It was the captain who'd sewn up Thomas's arm, handy with a needle from a lifetime of mending nets. Thomas's story came out, and Elberta, a lovelorn woman who still missed her husband though he'd been deceased eleven years, convinced the captain to provide Thomas passage back to England.

In exchange for his passage, Thomas was to serve as the captain's cabin boy—merely a pleasant name for galley slave. To the captain's delight, he learned that Thomas could read and even write—though with extreme difficulty, due to his burned fingers and broken arm. But Thomas's worst writing was better than the captain's, so he entered the log accounts each night with the captain dictating.

"Torr! Blast it, boy, where are you? Torr!"

Thomas scrambled out of his hammock and onto the deck.

"Are you gonna sleep all day, you no-good whelp?"

It amazed Thomas how congenial the captain had been whenever he was around Elberta. His sailors never saw that side of the captain.

"Get the portolano!" the captain bellowed.

Thomas ran into the captain's cabin and grabbed the book while, above him, sailors scurried on ropes and masts, unfurling the square sail.

Standing next to the captain, Thomas read aloud from the book, which listed coastal landmarks, harbors, and anchorages with distances and bearings and notes on tidal streams.

A fresh breeze rose up to fill the sails. The tide carried them out of the harbor and into the open sea. This was the job Thomas liked best on ship because with the passing of each landmark, he knew he was closer to home and Felice.

⚜

AN ENGLISH LANE. THE sun against his skin. Fresh air and plenty of room to stretch. How long had it been since he'd left English soil? Two and a half years. It seemed longer than that. How many English seasons had passed? He wasn't sure. He tried to piece it together, but succeeded only in confusing himself. Traveling had jumbled everything together.

What he did know was that the last five days had been heaven for him. Having been deposited along with the merchant's cargo by Captain Wilford in Portsmouth, he had begged rides and walked the distance between the seacoast and Fearnleah. England, in the fall. The air was so moist compared to Italy, Thomas felt himself shiver. He would adjust. This was home. And Felice was waiting for him. God alone knew what else awaited him, but he would take that in stride. By the grace of God, he was alive, he was almost home, and whatever came his way, he and Felice would find a way to face it together.

Thomas had no plans other than to marry the girl he loved and never leave home again. If he did nothing else but spend his days with Howel in the field, he would count himself the most blessed of men.

Of one thing he was certain. He wanted nothing more to do with Bible translations and churches and politics and theology and chants and lords and bishops and cardinals. He'd had his fill. Let them fight among themselves. The sooner all of them forgot the name Thomas Torr, the better. He couldn't fade into meaningless obscurity fast enough to suit his taste.

He thought it wise, at least at first, to enter Fearnleah as inconspicuously as possible. So the closer he got to the village, the more careful he was to avoid contact with other travelers. The fewer people who knew he was back in England, the better.

Thomas's heart escalated into a brisk trot as the homes on the edge of the village came into view with their thatched roofs and gardens and goats and ragged children playing fanciful games. This first glimpse of home warmed his insides in a way Rome never could, for all of its marbled majesty. It was late afternoon. He would be home in time for supper.

He took the longer route along the western edge of the village rather than pass through the heart of the population. And as a final rise separated him from Howel's house, he could barely contain himself. His skin became gooseflesh; tears welled in his eyes. It seemed like an eternity since he'd been home. So much had happened since he'd left. Most of it bad. He knew now, for certain, he never should have gone to Italy.

Climbing the rise, he nearly broke down and sobbed at his first sight of home. The house itself was shaded by the rise upon which he stood. A thin column of white smoke rose through a hole in the roof and twirled skyward. He wondered what Felice was cooking. What did it matter? Whatever it was, it would be the best tasting meal he'd ever had, simply because it had been prepared by her hands.

Chickens pecked aimlessly near the front door. Felice's perennial herbs were growing nicely in the garden. A movement in the corner at the base of the fence caught his eye. A rabbit was burrowing under it. Thomas grinned. Felice would not be pleased about that.

With the sun low in the sky, Howel would probably be home shortly. Thomas wanted to spend a few moments alone with Felice before her father arrived. Not that he didn't miss Howel too. If there was anyone whom he'd missed nearly as much as Felice, it was her father. Thomas couldn't ask for two better people with whom to share his life. And wouldn't the big ploughman be surprised when he opened the door tonight and saw Thomas sitting there?

With a contented sigh, Thomas started down the ridge. Then, abruptly, he stopped. Another movement caught his eye. This one much larger than a rabbit. Someone was emerging from the forest.

It was Felice!

But before Thomas's heart had the chance to skip a beat, he saw that she was not alone. A man was walking with her.

With her. Not beside her, with her. Thomas knew this because their hands were linked and swinging in unison between them.

Thomas squinted his eyes to see who was holding hands with his Felice. The fading sun and his poor eyesight made it difficult for him. But not so difficult that he couldn't identify a nobleman's clothing.

Kendall!

From atop the rise Thomas watched the two of them as they approached the house. They seemed in no hurry. Nor did they seem to be occupied with anything else save each other.

As they reached the door, Felice turned to Kendall.

The next moment was the blackest moment of Thomas's life. Nothing Bishop Pole or the cardinals or the Pope himself could ever do to him surprised him as deeply as he was surprised by what he witnessed. No pain was as great—no pierced arm, no burned fingers, no bruises and cuts from the fall, no stitches in his arm without anything to deaden the pain could hurt as much as he hurt at this moment.

In horror, Thomas watched as Felice placed her arms around Kendall's neck. He drew her to him. They kissed. At length. With passion.

They separated slightly and spoke words that Thomas could not hear, but he didn't have to hear them to understand their meaning. For barely had the last word been spoken between them when Felice and Kendall kissed again.

While their first kiss had pierced Thomas's heart like a knife, the second kiss twisted the knife mercilessly. He could not stand there and watch it any longer. It would kill him to see any more.

Turning away from the only home he knew, Thomas let the momentum of his own weight carry him down the hill. He placed one foot in front of the other, but he had no idea where he was going.

THE INCESSANT BUZZING OF flies woke him. He stirred. Remembered. And refused to open his eyes. There was no reason for him to get up. There was no reason for him to live.

Thomas could feel the sun beating down upon his back. His cheek was pressed against dry leaves. And there was a curious tingling sensation the length of his good arm.

He raised his head to look at the arm. As he did, leaves stuck to his cheek and temple. He didn't bother to brush them off. What for? He had to blink several times before the arm came into focus. When it did, he understood the sensation. A trail of ants had formed a highway from elbow to fingertip.

With a moan, he let his head drop to the ground. Ants. Flies. People. Life. What did he care?

Something nudged him in the side. He didn't move. An animal of some kind most likely. Couldn't it tell that he was dead?

He felt a second nudge like the first. Without looking up, he shooed whatever it was away.

This time it was a kick. A leather-booted kick, forceful enough to knock the wind from his lungs and turn him face upward.

Doubled over in pain, he blinked back the sun's bright light to get a look at his attacker. There were four of them. Their features obscured by the light, they towered over him like trees.

"Had a fight with the ol' wife, have we?"

"Or possibly a wee too much to drink?"

Thomas shielded his eyes to get a better look. It didn't help much.

"I have no money," he said. "Nor any relatives with money if you're thinking ransom. And if you're Good Samaritans? Go away and leave me alone. I don't want any of your goodwill."

He rolled back into his sleeping position.

Another kick to his side turned him face up again. That answered one question at least. They weren't Good Samaritans.

"What are you doing here?"

This voice was different. It had authority.

"Nothing to harm anyone," Thomas said. "I was sleeping."

"Stand up like a man."

Out of habit, Thomas leaned to his right. He winced back the pain as his right hand touched the ground. He shifted his weight to his left side, planted a hand, and managed to get up. Rather clumsily, but he was up.

Now that the sun was no longer behind his attackers, their features came into focus. Two he didn't recognize. Two he did. And from their expressions it was clear they recognized him too.

"Lookee what we have here!" said a man with a large, ugly scar on his left cheek that had cut his eye as well, leaving it closed.

"This is a curiosity," said the one with the authoritative voice. "It looks as though we have captured a dead hero. Amusing, don't you think? He doesn't look very dead to me! Does he look dead to you?"

Scar Face sized up Thomas. "Give me a moment or two with 'im. I could make him look real dead."

This prompted laughter from the other two men.

Thomas struggled to clear his head. "Cayle, we have no business with each other."

The broad-shouldered carpenter grinned appreciatively. "Ah! Master hero remembers me. I'm flattered. What with his consorting with lords and bishops and Popes, he even has time to remember the insignificant common people."

The inside of Thomas's head felt like it was stuffed with the leaves he'd slept upon. And the more he tried to clear them away, the more packed they became; and the more packed, the more painful, until his head hurt so badly he could barely see straight. The last thing he wanted to do right now was match wits with a carpenter-turned-revolutionary.

"This is a puzzle," Cayle said. "I have to ask myself, why would a hero be sleeping out in the open without so much as a weapon, without provisions, and within a short distance from the very town that has venerated him?"

Cayle's two nameless associates jumped in eagerly with answers.

"He got drunk and couldn't find his way 'ome!"

"I still say 'is wife tossed 'im out. From what I 'ear, 'eroes make lousy lovers."

Cayle laughed at this. He leaned toward Thomas and sniffed. "There's no odor of ale on him," he observed. "As for his amorous abilities . . ."

"'is *what* abilities?" one of the two asked.

His friend shoved him. "You *are* daft, aren't you? 'e means 'is value as a stud."

Raising his index finger, Cayle said, "But, my good fellows, you are overlooking a key characteristic of this man. You are forgetting that this man is dead. Our good Bishop Pole declared him so."

This was news to Thomas. So Pole had returned to England. And he believed Thomas was dead. If that was so, then ... He winced. It hurt to think. His bad arm was throbbing; his good arm itched from ant bites; the cold and dampness of the earth had seeped into his joints; and his stomach felt like it was caving inward.

Scar Face reached forward and shoved his shoulder. His right shoulder. Had he stabbed it with a knife it wouldn't have hurt more.

"Though I don't make it a practice to touch dead men," Scar Face said, "this one feels alive enough to me."

A different feeling was stirring inside Thomas. Anger. He was tired. Aching. And now angry. He had nothing these men wanted. And they had nothing he wanted.

"Care to enlighten us with the truth?" Cayle asked.

"No," Thomas said curtly. "Now, if you don't mind, I'll be on my way."

He lowered his head and attempted to pass between Cayle and Scar Face. Planting the flat of his hand against Thomas's chest, Scar Face shoved him back.

"You're not going anywhere!" he said through clenched teeth.

The four of them closed ranks around him. No longer was there any sign of merriment on their faces.

He addressed Cayle, easily the most intelligent among them. "I told you. I have no money. I have nothing to my name. Now let me pass."

Again he tried to step between Cayle and Scar Face with the same result, only harder. Thomas stumbled and fell on his backside. The impact jarred his aching head and stirred his simmering anger to a boil.

Pushing off with his good hand, he shouted and launched himself at Scar Face, plowing into his chest and bowling him over. The two of them tumbled to the ground.

Driven by pain and rage, Thomas yelled and pummeled Scar Face's midsection. With his first blow he could hear a rush of air expelling between the man's lips.

Hands grabbed him from behind and hauled him up. Somehow, Thomas managed to break free. Through his pain, his bad eyes, and the rising dust all around them, he could barely see. So he swung blindly with his good hand, first one direction, then another, then another.

He heard a whack and felt a sharp pain followed by a thud. He'd connected with someone. Knocked them to the ground.

"That'll teach you to—"

The next instant his eyes clamped shut. Reflex. Just when he thought the pain in his head couldn't get any worse, there was a thud and lightning struck between his eyes.

He felt his knees give way. Then, his equilibrium. He fell forward and raised a cloud of dust as his chest and face hit the ground.

The last thing he heard came from a voice directly over him: "Now why would he go and do a fool thing like that?"

TWELVE ⬌

CHICKENS. NO, GEESE. FROM the sound, Thomas concluded he was sitting in the midst of a gaggle of geese. His eyes were closed and his head pounded mercilessly. He became aware enough to know that he was sitting upright with his legs outstretched and with something hard jabbing into his back. All around him was a din of cackling with an occasional honk.

His head lolled to one side, threatening to send him back into the darkness from which he was emerging. Thomas fought the dark pull. His eyes fluttered, but saw nothing other than unfocused daylight. Then there were the geese sounds, the cackling and honking . . . but was it really honking? He listened harder. No, not unless geese had learned words . . . wait . . . not geese . . . children . . . children shouting, screaming.

The longer he listened the more distinct the sounds became. Too distinct at times. The louder ones hit his head like hurled rocks; the ear-splitting sound of children squealing in play, babies crying, people shouting or just talking. He added to their sound with a moan of his own.

His eyes made a second attempt to open. This time, after fluttering, they remained open and eventually focused. The image that clarified before him was that of Cayle seated on a rock. Sewing.

Thomas stretched his stiff neck and arms with a loud verbal complaint. He leaned forward. A glance backward revealed that the protruding pain in his back came from a jagged rock. His legs, devoid of feeling until now, began to tingle.

"It's your own fault," Cayle said, looking up from his sewing.

"My fault?" Two words. Both painful and difficult to say with a mouth and tongue as dry as cloth.

"It was foolish of you to attack Kleef."

"Kleef."

"The one with the scar on his cheek."

"I was defending myself. You were robbing me."

"Robbing you? Come, now. How can you accuse us of robbing you when by your own admission you had nothing of value?"

"You meant to harm me."

"If we had meant to harm you, why would we have brought you here?"

Thomas looked all around him. A succession of hills, grassy and rock strewn, stretched to the horizon. Crude shelters were erected against the larger rocks. Women busied themselves around boiling pots, some with little ones strapped to their backs or carried on their hips. Men could be seen fortifying shelters and repairing weapons. Older children supervised younger children with varying degrees of success. Sheep and goats and cows were bunched here and there; chickens wandered about idly. It was the kind of village scene one would expect to see in any of a hundred locations in England with one difference: this village had no buildings or cultivated land.

"All right, here's a harder one for you then," Thomas said. "If you didn't mean to harm me, why did that ox—what's his name? Kleef?—nearly cave in my ribs?"

"You'll have to excuse Kleef. He gets a little zealous at times. Doesn't comprehend his own strength."

Thomas couldn't help staring at his captor. Broad-shouldered, muscular, tall. Yet his large hands deftly manipulated a needle and thread. This image wasn't in keeping with the revolutionary, marauding, former Lord of Misrule.

"Why are you doing that?" Thomas asked.

"What? Sewing?" Cayle held up the pants and peered at Thomas through the half-closed hole. "It would be rather indecent of me to run around the countryside with a hole in my breeches, don't you think?"

"I mean, isn't there someone to do that sort of thing for you?"

"We each take care of our own things. And we each contribute according to our abilities for the greater good. Now it's my turn to ask a question. What's your story? Aren't you supposed to be dead?"

"That's two questions. Mind if I stand?"

Cayle shrugged. He watched as Thomas used the rock behind him to pull himself up with a few grunts and groans.

"Sarah!" Cayle shouted. The strength of his voice hammered against Thomas's head, prompting a reflexive wince. "Bring me a cup of ale for our guest here."

A black-haired young lady who was tending a half-dozen goats sprinted up a hill and disappeared over the summit. Several moments later she was back with a mug of ale, which she offered to Thomas along with a shy smile. Thomas thanked her and drank. His throat was so parched, the first swallow was nearly completely absorbed by the passageway without a drop reaching his stomach.

The young lady, very comely but dressed in nothing more than rags, left them immediately.

"Now, are you going to answer my questions?" Cayle asked.

"I just returned from Rome," Thomas said.

"On your way back to Fearnleah?"

It was an innocent question. Yet it brought to mind Felice and Kendall standing in front of the house. Embracing. Kissing. The wound in Thomas's heart was ripped open afresh. He didn't answer the question.

"Then tell me this," Cayle said, unaware of the pain his previous question had caused. "Why is Bishop Pole telling everyone you're dead?"

"Because he thinks I am."

Cayle lowered his sewing. Thomas's answer intrigued him.

At Thomas's request, Cayle related to him the story Pole was spreading throughout the countryside. He told Thomas about the purported confession. He also mentioned Bailiff Bromley's increased efforts to suppress the spread of the English version of the Bible. In return, Thomas narrated the events as they actually happened, including his appearance before the cardinals, the events in the catacombs, and his passage home aboard an English merchant ship.

"So what will you do now?" Cayle asked. "Go home to that pretty young thing I saw you with at Lord Harborough's manor?"

Thomas attempted to fend off the jab by drinking the last of the ale. His defense proved inadequate. Cayle's reference to Felice hit him hard. "There is no longer anything there for me," he said.

Maybe it was good for him to say the words. They helped him face the truth.

Cayle nodded knowingly. "Things changed in your absence, did they? Happens all too frequently."

Thomas knew that to be true; he had just never thought it would happen to him and Felice. How could she do this to him? Even considering that she must believe he was dead, how could she kiss Kendall so soon afterward? Something must have been there between them all along.

"When do you plan to unmask the devious Bishop Pole?" Cayle asked.

"What?"

"Certainly you're going to expose him."

Thomas shook his head.

"What?" Cayle shouted. He slid off the rock in disbelief. "You're going to let him get away with it?"

"What does it matter? My life is ruined regardless. I want nothing to do with him or anything related to him."

"And what about what he does to others in your name? Don't you care about them either?"

Thomas hung his head. "I don't care about anything anymore."

Cayle snorted in disgust. For a time he returned his attention to his sewing; the stabbing motion was much more pronounced.

"Where will you stay?" he asked.

Thomas shrugged.

"You can stay with us if you desire," Cayle said.

Thomas looked around him and slowly shook his head. He didn't want to be around anyone right now. All he wanted was for everyone to leave him alone, and he would be happy to return the favor.

A raised eyebrow was Cayle's response. He continued sewing.

Thomas plunked the empty mug atop the rock. "Am I free to go?" he asked.

"I already told you. You're not our prisoner."

"Well then, I'll be going." Thomas looked one way, then another, unsure as to where he was. Not knowing where he was, he didn't know in which direction to head. But then, did it matter? He had no place to go anyway. So he headed down the hill.

"I once was like you," Cayle said to his back.

Thomas stopped and turned.

"At the time, my world was limited to the confines of my family's carpentry shop. If something happened outside the shop, as far as I was concerned it didn't happen at all."

Thomas turned warily. "What made you change?"

"Without asking my permission, the world charged into our shop like an enraged bull, and I was helpless to stop it. The bull came in the form of Bailiff Bromley when he commissioned my father to add a room to his manor."

"On the eastern wing," Thomas said.

Cayle looked at him surprised. "How'd you know that?"

"I lived there at the time. I was Kendall's study partner."

Cayle grunted, then continued. "It took my father a week longer than the agreed-upon completion time to finish the job."

"I remember. Bromley was furious."

"He refused to pay my father for the work he'd done."

"From what I heard, an agreement had been written into the contract to the effect that if the job was not completed on time, Bromley was under no obligation to pay. I remember that because I never understood why a man would agree to a contract like that."

"My father signed that contract because he needed the money to feed his family," Cayle replied. "And because he knew he could complete the job in the required time."

"But he didn't."

"No, he didn't. And do you know why?"

Thomas shook his head.

"Because Bailiff Bromley caused the delay. He saw to it that the delivery of the timber was held up for nearly a month."

"And when your father learned of this?"

"First he confronted Bromley. Then, he went to Lord Harborough."

"What did Lord Harborough do?"

"Nothing."

"Nothing! Why not?"

"My father couldn't convince anyone to testify against Bromley. So Lord Harborough dismissed my father's charges for lack of proof."

Thomas grunted. This kind of story was all too common.

"Two months later he charged my father with sedition against the Crown. The charges were completely fabricated. He had my father taken to London for trial, where he was condemned and sent to prison. He died there within a year. After my father's arrest, I couldn't land any jobs. Who wants to hire the son of an insurrectionist? So, we were forced to sell the shop. My mother died of pneumonia a month later."

"I'm sorry."

"It's amazing to me now, but even then I accepted my fate. That's just the way things are, I told myself. If I were the son of a nobleman, it would be different. But I wasn't. So that was that.

"Then, one day, I heard a traveling preacher. One of them Lollard fellows. He spoke about Moses and the people of Israel in bondage in Egypt, and how Moses led them out of slavery and gave them their own land."

Thomas stared at the grass as his memory stirred. He spoke softly, "'And the Lord said, I have surely seen the affliction of my people and have heard their cry; for I know their sorrows, and I am come down to deliver them.'"

Cayle gazed at him with wonder. "You know the story?"

"I've translated the passage."

"Then you know the work of the Lollards?"

Thomas nodded.

Cayle scrutinized him for a long time. Then, with the expression of an excited child, he said, "Come with me."

Without looking back to see if Thomas was following, Cayle led him through the maze of tents and fires and animals. Men glanced up from their work and women from their fires as they passed by; children stopped their playing to gape at them openly. Kleef was among those watching them. He snarled as Thomas passed by.

Upon reaching a lean-to atop the highest of the hills, Cayle tossed his unfinished breeches aside. Reaching into the back of the lean-to he pulled out a book and handed it to Thomas.

It was an English translation of the Bible.

"Where did you get this?" Thomas asked.

"It belongs to the traveling preacher I told you about."

It was with mixed feelings that Thomas opened the Bible, thumbing its pages at random. He held in his hands everything he loved and hated.

"It was from stories I heard from this Bible," Cayle said excitedly, "that I began to realize that our times are not so different from those of Moses. His people were slaves to the Egyptian taskmasters. Our people are slaves to wealthy English nobles, and our taskmaster is Bailiff Bromley. All these people you see? Every one of them has had his home and farm or livelihood taken from him at the whim of a nobleman or the bailiff—they couldn't pay the taxes, they wouldn't bend to the nobleman's wishes, or just out of pure meanness. These are the oppressed."

Thomas looked out at the people populating the hills. It was easy for him to see the resemblance between them and the tribes of Israel wandering in the wilderness. It was also easy for him to identify with their status as victims. Hadn't his entire life been determined by the sexual whim of a nobleman?

"Whether you want to admit it or not, Thomas, you're one of us. From what you've told me, you've experienced firsthand the heavy-handed authority that rules this land, whether it be King or Church."

Thomas closed the Bible. "I should be on my way," he said.

Cayle reached over and opened it again. "Are you telling me that this book offers these people no hope?"

Thomas looked away, not wanting to admit the truth.

"Isn't there something in there about the words of this book setting people free?"

"'And ye shall know the truth, and truth shall set ye free.'" The words came out unbidden. Without thought, they were there on Thomas's lips. The immediacy of their appearance pleased Cayle and frightened Thomas.

"And what about the story of that little shepherd besting a warrior giant? That's in there, isn't it?"

"David and Goliath."

"So when it comes to the powerful English nobles and bishops and these people scattered on the hills, which do you think is David and which is Goliath?"

"It's not that easy," Thomas said.

"Isn't it? Or do you just not want to see it?"

Again Thomas closed the book. "Why are you doing this to me?" he asked. "I have nothing to offer you that you don't already have."

"We need someone who knows what's in this Bible and who can teach it to the people in a way they can understand it. Believe me, Thomas, it unites them in ways you cannot begin to imagine."

"That's the work of your Lollard friend. Let him teach the people."

Cayle sobered. "He's in a London prison. Bromley's work. Though we could not save our teacher, two men gave their lives to keep this book from getting into Bromley's hands."

Thomas was not immune to the charisma and passion of the man opposite him. He understood why so many people had allied themselves with him. But Thomas was not about to be one of them.

"I'm sorry," he said, handing the book back.

Disappointment and irritation were evident in Cayle's features. It was short-lived. A commotion in the distance caught the leader's attention. He glanced over Thomas's shoulder to see what was happening.

Thomas thought to use the distraction to his benefit. He stood. "I really must be going now," he said.

"Yes, I suppose you must," Cayle said, standing. "Could I persuade you to do one thing for me?"

"What's that?"

"As you are running, would you carry this with you and protect it?" He shoved the Bible into Thomas's chest without taking his eyes off whatever was happening behind Thomas.

"Running?" Thomas asked. He turned to see what Cayle was looking at. A line of horsemen followed by several rows of foot soldiers were descending upon the camp.

"Bromley's men," Cayle said, grabbing a few of his belongings.

Thomas stood there. Frozen.

"I suggest you run," Cayle said. "I doubt that they'll give you a chance to explain that you're really not one of us."

With that, the leader scampered down the side of the hill, shouting directions to all within earshot as he went.

Thomas groaned. He turned and ran, halfhearted at first, then after glancing over his shoulder and seeing the upraised weapons and hearing the thunderous pounding of an entire line of horses' hooves, he gripped the Bible and ran with all his might.

How clever of Cayle to shove the Bible into my hands, he thought. *If I escape being killed, it will be I who will spend the rest of my days in a London prison. I'll probably share a cell with his Lollard friend.*

The snort of a horse warned him that a soldier was close behind him. He turned in time to see the raised sword stained with red. Then, his toe caught the edge of a rock and he tumbled just as the swoosh of the sword split the air over his head.

The horseman didn't turn back. There were plenty of charging soldiers behind him to capture or kill those he missed.

Sprawled on the ground, Thomas looked back. The ground lay littered with bodies. Men. Women. Children. Animals. Soldiers hacked. People died.

Scrambling to his feet, Thomas clutched the Bible and ran with all his might. His head pounded; his lungs burned; and his legs began to waver. He didn't know why he was running. He seriously considered stopping. All he had to do was turn and meet his fate. Then it would be all over for him. So simple. So easy for a man who had nothing to live for.

❧ ❧

AS THE BEEFSTEAK WAS set before him, Bishop Pole clapped so hard his hands hurt. He leaned over the plate and sniffed.

"Ground cinnamon!" he cried. "Marvelous!"

He applauded again. Seated across from him, Kendall was no longer amused at this all-too-familiar display. Bromley sighed an irritated sigh.

"I must speak with the cook." Then to his host, he said: "May I? May I speak with the cook?"

Bromley shrugged with indifference.

To the server, the bishop said, "Please fetch the cook for me. Tell him one of his greatest admirers wishes to speak with him."

With an upward flutter of a hand, Bishop Pole assisted the aromas as they rose from the plate into his eager nostrils.

The cook, a short man with graying hair, approached the table, wiping clean his hands with a cloth. His step was hesitant; his eyes glanced frequently at the head of the table for signs of displeasure.

As soon as the man was within reach, the bishop pulled one of the cook's hands out of the cloth and cradled it between his own. He patted the hand reassuringly.

"Never before has it been my privilege to sit in front of such a delightful piece of meat," he gushed. "And before tasting this culinary marvel, I must ask you what you used to make this exquisite basting sauce."

"My ... my basting sauce?" the cook asked, shooting another nervous glance at Bromley.

"Yes, my good man. What ingredients?"

"Well, your excellency ... I use red wine vinegar ..."

"Yes! Of course!"

"... and orange juice ..."

"Orange juice? A stroke of genius!"

"... and red wine ..."

"Yes, yes, of course, red wine!"

"... and a pinch of ground black pepper."

"I can smell the pepper," cried the bishop. "Oh, this is lovely! But there's one more ingredient I can't quite identify...."

The cook appeared flustered. "Oh, yes. Forgive me, your Excellency. I also used a pinch of ginger."

"Ginger!"

The bishop threw his hands into the air and rose from his seat with ecstatic delight as he shouted the word.

"Thank you, my good man," he said to the cook. "You are a craftsman of the highest order. Bless you. Bless you!"

The cook nodded his thanks and eagerly backed out of the room.

While the bishop's knife hovered over his steak, searching for the choicest place to cut, Bromley whacked off a hunk of meat and tossed it in his mouth.

While chewing, he asked, "Are the arrangements complete for Cardinal Barberini's arrival?"

Bishop Pole grimaced as his quest for the perfect place in which to make his incision was interrupted. "Yes, yes," he said, irritated. "Everything is ready."

"And the King's emissary? I assume he'll be lodging with Lord Harborough?"

The bishop had just placed knife to meat when the second question interrupted him. He straightened himself. "Yes. Lord Harborough insisted. Everything is as it should be. Now if you'll excuse me a moment, this filet is demanding my attention."

"Then everything is in order for Sunday," Bromley stated.

Bishop Pole ignored him.

"Likewise Monday's accommodations? The entourage will proceed to London for an audience with the King?"

The bishop sat back in his chair, his beefsteak untouched. "Yes, my dear Bromley. I've seen to everything myself. Following the worship service on Sunday at Coventry, we will proceed to London where King Richard will receive us. It promises to be one of the greatest days in English history as King and Church unite against a common threat based on Dr. Wycliffe's heresy. Now, may I give this exquisite piece of meat the respect it deserves?"

Bromley's response was to hack off another bit of beef and chew it unceremoniously while the bishop made his third approach to the beefsteak.

"Then, you're not concerned about the rumors?" Bromley asked, still chewing.

"Rumors?" the bishop cried.

"About Thomas Torr."

Even Kendall, who had to this point been a disinterested participant in the discussion, stopped eating and gave his full attention to his father.

Bishop Pole made every effort to disguise the disturbing impact this news was having on him. "And what are these rumors saying about Thomas Torr?"

Bromley chewed and swallowed before answering. He cut another piece of meat. "That he's alive. . . ." He tossed the meat into his mouth. "And that he's here in England."

The bishop set his knife on the table. "Nonsense," he said. "What is the source of these rumors?"

Bromley shrugged. "Hard to pin down."

"Totally without substance," the bishop insisted. "Thomas Torr is dead."

"You're sure?" Bromley asked.

"As God is my witness."

Nothing more was said of the rumor during the remainder of the meal. But when the plates were cleared, Bishop Pole's beefsteak was carried away untouched.

❦

"Now you read it."

Felice handed the cloth strip to her father. The two sat next to each other at a table littered with cloth strips, quill pens, and an inkwell. They shared a single candle between them.

Stretching the cloth strip between enormous hands, Howel stared at the writing. He handed it back.

"You haven't finished it," he said.

"I know," Felice said with a grin. "Just read the words that are there."

"How do you expect me to read a verse that is not complete?"

"Just read one word at a time. I know your tricks. If I complete the verse, you'll recognize the first and last letters, then recite it from memory. This way I'll know if you're really reading it."

Like a little boy caught cheating by his tutor, Howel sighed heavily. He looked again at the writing on the cloth.

He read rapidly: "'Trust in the LORD with all thine heart....'" Handing the cloth back to Felice he said, "You thought I couldn't do it, didn't you?"

Felice stared at him with neither approval nor disapproval.

"Ha! I got it right, didn't I? Admit it!"

Taking the cloth from him, she printed the remainder of the verse on the cloth and handed it back to him.

Howel looked at it and frowned.

"Read it now," Felice said.

"Is this the same strip of cloth? Or did you switch it on me?"

"Read it."

With a note of resignation in his voice, Howel read: "'Train up a child in the way he should go: and when he is old, he will not depart from it.'"

He spoke the second half of the verse without looking at the cloth.

Felice searched for another cloth. When she found the one she was looking for she held it next to his.

"See the difference between the first two words? One is T-r-u-s-t and the other is T-r-a-i-n."

Howel leaned closer and stared at the words. After several moments of intense concentration, he slumped in defeat.

"All I know is that if I see the big T—"

"Capital T."

"—then it's either, 'Trust in the LORD with all thine heart; and lean not unto thine own understanding,' or 'Train up a child in the way he should go: and when he is old, he will not depart from it,' or 'Truly my soul waiteth upon God: from him cometh my salvation.' I need the ending g, t, or n to tell me which one it is."

"How is it that you can remember entire verses, but you can't understand that letters placed side by side form words?"

Howel shrugged. "I don't know. I guess I'm just a dumb ploughman."

Setting aside the pen, Felice took her father's arm and hugged his shoulder. "Anybody who can remember as many Scripture verses as you can isn't dumb."

"I say them over and over in my head when I'm in the fields. Sure colors my day different."

"Are you going to stuff the entire Bible into that head of yours?"

Howel grinned. "Somehow I doubt God will grant me that many years of life. In any case, I'll be content with whatever glimpses of truth he'll allow me to keep."

Felice pulled back to look at her father. "'Glimpses of truth'? Where did you hear that?"

"I didn't hear it. I thought it up."

"You did?"

"Is that not right? It came to me while I was learning this verse: 'Sanctify them through thy truth: thy word is truth.' The way I see it, that means the whole Bible is truth, right? And then that would make these scraps of cloth glimpses of truth. Wouldn't it?"

Felice squeezed her father's arm. "For an unlearned ploughman, you are an uncommonly wise man."

Later that evening, as Felice was clearing the table and Howel was sitting in a chair beside the fire, his feet propped up, dozing, she said, "Kendall came by today."

This elicited no response from her father. She didn't expect one. Kendall's presence at the house was common, almost daily now.

"He was wondering if we were going to Coventry on Sunday to see Cardinal Barberini from Rome. Nearly the entire village is going."

"Hadn't thought much about it," Howel said, "though I have given thought to Kendall of late."

Felice paused in her work to look up.

"I like the boy, in spite of his ancestry. I keep expecting to see some of his father in him. Either the boy keeps it well hidden, or it's not there."

"He's nothing like his father," Felice said. "Kendall is kind, and gentle, and he always treats me like a lady of nobility."

"Still, if Bromley did indeed sire the boy, he's got Bromley blood in him. It'll come out sooner or later."

"You're wrong," Felice argued. "Kendall hates the man his father is and what he does. Especially, what he does to you."

"I've given that some thought too," Howel said. "I believe it's Bromley's intent to steal you away from me."

"Father, I hardly think—"

"It makes sense. He couldn't win Lyssa from me, so why not her daughter? You look so much like your mother. By stealing you away, he finally has Lyssa in his house and his revenge against me is complete."

Felice went to her father and knelt beside him. "I would never let that happen," she said.

"It's all right, my dear. I've made my peace with this matter. Why should an ancient feud between two old goats ruin the lives of their children?"

The sound of a horse's hooves interrupted them. Whoever it was stopped right in front of their house.

BAM! BAM! BAM! BAM! BAM!

Howel motioned Felice to step toward the back of the house quietly. He grabbed a knife and approached the door.

BAM! BAM! BAM! BAM! BAM!

"Felice? Howel? It's me, Kendall!"

Father and daughter exchanged glances. Setting the knife on the table, Howel opened the door.

"I know the hour is late," Kendall said as he entered. "Please forgive me. I just had to get away from the manor for a while, so I thought I'd take a ride, and, well, I just happened to be riding by your place and thought I'd stop by for a while. I hope it's not inconvenient."

Howel indicated a chair, and Kendall sat. As they made small talk for the next few minutes, Kendall was more agitated than Felice had ever seen him. He couldn't seem to relax. Something was always moving; if his fingers weren't drumming, his knee was bouncing, or his foot was tapping. He was quick to laugh at things that weren't very funny. His uneasiness made Felice nervous.

"Well," he said, clapping a single clap. "The whole town seems to be talking about Sunday. You're going, aren't you? Of course, you are. How often do we get to see a cardinal from Rome and an emissary from London all on the same day?"

"We haven't decided yet," Howel said.

"Oh? Really? I just assumed . . . everybody else in the village is going . . . I guess I really shouldn't have assumed . . ."

"May I make you some tea?" Felice asked.

"That would be great! Wonderful. I could really use a cup of tea about now."

Felice prepared three cups of tea and set them on the table. Felice and Howel sat together on one side, Kendall sat alone on the other side.

He started laughing. "You should have seen the show Bishop Pole put on today at dinner. Well, you know how he is . . . no wait, you don't, do you? Since you've never watched him eat . . . but, it's really a show. And tonight he was in top form. Had the cook come out of the kitchen and everything." He chuckled as the image came to his mind. He laughed alone.

"What's on your mind, Kendall?" Howel asked.

"My mind? Oh, nothing. Really. Just thought I'd take a ride . . ."

The three sat and sipped their tea.

Slapping the table, Kendall jumped up.

"It's late," he said. "I . . . I really shouldn't have stopped by . . . it's just that I was out riding and . . . well, I already told you that."

He was at the door. It stood partially open.

Felice stared at him with a quizzical expression.

Howel said, "Son, are you sure you don't want to tell us what you came to tell us? You rode all this way."

Kendall's shoulders slumped. He closed the door and leaned against it. Even now, it took him several minutes to get out the first words. "It's only rumor," he said.

"Rumor?" Felice repeated.

"At the dinner table tonight, my father told Bishop Pole what he'd heard. He prefaced the news by saying it had yet to be substantiated. But the rumor was disturbing enough to drive the bishop's appetite away, which is significant in itself."

"Kendall, don't keep us in suspense," Felice cried.

"Whether it's true or not, I knew you would want to hear it."

"Kendall!"

He took a deep breath and said, "Thomas may be alive."

⋯⋯

FELICE LAY IN THE dark. Sleep was nowhere near her.

Thomas alive? Could it be true?

Her hopes rose within her, and, with them, a measure of pain. She was just getting to the place where she could think of Thomas without weeping. And now this. Of course, she wanted the rumor to be true. But what if it wasn't? It would be like losing Thomas all over again. She didn't know if she would be able to bear it.

"Felice?"

She sat up. "Yes, Father?"

His voice came from the darkness. There was not enough light in the house even to see his shape.

"Did I wake you?"

"No."

"I couldn't sleep either."

Felice pulled her legs to her chest and hugged them. She rocked herself back and forth.

Her father cleared his throat. "I'll be leaving, come morning," he said.

"Leaving?"

"Kendall said the rumor placed Thomas with the brigands to the north. Probably Cayle and his men. I'll wander up that way and take a look."

242

"No, Father. It's too dangerous. Remember what happened to Uncle Ives."

"I'll be careful."

"I don't want you to go."

"I know. But I have to go. If there's a chance . . ." His voice trailed off.

"Then, I want to go with you."

"No, it's too dangerous. If something were to happen to you, I wouldn't want to go on living. I couldn't stand to lose both Thomas and you."

"But I could—"

"No!"

This was his final answer. From the tone of his voice Felice knew that any argument beyond this point would be as productive as running headlong into a stone wall.

"I'll pack your things," she said.

"Thank you."

For the longest time nothing else was spoken. So long, in fact, Felice thought her father had returned to his bed.

"Felice?"

His voice was so unexpected it frightened her.

"Yes, Father?"

"If Thomas is alive. I'll find him."

THIRTEEN ❧

HAROLD, ME LOVE! 'AVE you seen a giant 'ereabouts?"

From a back room came a man carrying a cask as round as his own belly. Felice could only assume this was Harold. With a grunt, he lowered the cask. Wiping sweat from his brow with his fingers and flicking it aside he looked Felice up and down.

"You searchin' for giants, miss?"

"I didn't say he was a giant," Felice replied. "He's a big man and he's my father. Have you seen him?"

Felice had been secretly trailing her father since early morning when he'd set out from Fearnleah to find Thomas. It was deliberate disobedience, but she didn't care. She had to know if Thomas was alive.

At first, tracking her father had been a simple task, his size making him easy game. Add to that his behavior which, to Felice, was rather curious. He seemed to go out of his way to speak to everyone along the road. He would say something to them, pat a leather pouch tied to his belt, then continue on his way.

When her father had come to a clearing with a stone bridge and a small creek, Felice had to fall behind to keep from being seen. She bided her time, and when she concluded it was safe to continue, she ran to close the distance between them.

That's when she happened upon the fork in the road. Which way had her father taken? She looked for oversized footprints, but the ground was too hard to leave any telltale signs. She even tried running a short distance down each path in hopes of catching sight of him. But each road had too many twists and turns and by now he was a good distance in front of her. She would have to choose one.

She chose the left road. Several minutes down the road it became apparent that she'd chosen incorrectly. She found herself descending into a heavily wooded hollow with an increasingly narrow pathway. With a rising sense of panic, she retraced her steps to the fork and ran down the only other alternative. It led her to the tavern.

The interior of the tavern was dark and smelled of ale and male sweat. She stood with her back against the door, giving her eyes time to adjust. The few voices she'd heard when she first entered hushed at her presence.

As the room came into focus she saw three men seated at a heavily scarred wooden table. One of the men was a friar.

A large round woman with a face framed by unruly red hair paused with broom in hand to ask her what she wanted. That was when the woman called back to her husband, the bearer of the cask.

"Your father, you say?" Harold repeated.

"Have you seen him?"

The two men and friar stopped what they were doing, apparently preferring Felice's conversation to their own. The round woman leaned on her broom and listened too.

Harold scratched his nose. "Do you mean the man who's transporting money for Bailiff Bromley?"

Felice frowned. "Transporting money?"

"Quite loud about it, he was."

The friar nodded his head, confirming the tavern keeper's assessment.

Bewildered, Felice said, "I don't know anything about that. But my father is a tall man. Black hair. Broad shoulders. Huge hands."

Harold nodded. So did the friar. "Sounds like him, all right," he said. "Left here a short time ago."

Thanking them, Felice rushed to catch him. The brightness of the day hit her in the face the moment she stepped out of the tavern. Not waiting for her eyes to adjust to the light, she hurried blindly down the middle of the road. Then, just as her vision began to clear, she thought she saw a movement out of the corner of her eye. Unless she was mistaken, someone had ducked behind the tavern, but she couldn't say for certain.

She glanced in that direction, but saw no one.

Most likely her imagination, spurred on by guilt. Scant moments after her father had told her she couldn't accompany him, she had decided to disobey him. She just couldn't sit idly by waiting to hear if the rumor about Thomas was true.

Her plan was to follow her father from a distance until dusk, whereupon she would reveal her presence. He would be angry. She expected this. But what could he do? Send her home alone in the dark? That would give her the rest of the night to convince him to allow her to stay, which would be easier to do since she would already be there.

Her plan did not include losing him.

Ahead, the road appeared striped as sunlight combed its way through a row of trees. She had just passed the first tree.

Someone jumped out at her. A hand clamped over her mouth. A forearm slapped across her chest, holding her motionless. It had all happened so quickly, she didn't have time to scream.

Her fear passed quickly.

Eyes that had leaped open with alarm, calmed. She let herself go limp. She spoke into the hand. Her sentence was muffled beyond recognition.

Cautiously, the hand over her mouth was removed.

"I know it's you, Father," she said again.

The arm that pinned her down, relaxed. She pulled away and turned to face her abductor.

"What if I had been a highwayman!" Howel grumbled.

"I knew you weren't. The hand over my mouth looked and smelled like my father's hand."

"It could just as easily have been the smell of a highwayman's hand!" he insisted. There was a stern look in his eyes. He was angry.

Felice grinned. "And what does a highwayman smell like? Do you know?"

Howel didn't laugh. "This is no place for you," he said. "You're turning around and going right back."

A movement caught her eye. Behind her father, in the distance. Guilt hadn't prompted this movement. Someone had ducked behind the tavern. She was sure of it.

His back to the tavern, her father was unaware of the movement. "If you start back now you can reach—"

"Someone is following us."

Howel started to turn to see for himself. Felice stopped him.

"This is the second time I've seen him," she said in a whisper.

"What does he look like? Is he alone?"

Felice shook her head. "I've not been able to get a good look at him."

"Is there more than one?"

"All I've seen is one. But there could be others behind the tavern."

"Start walking," Howel said. "Don't look, just walk."

Howel started down the road. Felice fell in step beside him. "This is exactly why I didn't want you to come with me," her father muttered through his teeth.

They traveled about a mile until they came to a place where the road bent around a large boulder. As soon as they were out of the view of anyone following them, Howel shoved Felice behind an outcropping of rocks on the far side of the road and ordered her to stay out of sight no matter what happened, no matter how many men were following them.

Howel took a position behind the large boulder and prepared himself to jump the first person that appeared. Then, they waited.

When it seemed that more than enough time had passed without anyone coming, Felice peeked around the rocks. Her father motioned her to stay down.

Just then, a man rounded the bend.

Howel leaped upon him. The two rolled over and over in the dust. Quickly, Howel gained the advantage.

"Kendall!" Felice cried.

Howel pushed himself away from the man beneath him to get a better look. "Oh great! Another one!" he cried.

"Kendall, what are you doing here?" Felice stood over both of them, her hands set demandingly on her hips.

Groaning from the weight of the ploughman, Kendall replied, "I saw you leaving town this morning. Alone and without provisions. I thought you might be up to something unwise. So I followed you."

Howel climbed off the boy and helped him to his feet. "I couldn't have said it any better myself," he said. "And as it turns out,

Kendall did us a favor. Now there's someone to escort you back to Fearnleah."

"No!" Felice cried, shooting a frustrated glance at the dusty nobleman's son.

Kendall shrugged apologetically. "I'm sorry, Felice. I didn't know. It's just that I was concerned."

"Yes, you will go back home!" Howel said to Felice. "This is no place for you."

Felice stomped her foot. "I'll not go back!"

"You really should listen to your father," Kendall said.

Felice shook her head adamantly. "If you think for one minute I'm going back to Fearnleah to sit around and do nothing while—"

"Listen to me, young lady!" Howel shouted. "You're going to turn around—"

Silence.

It happened that suddenly. Men poured forth from behind rocks and trees in every direction and surrounded them. They were not soldiers, but they were armed. Some wore nothing more than rags and carried clubs. Felice estimated that there were at least two dozen of them, and not a friendly face among them.

One of them stepped forward. His left eye was closed with a gash that extended down his cheek. Felice recognized him as the man who had bullied Thomas during the vote for the Lord of Misrule at the winter festivities a couple of years earlier. With a staff, he reached out and tapped the pouch tied to Howel's belt.

"Let's have it," he said.

Howel made no move to untie the bag. He glared at the man with the scar.

"Don't make me cut you," Scar Face said.

"Like you did my brother?"

Scar Face reacted visibly. Cocking his head, he stared at Howel with alarm.

"Take a good look," Howel said. "My brother shut one of your eyes; I intend to shut the other."

Before Scar Face knew what had hit him, Howel was atop him pummeling him with blows.

"What is this nonsense? Get in there and stop them!"

The voice came from high up.

Men responded immediately, pulling Howel off Scar Face and separating the two. It took nearly twice as many men to restrain Howel, who had the clear advantage in size and strength.

Felice looked up to see who had given the order. "Cayle!" she muttered. The leader of the brigands stood atop the large rock.

Cayle made his way down to the road and stood before the restrained ploughman. He reached for the pouch tied to Howel's belt.

Howel made no attempt to stop him.

"Just as I suspected," Cayle said. He spilled the contents of the bag into the dirt. Dried beans.

Stepping closer to Howel, he said, "All this—the pouch, the ruse—just to get revenge?"

Howel showed no fear. Looking Cayle directly in the eyes, he said, "I did not come here for revenge."

"Good!" Cayle cried. "Because if you were seeking revenge, you are seeking it in the wrong place, with the wrong man."

The highwayman turned his attention to the other two captives, studying first Felice, then Kendall.

"So then, why the ruse?" He chuckled with a note of disdain. "And I must say it was one of the more obvious ruses I've ever witnessed. Had there actually been gold in that pouch, I would have been the most surprised man in all England."

Cayle's men laughed appreciatively. All except Scar Face.

"For what purpose then?" the leader of the brigands asked no one in particular. "This is indeed a puzzle. Why would a man involve his lovely daughter . . ." Leaning close and whispering to Felice, he said, "Yes, dear, I do remember you from Lord Harborough's winter celebration." Aloud again, he said, ". . . and, oddly enough, the son of our local bailiff in such an obvious ruse?"

"They have nothing to do with this," Howel said. "Your business is with me."

Cayle gave no indication he'd heard Howel. "Indeed, we haven't had a good puzzle like this since the day we stumbled upon . . ." He paused for effect. His next words were spoken directly to Felice. ". . . Thomas Torr."

"Thomas!" Felice shouted. "You know where Thomas is?" All of a sudden her knees felt weak.

Howel attempted to step forward. He was immediately yanked back. He said, "Cayle, answer me truthfully. Is Thomas alive?"

❧ ❧

THOMAS SAT BENEATH THE lean-to he shared with Cayle. Their temporary shelter was situated near the top of a gentle slope. He still didn't know what he was doing there. His greatest regret was that he hadn't taken a stand and let one of Bromley's raiders run him through. His fear of dying had saved him. But that was resolved now. Let Bromley's men come again and the result would be different.

The English Bible lay open on Thomas's lap. Cayle had taken a band of men to investigate a possible trap believed to have been set by Bailiff Bromley. Some fool was traveling down the road announcing to everyone that he carried a big purse. Either the man was insane or it was a trap. Cayle had gone to investigate. Thomas saw Cayle's absence as an opportunity to take a good look at the Lollard book.

With the flat of his good hand, he gently rubbed the surface of a page. The flesh side. Turning the page, he rubbed the hair side in similar fashion. The scribe who had penned this particular book should have spent more time smoothing the pages with pounce.

The text of each page was printed in double columns. It was not illuminated, but then the purpose of the Lollard Bibles was to get the Word of God to the masses. Colored ink illustrations were thought unnecessary. Thomas disagreed. The Bible was God's book. Only the best effort was worthy enough to receive . . .

He stopped himself. That was the old Thomas talking.

Leaning closer, he examined the page as best he could with his hindered sight. He spotted the prick holes that the scribe had used to score the page. The letters themselves had been inked with a practiced hand, though hurried at times. A pity.

He turned toward the center of the book. Psalm 121, the passage in which Dr. Wycliffe had emphasized the translation of the perfect tense.

He never got to the psalm. The sound of approaching men distracted him. Glancing up, he saw Cayle and the others returning. Not wanting Cayle to see him reading the Bible, Thomas snapped the book shut and scrambled to his knees to return it to its place.

Emerging from the back of the lean-to, Thomas saw something that sent a shiver through him. Cayle and his band were returning, nothing unusual there. Cayle led the way, still nothing unusual. What was unusual was that three others walked with him; three who were not part of Cayle's assembly. One was much taller, the other was a woman, and the third a younger man dressed in the clothes of a noble.

No! It couldn't be!

Thomas stared as best he could into the distance. Howel! And . . . Felice? No! But it was. And who was that beside her? Impossible! Kendall! Of all the nerve! What were the three of them doing here?

Standing, Thomas glared down the slope in disbelief. His hands and knees trembled. He didn't want to see them. They had no business being here!

Thomas turned and ran.

He scurried up the slope where the grass gave way to rocky terrain. It was the assembly's planned escape route should Bromley's men attack again. On the other side of the crest there was a thick forest. Once they crested the hill and were out of sight of an invading force, it was thought they could disappear into the woods in any one of three directions—straight forward up a steep grade; left, which led to a river; or, right, which led into deeper and thicker woods. By the time the pursuers reached the edge of the woods, it would appear as though the forest had swallowed them up. The route would serve Thomas just as well.

Reaching the top of the ridge, Thomas stopped long enough to look back. A single person pursued him.

Howel.

Felice, Kendall, and Cayle stood side by side in the far distance and watched.

Turning, Thomas cleared the ridge and disappeared into the forest.

"What in heaven's name is he doing?" Cayle cried as they watched Thomas scamper up the slope.

When they had first spotted Thomas, Howel had set out after him. Kendall and Cayle had begun to follow, but Howel had ordered them to stay back. He'd go after Thomas alone.

Staring at Thomas's back, a feeling of disbelief and confusion moved over Felice like a fog. Her Thomas really was alive! But why was he running from her? And what was he doing here with these people? And why hadn't he come home?

Relieved. Confused. Tired. Hurt. Felice succumbed to her mounting emotions. She slumped down onto the grassy hillside and stared dumbly at the fleeing figure.

And, as was so often the case, Kendall was there to comfort her.

Thomas crouched behind an ancient stone wall, the crumbled remains of a once-grand castle. Doing his best to still his heaving chest, he listened for the sounds of his pursuer. Upon entering the forest, he had continued straight up the hill, figuring that the steady climb and his youthfulness would give him an advantage. The castle remains, an unexpected find, provided an ideal hiding place.

"Thomas! Why do you run?"

Howel's voice bounced against trees and stone, making it difficult to fix his location. But Thomas had a good idea of where he was. He doubted that the middle-aged ploughman could have flanked him.

Slowly, Thomas raised himself until his eye cleared the top of the wall. He spotted Howel—bending over, his hands resting on his knees, his head down, catching his breath. A sizable distance lay between them. Better still, Howel was shouting in the wrong direction, toward the river. The ploughman straightened himself. Thomas ducked down.

"Thomas! It's your father!"

Thomas winced. Howel's words hit him hard. He owed so much to this man. It was Howel who had found him in the forest when his mother died. It was Howel who had taken care of him—first at Lord Harborough's request and then again when he ran away from Bailiff Bromley. It was Howel who had clothed and fed and sheltered him, never once complaining that Thomas spent all of his time on his studies. The man had been more of a father to him than many blood fathers were to their children.

"Why do you run from your aged father who loves you? I mean you no harm!"

No harm. Thomas had never known a gentler man.

"Felice is with me. We thought you were dead."

Thomas closed his eyes and fought the emotions that welled up inside him. He wished he *were* dead. In a sense, he already was. All his hopes and aspirations regarding the English translations lay dead in a catacomb shaft in Rome; the rest of him had died the day he saw Felice kissing Kendall. What else was there? His life was gone. His flesh remained, but there was no longer any spark of life in it.

"I know I'm just an ignorant ploughman, Thomas. I don't pretend to understand what has happened to you. Why you never came home. Why you feel you can't face Felice or me. But you've always been good at explaining things. Help me to understand, Thomas. Help me to understand."

Tears streamed down Thomas's cheeks. He did not want to hurt this man. He placed his hands over his ears.

"Thomas, if you want us to go away, we will. By coming to look for you, we never meant to hurt you. It's just that we heard you were dead, then we heard you were alive. We had to find out for ourselves. At least, now we know you're alive."

Despite his initial effort, Thomas was still able to hear. He pressed harder until the only sound he could hear was that of his own breathing. His chest racked with sobs. He drew so far within himself that nothing else existed except his own miserable existence wrapped in a black void. He waited there until he thought it was safe. Then, slowly, he eased his hands from his ears.

". . . leave now. But Thomas, I want you to know this: I have always thought of you as my own son. And I always will. Nothing you have done will ever change that."

There was a rustling sound. Howel was leaving.

❧ ❧

KENDALL ASSISTED FELICE TO Cayle's lean-to. Felice had yet to take her eyes off the ridge over which both Thomas and her father had disappeared. Prompted by Cayle's questions, she explained the unique relationship that existed between her, Howel, and Thomas. She was very much aware that Cayle was openly staring at her as she talked, also that Kendall was uncharacteristically withdrawn. Still, she couldn't bring herself to look away from the ridge.

She saw movement.

A single head, then another appeared.

Felice was on her feet and running toward them before either Cayle or Kendall got a good look at the ridge.

A beaming Howel stepped to one side just as she arrived.

"Thomas! Thomas! Thank God, you're alive!"

Felice flew into his arms, her momentum causing them to teeter for a moment. Felice covered Thomas's face with kisses. He was noticeably restrained. Sensing something was wrong, she stepped back and took a good look at him.

"Oh, Thomas! Your arm!"

He was cradling it against his side, still protecting it. A maternal expression formed on Felice's face as she examined it.

"You poor boy!" she cried. She kissed him again.

This time she noticed he didn't kiss back. She looked into his eyes. They were coldly indifferent. Almost hostile. What was wrong? Why was he acting like this?

"Thomas?"

Before he had time to respond, Kendall and Cayle joined them. Kendall's greeting was lukewarm at best; Thomas's was cold.

What had happened to Thomas to make him act like this? Felice smiled reassuringly at him. Whatever it was, he would tell her eventually. And she would listen. They'd been apart for over two years. It was obvious that he'd been hurt. She would be patient. All they needed was time together. Then, everything would be like it had been before between them.

She took him by the hand and walked with him back to the lean-to. It was like walking with a stranger. A thought came to her. She rejected it. Stubbornly, it returned.

This was not her Thomas!

◄§ §►

HE SAT IN SILENCE. Sullen, dispirited silence. He told himself he was merely observing.

As the sun sank behind the hills, Thomas watched as Felice moved among the others, serving them roast mutton fresh from the spit. When she was at the spit, Cayle's gaze caressed her wolfishly. When she drew near to serve him, he nearly ended up with a hunk of mutton in his lap for paying too much attention to her and not enough to what he was doing.

Kendall could have been her shadow. Everywhere Felice went he was there with her. Helping her. Talking to her. Laughing with her. Much of their conversation was over shared experiences. It was obvious that they'd spent a lot of time together over the past two years.

When Felice brought Thomas his portion of meat, he avoided looking at her. He expressed his thanks with little more than a grunt.

Howel, who had made himself useful by turning the spit, plopped next to Cayle and attacked his piece of meat hungrily. It was dark now. The fire cast shadows against the backdrop of the lean-to.

"Back on the road," Cayle said to Howel. "Why did you attack Kleef?"

Howel's face, which had been amiable until now, clouded with anger. He chewed, swallowed, then said, "He killed my brother."

Cayle shook his head. "No. Kleef stabbed your brother, but only after your brother cut him across the face."

"You were robbing him!"

"We were set up. Just as he was."

"Set up?"

"By Bailiff Bromley."

Howel wiped his mouth with the back of his hand. Cayle had his attention.

"I don't know how well you know the bailiff . . ." Cayle glanced at Kendall. The boy gave no indication he was aware of this line of conversation. He sat next to Felice whispering things back and forth to her.

Howel replied, "I know Bromley all too well."

"Then you know it is not beneath him to use people like pawns, to manipulate them to his advantage."

"I'm listening."

"Bromley hired four men to approach your brother."

"You were one of the four?"

Cayle shook his head. "No. But later, when they told me what they'd been hired to do, it sounded peculiar, so I joined them, hoping to keep them out of trouble."

"What do you mean they were hired to 'approach' him?"

Cayle sighed. His downcast gaze gave evidence that he was finding it difficult to admit his part in this. He said, "Bromley told the men he suspected your brother was stealing from him."

"Ives would never do such a thing!" Howel thundered.

"How were we to know that?" Cayle shouted back. "We were to masquerade as highwaymen. The instructions were that we were to offer him a portion of the money if he agreed to hand it over readily."

"And if my brother resisted?"

"We were to press him at first, but if it looked like he was acting in Bromley's best interests, we were to let him go. Let him think he'd escaped."

"What went wrong?"

"Your brother caught us completely by surprise. Before Kleef could speak a word your brother pulled a knife and charged him like a bull. Cut him badly. Well, you saw. Kleef flew into a rage and by the time we were able to separate them, your brother had gotten the worst of it."

Howel shook his head stubbornly. "Your story doesn't ring true. My brother would have more sense than to attack against superior numbers. Besides, he had no great love for Bromley. He would have sacrificed the money willingly."

"You don't understand," Cayle said, leaning toward Howel like a teacher would to a student. "It was a setup all around. Your brother wasn't carrying any money!"

"What?" Howel cried.

"There was no money in the pouch—though of course he thought there was."

"Then what? Why?"

"I learned afterward, from one of Bromley's house servants, that your brother was promised half of the money in the bag if he delivered it successfully. Bromley told him there was a band of four drunken men who had been unsuccessful in several attempts to rob carriers. Not to be afraid of them. Strike first and they would run away."

Howel frowned, taking all this in.

"Like I said. Bromley set us all up."

"But why my brother?"

"He wasn't after your brother. He was after me."

"But you said you weren't involved initially."

"He was after me through some of my men. Up to that point, he had no good cause to arrest me. I was a nuisance with a following, but that was all. After the incident with your brother, Bromley was able to brand us as brigands. Now, the entire countryside thinks we're nothing more than a band of highwaymen. Plus, he now has reason to hunt us down."

Felice began listening to the conversation halfway through. She asked, "If that's true, then why didn't he arrest you at the winter festival?"

"Christ's Mass eve is a popular celebration. Lord Harborough held him back. He was afraid that if we were arrested in public during such a festive occasion, the villagers might become sympathetic to us and our cause."

Felice was aghast. "You were enjoying Lord Harborough's protection that night, and yet you used the occasion to speak against him as you did?"

Cayle bristled. Apparently he wasn't used to being challenged in his own camp. His voice rose defensively. "You caught me red-handed!" he said sarcastically. "I'm guilty of bad manners. Now compare that to Lord Harborough's annual hypocrisy! What do you think he is doing every year with that festival? For one night he placates the villagers in hopes that they'll forget all about the wretched conditions in which they live for the rest of the year. One night's penance for a year's worth of sin. Now you tell me, which of us is the greater sinner?"

Thomas grunted. He had something to add. Everyone's attention shifted to him. "Lord Harborough told me as much himself. That very night," he said. "His exact words were that one night of generosity puts the villagers in a good mood for most of the year. He went on to say that it was quite a bargain for him."

"There you have it!" cried a vindicated Cayle.

Felice conceded the point but looked none too happy about it.

Cayle turned to Howel. "Bromley sacrificed your brother like a pawn in exchange for a stronger political position."

"It wouldn't be the first time," Howel replied. He was angry. His jaw was clenched, he stared hard at nothing when he spoke, and he was squeezing his mutton so tightly the juice was running down his arm and dripping from his elbow.

"He's not above using his own son." It was a new voice in the conversation. Tossing aside a scrap of meat, Kendall continued, "My father all but ordered me to court Felice."

Felice blushed. Cayle grew an amused grin. Kendall shot a nervous glance at Thomas but was unable to look him squarely in the eyes.

"For what purpose?" Cayle asked.

"For revenge against me," Howel replied for him.

Kendall nodded. "That's true. But there's another reason. He thought that if I was able to steal Felice away from Thomas, it would prevent her from complicating plans he and Bishop Pole had for Thomas."

"Your father told you this?" Felice asked.

"I overheard him and the bishop."

"And that's why you've been coming around to see me all this time?"

"No, no!" Kendall cried, genuinely injured. "I came because..." He had gone too far. Now the eyes of the other four persons were on him.

"Go on," Cayle urged the boy. He was enjoying the unexpected entertainment.

Finding a measure of courage, Kendall looked earnestly at Felice. "I think you already know this, but I came to see you because I . . . I love you."

Felice's face turned scarlet. She glanced nervously at Thomas.

He could feel his face flush with anger. He fought the red tide and told himself he didn't care any longer. This may be news to Cayle and possibly to Howel, but it wasn't to him.

"How much more of Bromley are we going to take?" Cayle said, guiding the subject back to the bailiff. "He is the very reason we must stick together. Don't you see that? Unless we resist men like him, they won't stop until we are all their slaves."

Howel and Kendall stared at him with interest.

"With enough of us banding together, each contributing as he is able, we can speak with one voice and the nobles and the King will be forced to listen to us."

"We'll have rebellion," Howel said.

"I'm not talking about doing away with law. I'm talking about new laws that protect us from those who know no other law but themselves."

"Rising up against the nobles and the King is wrong!" Howel said. "It is God who makes some men nobles and other men peasants."

"Ha!" Cayle cried excitedly. "I used to think so too! After all, that's what we have been taught to think since the time we were born, isn't it? But it's not true!"

"And what makes you think you know better than the scholars?" Howel asked.

"I learned it from God Himself!" Cayle said. Leaning back into the far reaches of the lean-to, he pulled out the English Bible.

Once they recognized what he had in his hands, all eyes turned to Thomas.

"It's not mine," Thomas said, deflecting their thoughts with upraised hands.

"No, it's not," Cayle said. "I can't even get him to read it. But if what you are saying is true and some people are born to be the servants of others, why did God deliver His people from the oppression of the Egyptians and lead them to a land of freedom?"

Howel looked to Thomas. "Is this true?" he asked.

Thomas looked away. It was obvious what Cayle was doing. The wily leader was trying to pull him into this discussion, and Thomas wanted no part of it. However, thinking it would be easier to answer just one question than to explain his objection for doing so, he conceded, "Yes, God rescued His people from Egypt and led them to the Promised Land."

"See? That is the truth!" Cayle said. "And the Bible also says that once we know the truth, then we will have freedom."

Again, all eyes turned to Thomas.

This time, he didn't respond.

Felice looked at him with a disappointed expression.

"Does the Bible say that, Thomas?" Howel prompted.

Thomas turned his head aside. They were trying to force him to be something he no longer wanted to be. The book in Cayle's hands and all it represented had caused him nothing but trouble.

"Thomas?" Howel asked again.

A feeling of resignation swept over him. If anyone else was asking him, he wouldn't have answered.

"Yes," he said. "To quote directly: 'And ye shall know the truth, and the truth shall make you free.'"

Howel looked at Cayle with newfound respect. "So then, what do we do?" he asked.

"For one thing, we keep out of Bromley's reach. Then, we teach people these Bible truths, just as the Lollards are doing. And we look for opportunities to expose the nobles' greed and arrogance."

"Opportunities such as . . . ?" Howel asked.

"Such as the one at hand this Sunday at Coventry."

"Coventry? Bishop Pole? What do you plan to do?"

"Alas, nothing. We have a chance to refute the document Bishop Pole is parading around renouncing the English Bible, the one allegedly signed by Thomas Torr. And to unmask the good bishop himself. To tell everyone the truth about the events in Rome. To tell them how the cardinals and bishop nearly succeeded in killing Thomas."

All eyes turned to Thomas.

Howel asked, "What is stopping us?"

"Do you want to tell them, Thomas?"

One by one Thomas looked at the faces of those sitting around the fire. They awaited his response.

Getting up, Thomas walked into the darkness.

"Thomas!"

He heard her but didn't stop.

"Thomas, wait!"

He kept walking.

Catching up with him, Felice grabbed his arm. She swung him around.

"Thomas! What is wrong with you?"

"Nothing."

"There most certainly is something wrong! It's like I don't even know you!"

Thomas looked aside. "Maybe you don't."

They stood in silence opposite each other. A lover's moon rose overhead bathing the hillside in a soft light.

Her next question was softer, more conciliatory. "What happened to you in Rome?"

Without looking at her, Thomas replied, "I learned that I'd been fooling myself all these years."

"Fooling yourself?"

"Yes, fooling myself! The cardinals and bishops will never allow us to keep the English Bible! They'll come after us until every one of them is destroyed."

"Then, we'll just make more of them."

"Yes? And how are we going to do that? With what funds?"

"Surely, there are some godly men who aren't afraid of—"

"Godly men? That would be a small group. And even if we had the materials, my eyesight is so bad I can barely see you! And this?" He lifted his bent right arm. "I'm not exactly in condition to print Scripture any more."

"I can be your hands," Felice said. "I've been practicing! Every night I practice!"

"Then you've been wasting your time."

Felice took a step back. "You've changed," she said. "It's not like you to give up."

Thomas felt the ire climbing up the back of his neck. "Haven't you been listening to me?" he shouted. "The men who oppose this English translation are powerful men! Not only will they burn every manuscript they find, but they won't hesitate to kill every person they find who is translating or distributing it! They've already tried to kill me once! I'm not about to give them another chance."

Felice didn't reply.

Good, Thomas thought. *Maybe she's beginning to understand a little of what I've been through.*

The silence between them lasted so long Thomas glanced up to see what she was doing. What he saw was her cold stare of displeasure.

"If you ask me," she said, "they did kill Thomas in Rome. Because the Thomas I knew is not the self-pitying coward standing before me."

Thomas said nothing. She merely confirmed what he already knew: Thomas Torr died in Italy.

"Will you at least answer this for me?" Felice asked. "Why didn't you return home? Why did you let us go on believing you were dead?"

"I did return home."

This confused her. "You mean you returned to Fearnleah but not our house."

"I returned to the house," Thomas insisted.

"When? How come we didn't see you?"

"Maybe you didn't see me because you were too busy kissing Kendall."

A hand flew to her mouth. "Oh, Thomas! I . . . we thought you were dead!"

"You seem to have recovered from your grief. But then, you had someone there to help you. Didn't you?"

Now it was Felice who was defensive.

"Don't you dare speak ill of Kendall!" she cried. "He has been a trusted friend and always a gentleman!"

"And, of course, the mark of a true gentleman is one who takes advantage of an emotional, distraught woman."

Thomas's eyesight may have been restricted but not so much that he couldn't see the anger that sparked in Felice's eyes.

"At least Kendall's not a pathetic, self-pitying coward," she said.

"Then everything has worked out fine for you, hasn't it? You've ended up with a better man, a richer man. Thank God! When you might have been stuck with an invalid coward for the rest of your life!"

Felice shook with anger. Her lips trembled as she fought back tears. She started to say something, then shook her head and stalked past Thomas, returning in the direction from which they'd come.

Thomas's chest tightened until he could barely breathe. His jaw ached from clenching it so tightly. He continued up the slope until he found a rock upon which to sit. A valley of tents, bluish-white in the moonlight, stretched before him, but he saw none of them as a hundred hellish thoughts burned in his head.

He sat on that rock muttering to himself until late into the night.

FOURTEEN ❧

ISHOP WILLIAM POLE SAT regally in his chair. Stretched out before him, Coventry Cathedral was filled beyond capacity. And why shouldn't it be? It wasn't often peasants got a glimpse of such an impressive gathering of luminaries. Sharing the platform with him were Cardinal Barberini from Rome; Lord Edgar Suffield, King Richard's personal emissary; Lord Harborough; and Bailiff Bromley.

He had done it! Secular and ecclesiastical authorities shared the same platform. It was a glorious day for England and the Church. It was the proudest day of his life.

This gathering was the culmination of the local tour of Thomas's written confession. Everywhere he and Bromley had displayed the document—Naseby, Crick, Dunchurch, Bulkington, Rugby, even Lutterworth—it and the story behind it had been well-received. The portrayal of Thomas as a local champion of orthodoxy was swaying popular opinion against the English translation. His untimely death gave him martyr status with the crowds. Everywhere the bishop journeyed, he heard reports of Lollards being openly attacked in the fields by villagers. English translations were seized and burned.

Reports favorable to the confession came also from high sources in Rome and London. Eager to capitalize on these reports, Bishop Pole had used his newfound notoriety to arrange for a meeting between ecclesiastical and secular heads of state. Everything he had hoped for was coming to pass. And, as he had anticipated, the key to it all was Thomas.

He thought of the boy with a pang of regret. The rumors of Thomas's reincarnation in England had, of course, been proved to be just that: rumors. He'd been utterly foolish to give them credence, if only for a short while.

He had, of course, once hoped that Thomas's life would be the pivot upon which these great events would turn. The fact that they turned on his death at least gave meaning to the boy's tragic demise—no, more than meaning. Historical significance.

Cardinal Barberini sat on the bishop's left. Recently arrived from Rome, the original purpose of his trip had been to follow the bishop back to England and bring pressure on Parliament and the king regarding the renegade translation. But with Bishop Pole's favorable report, his presence was now viewed as largely ceremonial. At today's festivities he would bring greetings and a blessing from the Pope.

Seated next to the Vatican representative was the elderly Lord Edgar Suffield, a nobleman respected by both King and Church. He was the Crown's representative. Following this ceremony he would lead the entourage to London for an audience with King Richard himself.

Oh, Thomas, the bishop thought, *do you realize how much your sacrifice has accomplished? It is only fitting that your name be extolled throughout all England. I pray that you have forgiven me, my son. That you now see that the greater good has been served. For in all honesty, in spite of these advances, I miss you terribly. I miss our discussions. I miss teaching you. Singing with you.*

The high range of young male voices reverberated among the cathedral arches as the chancel choir sang:

Alleluia. Alleluia. Beatus vir,
qui suffert tentationem:
quoniam cum probatatus fuerit,
accipiet coronam vitae. Alleluia.

The song, together with the memory of Thomas, brought tears to the bishop's eyes. But he brushed aside the emotion. The time had come for him to honor his son once more.

Holding Thomas's confession in his left hand, Bishop Pole smoothed his robe with his right and waited for the final alleluia to fade. This was his moment. The moment he'd waited for, prayed for, lived for. And he was going to cherish it.

"Psst! Psst!"

The insect sound came from beside him. Cardinal Barberini was motioning him toward the pulpit. So typical of Barberini. Always having to be in control. Directing people. Telling them what to do. Where to go. What to say and how to say it.

Bishop Pole ignored him—partially out of spite, but mostly because he wasn't about to rush this ceremony of a lifetime for some meddlesome Roman cardinal. The bishop piously bowed his head, as though to pray. Of course, he didn't pray. He counted to ten. Slowly. Just long enough to irritate the cardinal, which it did. He could hear the cardinal fidgeting impatiently beside him.

Smoothing his robe once more, Bishop Pole rose majestically and mounted the pulpit. He did not begin immediately. Instead, he slowly scanned the congregation, basking in their upward gaze. His opening remarks were the same words he had used so successfully in the other towns.

"I begin on a sad note," he said. "Although by now I'm sure most of you have already heard, today we mourn the loss of one of our own. One of the brightest, most promising young men it has been my good fortune to know. I speak of Thomas Torr, who departed with me on a journey to the Vatican but who, for reasons God alone can fathom, died needlessly before—"

Thomas?

A sharp inhale cut off the sentence, prompted by the bishop's sudden and startling glimpse of what appeared to be Thomas seated among the congregants. It had been only a glimpse. But the resemblance!

The bishop scanned the area of the crowd in which he thought he'd seen Thomas. His search was fruitless. Men. Women. Children. Peasants all. But no Thomas.

The pause in his oration had grown so lengthy that it was becoming awkward. Taking a deep, calming breath, the bishop continued, his gaze constantly gravitating back to the area in which he thought he'd seen his dead son.

"Thomas was killed when he lost his balance and fell down a deep shaft while we were exploring the catacombs of Rome. I wish

I could convey to you the excitement of this young man in that historical city. We had gone to the catacombs because Thomas wanted to worship at the final resting place of some of the great early—"

There! Thomas!

The bishop gripped both sides of the pulpit. His heart pounded. His eyes strained. Sweat trickled down his temples onto his cheeks.

It *was* Thomas! He knew it! But once again, Thomas had disappeared.

"Bishop Pole, are you ill?"

The voice came from behind him. Barberini. Just like the cardinal, looking for the slightest excuse to step into the pulpit, to rob the bishop of his greatest triumph.

"No, I'm—I'm fine," the bishop replied. "I can continue."

He turned again to the congregation. His eyes were drawn to the area where twice he thought he'd seen Thomas. Like before, Thomas wasn't there.

The bishop continued, "At . . . at least Thomas did not die in vain, for his work in Rome has left a spiritual legacy that will shape England for generations to come." He paused. "Forgive me, but mere words fail me. For I wish I could convey to you the scene of our bright young scholar engaged in theological debate with the most brilliant minds at the Vatican."

He went on to describe how Thomas learned the error of Dr. Wycliffe's English translation of the Bible and how he eagerly embraced the truth taught by the cardinals, chief among them being Cardinal Barberini, now seated on the platform. At this point the bishop turned and acknowledged the presence of Cardinal Barberini, who returned the acknowledgment with a courteous nod.

The bishop described how Thomas dramatically demonstrated his opposition to the Wycliffe version by burning the copy he had carried with him from England to Rome.

Holding high the document containing Thomas's confession, the bishop said, "This is Thomas's confession, signed by him and witnessed by two of the most powerful cardinals of—"

What happened next caused the bishop's heart to stop cold. His upraised arm faltered. His breath was cut off. His eyes were fixed with horror.

WELL BEFORE THE SERVICE began, Thomas had slipped into Coventry Cathedral with Cayle at his side. A dozen or so of Cayle's followers surrounded them, providing a buffer between them and other congregants to keep anyone from getting a good look at Thomas. To further conceal his identity, he wore a liripipe, a long hanging cloth attached to a hood, which wound around his head and fell loosely to his shoulders. The liripipe veiled his face.

A feeling of apprehension weakened Thomas's knees as they entered the cathedral. He worried about the outcome of their course of action. If they were caught, it would be prison for them all. Even if all went as planned, the outcome might prove to be disastrous, for Thomas would find himself once again cast into the center of controversy.

Which of the two was worse? He didn't know. One side of him wished he *would* get caught. If he was jailed, at least he could live out his days in obscurity.

They took their place. As the dignitaries filed onto the platform he felt a chill.

Bishop Pole!

It was the first time he'd seen the bishop since the catacombs, the day the man tried to kill him.

Beside him was Cardinal Barberini, the man who, under pretense of wanting to read Dr. Wycliffe's translation, had ripped it and burned it while a restrained Thomas was forced to watch.

Also on the platform was Lord Harborough. Patron or oppressor? Which was he today?

Then there was the most unnerving realization of all, one for which Thomas was unprepared. His father was seated on that platform. Only he didn't know which man it was—Lord Harborough or Bishop Pole?

The boys' chancel choir began to sing a Gregorian chant.

Alleluia. Alleluia. Blessed is the one
Who endures temptation:
When he has been proven,
He shall receive the crown of life. Alleluia.

The music that had once saturated him with holy ecstasy now grated his nerves and set him to shaking. His hands felt chilled and clammy. This was the music that haunted his dreams. It was the eerie sound of the bishop's voice falling like leaves, drifting down the catacomb shaft; these were the tones uttered over him like a funeral prayer while he lay crumpled, suspended between this world and eternity, conscious, then unconscious, never knowing which of the two realms would ultimately claim him; unaware of time; afraid to move, to breathe, lest he give himself away, whereupon the chanting would cease and death would descend the shaft to finish the job that was only half-done.

"Thomas! What's wrong?" Cayle whispered.

A ragged breath brought Thomas back to the present. "I'm all right," he lied.

A significant silence followed the end of the choral selection. The lack of movement on the platform only served to draw everyone's attention to it. Finally, Bishop Pole ascended to the pulpit. This was Thomas's cue to disappear. He slumped low so that the bishop would be unable to see him.

This bit of drama was Cayle's idea. He thought it best not only to confront the bishop, but to disturb him, to shake him by countering his presentation with one of their own.

"I begin on a sad note," the bishop said. "Although by now I'm sure most of you have already heard . . ."

Thomas waited for Cayle to nudge him. When he felt the nudge Thomas sat up straight. He stared directly at Bishop Pole, attempting to catch the bishop's eye. He did.

The bishop's gasp was audible.

Thomas then slipped out of sight while Cayle and the woman seated on Thomas's left leaned closer together to close the gap between them. From his low position Thomas couldn't see what was happening, although he could hear Cayle chuckling.

After a time, the bishop began speaking again. "Thomas was killed when he lost his balance and fell down a deep shaft while we were exploring the catacombs. I wish I could convey to you . . ."

Thomas waited for his cue. Cayle nudged him again. Again he sat up straight, this time pulling back his liripipe to reveal more of his face.

Bishop Pole looked directly at him. Their eyes locked. The bishop gasped. He grabbed the pulpit to keep himself from toppling over.

Again Thomas ducked down.

Murmurs of whispered concern floated back and forth over the congregation. This second interruption lasted longer than the first.

"What's happening?" Thomas whispered to Cayle.

Cayle reached down and patted his back. Patience.

The bishop's voice could be heard again. "At . . . at least Thomas did not d-die in v-vain, for his work in Rome has left a spiritual legacy that will shape England for generations to come. . . ."

Thomas found it difficult to wait for the next signal. His position was uncomfortable, but even more uncomfortable was Bishop Pole's account of the events in Rome. A spirited theological debate? It had been more like a mugging! He cringed when he heard Pole describe how he had acquiesced to the superior wisdom of Cardinal Barberini. Then he burned with anger when Bishop Pole credited him with the destruction of the Wycliffe Bible. Until now, he'd been reluctant about participating in this demonstration. No more. He was glad now that Howel had talked him into helping expose the bishop.

The bishop's voice boomed, "This is Thomas's statement, signed by him and witnessed by two of the most respected . . ."

Cayle's elbow jammed into Thomas's ribs. Lest Thomas miss the cue, he looked down at him and whispered, "Now!"

Thomas stood tall. He yanked back his liripipe. At the top of his lungs he shouted: "That document is a forgery and that man is a liar! I ought to know. My name is Thomas Torr!"

Bishop Pole's eyes bulged with horror. The arm that bore the confession sagged. Nonsensical mutterings fell from his lips.

Without exception, the luminaries were on their feet. Thomas had to speak quickly before they could gather their wits.

"Take a good look at me!" he shouted. "No, I am not dead. So why would our Bishop Pole testify to my demise? I'll tell you why. Because he left me for dead at the bottom of that catacomb shaft, bleeding from a knife wound he gave me when he attempted to murder me!"

He lifted his injured right arm as evidence.

Bishop Pole had sunk so far behind the pulpit he could no longer be seen. The congregation was coming alive with noise and movement. Thomas knew that he would have to get his message across quickly or it would be drowned out by the escalating din.

"Listen to me! Listen to me!" he shouted. "Everything you have heard about my journey to Rome is untrue! I did not burn Dr. Wycliffe's Bible; on the contrary, it was taken from me and burned against my will! As for the confession, I did not sign it and I do not agree with it!"

The cathedral erupted with shouts. Cayle grinned at Thomas in triumph. They'd done it! They'd needed to do something so startling, so gossip-worthy, that it would spread from town to village like wildfire and undo all the damage Pole and Bromley had done to the cause of the English translation.

"Calm yourselves!" The bass voice thundered from the front of the cathedral loud enough to be heard over the din. Cardinal Barberini had moved into prominent view. "In the name of all that is holy, have reverence for the house of God!" With an upward sweep of both arms, his bright red robe did even more to gain people's attention than did his voice.

"If you fear your immortal souls, you will listen to me!"

With astonishing suddenness the storm of noise and agitation calmed. Cardinal Barberini had reestablished control—with himself in charge.

He used the silence to fortify his authority. Once he had everyone's attention, he didn't say anything immediately; instead, he paced back and forth glaring at them with the expression a parent uses when disappointed with a child. When he spoke, he addressed Thomas directly.

"This is quite a surprise you pulled on us, Thomas," he said. "Indeed, we thought you dead. And though I am the first to rejoice that you are alive, I fear that your tumble down that shaft not only injured your body, but your mind and judgment as well."

Behind him Lords Harborough and Suffield assisted Bishop Pole to his feet; he still could not stand without assistance. But the most telling sign that he had not yet recovered from the shock of seeing Thomas alive were his terror-filled eyes. They remained locked on Thomas.

Bromley stood apart motioning to his men to guard the doorways.

"And I have to ask myself," Cardinal Barberini pondered aloud, "why would a young man who is believed to be dead not come forward immediately and let the truth be known? Why would he allow his beloved mentor to grieve needlessly for months? Why would he sneak back to England? And why would he now come forth in such a way so as to injure grievously the bishop who befriended him? Can't you see what your sudden appearance has done to this good man who has treated you with nothing but kindness?"

The cardinal motioned toward Bishop Pole, offering up the still-shaken bishop as evidence.

"Say something!" Cayle cried. "He's turning the table on us!"

Cardinal Barberini didn't give Thomas the chance. "I am forced to conclude that a young man who returns pain and suffering for love is either mentally addled from his injury or else his motives are so dark and mean-spirited a decent person would shudder upon hearing them. Which is it, Thomas? What do you have to gain from this cruel plan?"

"The truth is—" Thomas shouted.

"The truth is!" Cardinal Barberini shouted over him.

In the battle of voices, Thomas was woefully overmatched.

"The truth is," Cardinal Barberini said again for emphasis, "that though you may refute the events that took place in Rome. And though you may even get a few ne'er-do-wells and drunks to take your word over that of a cardinal and a bishop ..." He paused to enjoy the smattering of chuckles his comment prompted. ". . . You cannot refute this!"

Cardinal Barberini bent to retrieve the confession paper from the floor. Holding it up for all to see, he pointed to the bottom of the page.

"Signed by Thomas Torr!" the cardinal boomed. "And witnessed by . . ." He looked at the paper with a comical expression. Confident that he had won back the congregation, he was toying with Thomas. "Why, is that my name? My signature? So it is!" Dramatically, he held the confession high over his head. "As God is my witness, I watched as this man, Thomas Torr, put pen to paper and signed his name on this confession."

Thomas had once again become the center of attention in the dispute over Dr. Wycliffe's English translation of the Bible, the very position he had dreaded. And from the expressions of those who were crowded around him, it was clear his dramatic victory was short-lived. The cardinal was winning the crowd over.

"We'll be lucky if we get out of here alive," Cayle muttered.

Cardinal Barberini waited.

Thomas smiled.

The cardinal had overplayed his position. He'd had Thomas cornered, but in his moment of triumph, he'd succumbed to his own arrogance and made a fatal mistake.

"I did not sign that confession," Thomas said calmly.

Cardinal Barberini looked down upon him with growing impatience. "My son, give glory to God. And be aware that the words you speak next may imperil your immortal soul. For you have already borne false witness against a bishop of the Church. Is it your intention to multiply your sin by calling a cardinal from Rome a liar?"

A chorus of gasps came from every corner of the cathedral.

Thomas fumbled around inside his gypon until he found what he was looking for. With his good hand he held up a worn and tattered piece of cloth.

"I carried this with me to Rome," he cried. "On it, there is writing. It is this very strip of cloth that Bishop Pole used in Fearnleah when he first presented my alleged confession. In the presence of witnesses he used it as proof that the signature on the confession was genuine. And, sure enough, if you were to put the two side by side as he did and match them up, you would come to the same conclusion. There is little doubt that the writing on this strip of cloth is identical to the signature on that petition."

Cayle was aghast, as was the congregation. "What are you doing?" he cried.

Cardinal Barberini wore an amused expression, but one that was tinted with concern.

The congregation grew restless. There were shouts calling for Thomas's arrest, calling him a hypocrite, urging him to beg the cardinal's forgiveness.

"Hear me out!" Thomas shouted. "Hear me out! While I admit that this cloth belongs to me, I tell you now that the words that appear on it were written by a different hand. This is not my hand-writing!"

An eerie stillness settled upon the congregation.

Cardinal Barberini appeared dumbfounded.

Cayle cried to Thomas, "Keep going! Keep going!"

"As proof, I can produce a mountain of similar pieces of cloth written by this same hand. And I can produce a second mountain of cloths written by my hand which will conclusively prove that the signature on the confession is not mine!"

The tide had turned. The crowd's attention was shifting back to the cardinal and it was not favorable. Thomas pressed home his point.

"So I have to ask myself," he pondered aloud, borrowing the cardinal's technique, "why would someone manufacture a document signed by a person whom they believe is dead? And how would they do such a thing? I can only conclude they would use what they assumed to be a sample of the dead man's handwriting and forge his signature! Only in this case, the dead man wasn't dead. And the handwriting sample wasn't his!"

Cardinal Barberini whirled around to face Bishop Pole. The guilt-laden expression on the bishop's face was as good as a confession.

Bailiff Bromley jumped forward. Pointing at Thomas, he yelled, "Seize that man!"

Armed men invaded the cathedral at every doorway.

Thomas looked every direction for an avenue of escape. He looked to Cayle. The revolutionary was shaking his head. Every route was guarded.

Cayle and Thomas had discussed this very contingency, and they were prepared for it. Cayle's men were armed. They merely awaited his signal. But it had been agreed that their cause would be little served by bloodshed in a cathedral. Cayle had promised that force would be used only as a last, desperate measure. Had that point been reached?

"This way!"

Thomas didn't recognize the voice, nor the rugged, filthy hand that grabbed him and nearly pulled him off balance. The man's face was as filthy as his hands. Squinty eyes and blackened teeth were separated by a bulbous nose. Yet, despite the man's appearance, he plowed a way for them through the crowd.

"Make way for Thomas Torr!" he cried. "Make way for Thomas Torr!"

It was as though the waters of the Red Sea had been rolled back, for a path miraculously appeared. Thomas and Cayle followed close behind their soiled escort.

Bromley's men angled toward them, threatening to cut off their route.

"Don't let them take Thomas Torr!" shouted the escort. He pointed at the converging guards. "Stop them! Don't let them take Thomas Torr!"

The soiled man commanded the army of congregants, and they obeyed. Instantly, thick knots of humanity formed in front of Bromley's men, blocking their progress. As a river breaks through a dam, so people spilled out the doorways, sweeping Bromley's men aside.

The next thing Thomas knew, he and Cayle were outside the cathedral running free as the crowd of humanity closed in behind them, swallowing up their pursuers.

❦

"MASTERFUL!" CAYLE CRIED. "YOU should have seen him! Thomas was masterful!"

Thomas felt his face color. He didn't mind. He hadn't felt this good in a long time.

Howel, Felice, and Kendall were seated around a table littered with cloth strips, parchment, and writing instruments. A slim, gray-bearded man sat with them. A Lollard. Thomas and Cayle were regaling them with their exploits at the cathedral.

"You should have seen Bishop Pole's face when Thomas stood up!" Cayle said. "The man never said another word. Never recovered!"

"So the whole thing went as you expected?" Howel asked. "You had no trouble?"

The possibility of conflict with Bromley had been Howel's foremost concern. He had desperately wanted to accompany them to the cathedral—but so had Felice, and the only way Howel could get his daughter to stay behind was for him to stay with her to make sure she didn't follow.

Kendall had also offered to go. Cayle had decided against it, unsure how the boy would react face-to-face with his father.

"It didn't go exactly as we expected," Thomas said. He explained how Cardinal Barberini had nearly turned the tables on them.

"At that point," Cayle chuckled, "I was preparing myself for life in a London prison."

"I've faced Cardinal Barberini before," Thomas said. "He's not a man you want to oppose very often."

"You should have seen Thomas!" Cayle cried. "He handled the situation masterfully! It was beautiful! One minute I thought we were sheep fodder. The next thing I know Thomas landed a knockout blow!"

"What did you do?" Felice asked.

Pleased with himself, Thomas reached into his gypon and pulled out the cloth strip. He said, "I used the weapon you gave me." To the rest of them, he explained, "Before we left for Coventry, Felice returned this strip to me, which the bishop had handed to her at Fearnleah."

"Oh, fine! Now you tell me!" Cayle cried. "Couldn't you have informed me about that little wonder before I nearly died of apoplexy?"

"I did feel sorry for Cardinal Barberini, though," Thomas said.

"Sorry?" Cayle cried. "He nearly helped Bishop Pole bury you alive for a second time!"

"But I truly believe he was convinced that the signature on that confession was mine," Thomas replied. "It's my guess he had nothing to do with the forgery. Did you see the glare he gave Bishop Pole when he learned the truth?"

"How did you manage to escape?" Howel asked. "Surely Bromley didn't just let you walk away."

Cayle laughed. "That was the miraculous part! God sent us an angel!"

"An angel?" Felice said.

"He was like an angel, wasn't he?" Thomas laughed. "He was the ugliest, dirtiest angel you'd ever hope to see, but a rescuing angel nonetheless."

"What did he say to you just after we got outside?" Cayle asked.

"First, I asked him why he had helped us. Do you know what he told me? He said, 'If Bromley hates you, you've got a lot of friends.'"

"Did you get his name?" Cayle asked.

Thomas nodded and grinned. "Burford."

Cayle howled. "Imagine that! We were rescued by an angel named Burford."

Everyone laughed, all except Kendall, who sat in the corner with a sick expression on his face—his eyes fixed, Thomas couldn't help but notice, on Felice.

◦§ ◦

THAT NIGHT, THOMAS LAY on his back on the grassy slope and stared at the stars overhead, reviewing the day's events.

Howel ambled toward him. "Days don't get any better than this, do they?" he said, reclining next to Thomas.

"Don't get me wrong, I'm pleased with what we were able to accomplish, but I'll settle for a quiet afternoon in a scriptorium any time."

Howel looked over at him. "Do you mean that?"

"Mean what?"

"That you want to get back into the scriptorium."

Thomas took a deep breath. That's not what he'd meant, but Howel seemed to have a way of cutting through the fog of confusion and getting to the heart of a matter.

"Yes. I think I am."

Howel grinned. "Good answer. There's not another like you, Thomas Torr."

Thomas stared at the man who had been more a father to him than any other man. "Thank you for coming after me. On the hillside, and then the next morning, when you shamed me into going to Coventry."

Not only that. The big ploughman had shamed him into returning to the living—to fight for the things he believed in, no matter the odds, including Felice. The man was a convincing teacher. He had a lifetime of experiences to draw upon in his on-going battle with the powerful Bailiff Bromley.

"You would have come to that conclusion sooner or later," Howel replied. "I just helped make it sooner."

Thomas rested his head back and closed his eyes. He did it to hide his feelings. There was no other man on the face of the earth he respected more than Howel. This simple ploughman had more integrity than a hundred noblemen.

And as much as he admired Howel, he loved Howel's daughter. All of his feelings for her were coming back. He didn't want to lose her. He feared, though, that it might already be too late. Still, for all the excitement and adventure and feelings of vindication he felt about the Coventry affair, the part he treasured most was the proud and loving way Felice had looked at him as Cayle narrated their victory over Bishop Pole.

Howel interrupted his thoughts. "Kendall has gone home to Fearnleah," he said.

Thomas didn't answer. He thought, *You're right. Days don't get any better than this.*

FIFTEEN ❧

ELICE AND HER FATHER sat at the table in a house that served as a makeshift scriptorium. Felice sat next to the window, scoring a sheet of parchment as Thomas had taught her to. Howel fumbled mindlessly with the scraps of cloth that lay on the table, some with Scripture verses inscribed on them, others blank. A kindly summer breeze drifted into the room.

Howel said, "Bromley raided Crick three days ago. Made several arrests."

"Who told you that?"

"Gardner. He heard it from those two Lollards who passed through here last night."

"That makes three raids in one week," Felice said.

"These are good times for men like Bromley," Howel replied, "men who love to hate. Now that the restraints are off, he'll hunt until he drops from exhaustion."

Felice leaned forward to make three pin pricks in the parchment. Satisfied that she'd marked the parchment correctly, she looked up. "Are we safe here?"

Howel shrugged. "As safe as we can be in England."

The house in which they sat had been originally used as a refuge for Lollards. Cayle had learned of it while sheltering two of the itinerant preachers. More recently, however, since the destruction of the scriptorium in Lutterworth, the house had been turned into a makeshift scriptorium. Until now it had been a one-man operation. A man named Gardner, a former copyist for Dr.

Wycliffe, did the copy work. When Cayle heard of the house, naturally he'd thought of Thomas.

Despite Thomas's renewed commitment to further the cause of the English translation, Cayle nearly had to drag him to the house. But once the former translator and copyist got a whiff of the parchment, he was ready to roll up his sleeves and get to work.

"You look bored," Felice said to her father.

Howel looked around at the spartan interior of the Lollard house. "I miss our place, that's all," he said. "Our animals. Our routine. Sometimes I even miss the plowing."

Felice laughed. "You really are homesick, if you miss the plowing!"

Fumbling with the cloth strips, Howel asked, "Is there something I can do to help?"

"Not until the others return with the supplies."

"Why does it take four of them to get supplies?"

"Gardner wanted to introduce them to the monks at the abbey, so that in the future any one of them could be sent to get the parchment. Thomas especially wanted to go. He's always wanted to see how parchment was made."

Howel chuckled. "Gardner sure is taken with Thomas."

"He's just happy to have someone of Thomas's ability to help out here."

"Gardner was telling me this morning about hearing Dr. Wycliffe speak about Thomas. From what he said, the rector was quite impressed with him."

"Did you know that Gardner and Thomas shared a desk at the Lutterworth scriptorium?"

"So that's how he knows Thomas."

Felice nodded. "Thomas was telling me last night that Gardner was an expressionless copyist who spent more time correcting his mistakes than he did copying."

"He doesn't strike me as the careless sort."

"Thomas says he's changed. He says Gardner is a completely different person from what he remembers."

"Aren't we all," Howel mused.

Felice sat up and arched her back. A moan escaped as she stretched. Howel slumped further down in his chair.

"I should have gone with the others," he said.

Reaching across the table Felice patted his hand. "I'm glad you didn't. You're good company. Oh! By the way, Thomas heard some news about Bishop Pole."

This perked Howel up.

"Apparently, following the debacle at Coventry, the meeting between Cardinal Barberini and King Richard was canceled."

"That comes as no surprise."

"Also, Cardinal Barberini has left England to return to Rome. Seems he took Bishop Pole with him. Under guard."

"Under guard?" Howel exclaimed.

Felice nodded. "That's what Thomas heard."

Howel reflected on this for a moment. "So you and Thomas are speaking again."

"We never stopped speaking."

"That's true," Howel conceded. "If you call yelling speaking."

Felice didn't respond. She frowned and doubled her concentration on the parchment.

"What is it going to take for the two of you to work out your differences?"

There was a reluctant silence, then, "It's not a matter of working out differences. Like you said, we've all changed. We're not the same people we once were."

"You haven't changed so much you can just toss aside your feelings for each other."

"I'm not so sure."

"One thing hasn't changed."

"No? What's that?"

"You're both as stubborn as mules. And I think it's a shame you're torturing each other."

"I'd rather not talk about it."

Howel sniffed. He leaned his elbows on the table so he could gaze out the window. "All right, let's talk about Kendall then."

"No! We're *not* going to talk about Kendall!" Felice insisted.

"I think it's unfair of you to let Kendall think there might be something between you and him."

Felice flushed in protest. "I don't think I'm being unfair to Kendall!"

"Yes, you are. The boy thinks there's a chance you might marry him someday. And you and I both know that Thomas and you will marry."

"I don't know anything of the sort!"

"Yes, you do. You're just being pigheaded about it."

Felice had had enough. She dropped the parchment and awl onto the table and stood. Tears glistened in her eyes. "Thomas has given me no indication he still cares for me! As for Kendall—"

"Shhhh!"

"He's a kind and considerate friend."

"Shhhhh!"

Howel was standing now too.

"What is it?" Felice asked.

"Don't you hear it?"

"No."

"Listen!" he said.

She did. And what she heard caused her to hold her breath in fear. A distant rumble. Horses. Many of them.

Howel went to the door and opened it a crack. He slammed it shut. "Lord, help us."

Felice felt her pulse quicken. Her father's eyes darted side to side. Taking her by the shoulders he stared hard into her eyes. He muttered a single word. Only one was needed.

"Bromley!"

The door flew open with such force it swung back around and closed again. It slammed open a second time.

Armed and angry men poured into the small room until it was nearly packed. No one said a word, but without exception they focused their hostile stares at Howel. There was a shuffling of feet as a pathway was created, allowing one more man to enter.

"Good afternoon, Bailiff Bromley," Howel said.

The ploughman sat casually at the table, with a piece of parchment in one hand and an awl in the other.

Bromley looked surprised to see Howel. He said, "What do we have here? Cast a net far enough and one never knows what he'll catch."

"God willing," Howel replied, "you'll catch nothing more than a summer cold."

Bromley was not amused. "Where are the others?"

"Others? Look around you. Do you see any others? A single table. A single cot in the corner."

"I count four chairs."

"For guests," Howel replied. "Care to sit down?"

Bromley's eyes roamed around the interior. As they did, men shuffled, moved and leaned so that he could see. The bailiff checked under the cot, under the table, up in the rafters. Finding nothing, he leaned against the table and stared at the parchment, the scraps of cloth, and the tools. Picking up one of the scraps of cloth a sickening look crossed his face.

"How many times must I destroy these?" he seethed.

Howel didn't reply.

"Once a criminal, always a criminal. I should have arrested you years ago and been done with you. Where are the others?"

"If you think there are others because of these," Howel nodded at the cloth strips, "you're mistaken. They're mine."

Bromley snorted, sort of a half-chuckle, half-sneer. "So, you've learned to read have you? You'll have to introduce me to your tutor. I have an ox I'd like him to teach."

"You don't believe me."

"I know you. You're dumber than the dirt you plow."

Reaching across the table, Howel picked up one of the cloth strips. Stretching it between his hands, he said, "*'Truly my soul waiteth upon God: from him cometh my salvation.'*" He set the cloth strip on the table in front of Bromley.

Bromley read it. He scowled.

"Go ahead," Howel challenged him. "Choose any one."

Bromley accepted the challenge. He reached into the middle of the pile, selected a cloth strip, read it, and handed it to Howel.

Howel looked at it and said, "*'My flesh and my heart faileth: but God is the strength of my heart, and my portion for ever.'*"

Bromley's scowl deepened. Convinced it was a trick, he foraged in the pile again, selecting a third cloth strip.

Howel took it from him. With a smile, he said, "*'Sing unto God, ye kingdoms of the earth; O sing praises unto the Lord.'*"

With a growl that rose from deep in his being, Bromley snatched the cloth strip from Howel's hands. "Seize him!" he shouted.

At least half a dozen men jumped on Howel, pinning his arms behind him.

Howel offered no resistance. Shaking his head sadly at his lifelong adversary, he said, "Today's catch is rather pitiful. You've landed yourself the tiniest of fish."

Bromley grabbed a fistful of cloth strips and stuffed them into Howel's mouth. Moving within inches of his captive, he growled, "Congratulations on learning to read. You've just read your death sentence!" To his men, Bromley shouted, "Take him out of here!"

Howel was shoved out the door, bound, and loaded into a waiting cart. Still inside, Bromley overturned the table and cot, smashed the chairs, pounded walls, and tried to pry up floorboards. The more things he destroyed without finding anything, the angrier he became. With a final shriek of frustration, he stormed from the room, only to return moments later with a torch. The crackle of burning wood and the gathering clouds of smoke soon filled the room.

Through the tiniest of cracks, Felice watched in horror as the flames began to claim every inch of the house. Then, she heard footsteps. Had Bromley gone? Should she cry out? Straining to see, she caught a glimpse of something that made her gasp.

Kendall!

He surveyed the room quickly. Then ran out.

A short time later, the sound of horses' hooves could be heard riding off. Felice began to cough from the smoke of the fire.

THOMAS COULDN'T GET OVER how much Gardner had changed. Of course, with the scriptorium's rule of silence there had been little opportunity to become acquainted with any of the copyists, but the man who walked beside him was a completely different man from the one with whom he had once shared a desk.

Gardner explained. "It took the death of Dr. Wycliffe to force me to examine my life. I asked myself, 'Am I willing to die for what I'm doing?' When I finally resolved that indeed I was willing to die for an English translation of the Bible, I decided I'd better start living for it too."

The change was noticeably evident. The printed pages Thomas had seen in the Lollard house were flawless; the production of the books was efficient and professional. Even Gardner's personal appearance had changed. He was much neater, though he had aged and grown a gray beard. About the only part of him that hadn't changed was his bony, twig-like wrists.

The trip to the abbey had been without incident. Thomas had seen how parchment was made. His chief observation? The odors were much worse than he'd been led to believe. Gardner provided the introductions so that future purchases could be made without him. Even the journey itself had been pleasant. Getting acquainted with the new Gardner was more than enlightening; it became clear to Thomas that here was a man with whom he could work comfortably. Cayle kept the conversation lively.

As they drew near to the glen in which the Lollard house was situated, a column of smoke caught Thomas's eye.

Cayle saw it too. "Look there!" he cried.

The foreboding column rose just beyond a clump of ash trees. It was too wide and too black to be a controlled fire.

"The house!" Gardner shouted.

"Howel and Felice!" Thomas added.

Cayle proved to be the fastest of the three. He had already ducked through the burning door frame just as Thomas arrived. Flames had already claimed a major portion of the house. The heat turned his head.

"Thomas! Hurry! Felice is still in here!"

Using his forearm to shield his eyes, Thomas braced himself against the heat and charged into the burning room. Inside, the table and chairs and cot were black, charred, and falling apart, barely recognizable.

"Help me! Help!" Felice's voice was muffled and racked by spasms of coughing.

Cayle stood under burning beams, staring at the wall, puzzled. "She's behind the wall!" he shouted. "How did she get behind the wall?"

Gardner barged into the room. "It takes two men!" he shouted. He could barely be heard above the roar of the flames. He showed Cayle where to grip the wall.

Thomas knew what to do. He ran to the other end of the wall.

"I'll swing my end out," Thomas shouted.

As Thomas bent down to grip the wall he placed his ear against it. Felice's cries and choking cough could be heard all the louder.

He was swallowing smoke with every breath. A trio of coughs and wheezes mixed with the roar and whoosh of the growing fire. The heat pressed heavily upon them, sapping their strength. At the other end of the wall, Cayle bent down, gripped the wall, then jumped back, waving burned hands.

"Use your gypon!" Thomas shouted.

Cayle was ahead of him. He was pulling his shirt over his head. Wrapping it around both hands, he tried again.

"Straight up, then out!" a wheezing Gardner shouted.

"Hurry! Please, Thomas, hurry!"

With all his might, Thomas lifted. He felt the wall move a little. He pulled up harder, using every bit of strength he had. At the other end, his effort was matched by Cayle's, whose face was strained and red.

The wall came free. Thomas swung his end out by lifting and shuffling his feet, all the time shouting, "Felice! Over here! Over here!"

As soon as there was room enough, Thomas set the wall down and poked his head around the side. Behind the wall was a hiding place the length of the room and barely a foot deep. Pages of script, parchment, and an assortment of tools were on shelves, some had fallen to the floor. In the middle of it all was Felice. Coughing. Crying.

Thomas grabbed her hand and pulled her around the wall. Sweeping her into his arms he carried her out of the burning house. A good distance away there was an ash tree. There, he gently laid her on the ground.

"Where's Howel?" he shouted. "I didn't see him in there."

She fought a spasm of coughs to answer him. "They took him!"

"Who took him?"

"Bromley."

Cayle and Gardner ran in and out of the blazing house, rescuing as many printed pages and blank pages of parchment as they could.

Suddenly, Kendall appeared, running down the road toward the house. "What happened?" he shouted.

Thomas pointed to Cayle and Gardner. "Help them!"

Kendall nodded. He ran into the blazing structure and, like the other two men, brought out as many parchments and tools as he could carry.

"It's going fast," Thomas said. "I'd better help."

Desperate arms pulled him back. "Please, don't leave me," Felice cried. "Please, Thomas, I'm frightened." She buried her head against his chest and clung to him as though the fire was closing in around her.

⊰ ⊱

"Kendall? May I speak with you?"

"Felice! How are you feeling?"

The question itself seemed to prompt a residual cough. She had found him standing at the edge of the peasant encampment, which was situated at the base of the grassy slope. It was late. The moon was small and high overhead.

"Take a walk with me?" she asked.

The very offer prompted a huge smile. He fell in step beside her and they strolled across the field.

"I'm really sorry about your father," he said. "Maybe if I'd been there I could have done something."

The mere mention of her father brought tears to her eyes. She fought them back. Now was not the time.

"You saw it all?" he asked.

She nodded. "There was a crack in the wall."

Kendall grew nervous. "With a structure like that I imagine the smoke filled the room rather quickly," he said.

"Yes, it did."

A thin smile crossed his lips.

A moment of silence passed between them.

He stopped walking and turned to her. "I had to come back to you," he confessed. "Even though I know I no longer have a future with you now that Thomas has returned. I know it sounds foolish, but I just couldn't stay away."

Felice didn't reply. She let him do the talking.

"I've been trying to devise a plan to rescue Howel," he said. "I have a pretty good idea where my father might be holding him."

"Kendall?"

"Yes?"

"I saw you in the house."

Her words found their mark. He reacted visibly. "What do you mean?"

"After your father set fire to the house. You came back. I presume to make sure that I was still not in the house."

Kendall chuckled nervously. "That smoke must have really been thick to make you think you saw me there," he said.

"I know what I saw."

Kendall looked at her. His lips quivered.

A voice came from behind him. It was Cayle. "You told your father about the house, didn't you, boy?"

Kendall swung around. Coming out of hiding nearby were Thomas, Kleef, Gardner, and a half-dozen other men.

"Why, Kendall? Why?" Felice cried.

He inched away from the armada of men facing him. Turning to Felice, he pleaded, "You don't know how much I love you!" he cried. "How agonizing these last few days have been for me. At first it was different. I knew you loved Thomas more. I knew I never had a chance with you. But then he was gone and I had that chance. And even after we heard he was dead, I waited. I was patient. Finally, my dreams came true—I knew you loved me. You loved me! I know you did!"

He began to weep. "How could any of us know that Thomas would return?" he continued through his tears. "I thought all was lost. But then he was different, and you didn't like him. And we still had something between us. I . . . I didn't want to give you up!"

He looked from her to the men. His fear was escalating. He spoke more rapidly.

"I made a deal with my father," he cried. "Howel for Thomas. Your father can be rescued. It's Thomas they want!"

"We've heard enough," Cayle said.

Instantly, Kendall was surrounded by men. He sank to his knees, helpless.

Felice approached Cayle. She placed her hand on his arm. "Please, don't hurt him," she said.

"After what he did to your father?" Cayle cried. "And nearly to you!"

"He is not evil."

Cayle grimaced with disgust. He stood silently for long minutes, debating with himself. Finally, he said to his men, "Show the boy the road back to Fearnleah. And make sure he takes it!" Turning back to Felice, he said, "You realize, don't you, that this means we're going to have to move again."

Felice nodded. "Thank you."

Thomas moved to her side, saying nothing, simply standing beside her. She placed her head against his chest. And wept.

SIXTEEN &

*L*ORD HARBOROUGH REFUSES TO intercede," Thomas said as he pushed his way into the lean-to, then dropped to the ground, angry and defeated. Cayle tossed his traveling pouch to the back of the lean-to, equally disgusted.

Felice stirred a pot of stew and took in the news. She hooked the stirring spoon on the spit and joined them, wiping her hands with a towel.

"The coward!" Thomas shouted, pounding his fist against the ground.

Cayle interpreted, "Lord Harborough claimed he was taking a great risk just seeing us."

"'I'm only one man!'" Thomas cried, mimicking the whiny noble. "'What can one man do?'"

"He's not going to do anything to help us?" Felice asked.

Thomas shook his head. "He's afraid of Bromley! You can see it in his eyes!"

The day after Howel's arrest, he and Cayle had journeyed to Lord Harborough's manor, requesting a reprieve for the ploughman. Thinking back on it now, Thomas wondered if his chances would have been better if he'd gone alone.

He had been so sure that Lord Harborough would help them! Never once had he asked his lordship for anything, and yet he had always tried to live up to the nobleman's expectations of him. That in itself ought to count for something. Besides that, you would think his lordship would feel indebted to Howel for all that the ploughman had done over the years by raising Thomas. Maybe

Cayle was right. Nobles cared nothing for peasants except to use them to make their own lives comfortable.

As the events replayed themselves over and over in his mind, he remembered something Wycliffe had once told him: "I have at times placed my faith in men of power and wealth to assist and strengthen me during times of travail, only to be deserted by them. Foolishly, I looked to the hills. Thomas, trust the words of the psalmist. Put not your faith in kings or nobles or clergy. Put your faith in God alone. 'From whence cometh my help? My help cometh from the LORD ...'"

"Where does that leave us?" Felice asked.

"It looks like we're on our own," Cayle replied.

"It's time we stopped looking to the hills for our help," Thomas said.

⋐§ ⧽⋑

A WEEK LATER, THE morning selected for Howel's execution dawned clear and hot. Thomas felt that he would suffocate under the hooded cloak he wore. It was much too heavy for this kind of weather. He was aware, too, that many other people had noticed his unseasonal apparel. He wondered if Cayle and Felice were getting as many stares from the others who were traveling to the execution site.

He glanced at the two cloaked figures beside him. Their heads were bowed slightly. He couldn't see their faces to catch their eye. The disguises were proving to be an unexpected encumbrance. In fact, the only way he knew for sure Felice was walking between him and Cayle was because she was the shorter of the two.

For three straight days, he and Felice had argued. Thomas had insisted that she remain behind. It would be too dangerous. She had insisted on going, saying the only way they would stop her would be to bind and gag her. Even then, she'd warned, the ropes had better be new and thick. At the eleventh hour Thomas relented, deciding it would be better for her to be part of the plan from the beginning than to show up unexpectedly as a random element.

Something hit him in the chest. Looking down, he saw Cayle's long arm stretched out in front of Felice and him. They stopped. With a nod, Cayle motioned ahead. Not more than a dozen feet in front of them stood two armed guards, inspecting everyone who passed by. One man, who wore a liripipe, had it unceremoniously ripped from his head so the guards could get a better look at his face.

Motioning for Thomas and Felice to hold their ground, he turned and signaled Kleef who was trailing behind at a distance.

The scarred man hurried past them. He too was wearing a hood. He walked brazenly toward the two guards and attempted to pass without stopping. One of the guards grabbed him and reached for his hood. Kleef flew into a rage. He lunged at them, thrusting his scarred face into their faces and shrieking like a stuck pig.

In the tussle, one guard plopped onto his backside with a thud. The other had his hands full with Kleef. They wrestled for position, and just as the fallen guard was nearly up, the two wrestlers bowled him over. Now all three were on the ground.

Meanwhile, spectators passed by toward the execution site, hindered only momentarily by the sight of three men wrestling on the ground. Thomas, Cayle, and Felice were among those who continued on toward the execution site unchallenged.

The place of execution was a hill not far from Howel's house in Fearnleah, so Felice and Thomas knew it well. They had spent many a summer's eve atop the hill, watching the stars pop out all across the sky.

The execution site was arranged so that spectators would stand on a field that Howel had plowed every year for as long as most of them could remember. This year the field lay fallow.

The hill provided a natural platform for the event. Rising from the center of the mound was a solitary wooden post. Thick. Sturdy. Suitable for a big man. A huge pile of wood was stacked nearby. Two men stood guard atop the mound.

With Thomas in the lead, the hooded figures took a position just to the right of center. He glanced at Cayle to indicate that this was the spot he'd spoken of earlier, when they'd planned the rescue.

Beside him, Felice raised her head—and got her first sight of the execution post. She swooned. Thomas caught her.

"It's the heat," she said, quickly regaining her feet.

Thomas smiled assuringly. Though she insisted she was fine, he kept a supporting hand under her arm.

The crowd began filling in behind them. Cayle spent the time studying every direction, evaluating their chances of success. After several minutes, he looked at Thomas and nodded his approval.

Their rescue plan had two key elements: surprise and numbers. Of the two, surprise was the weaker hand. They conceded that Bromley might expect a rescue attempt. Still, he didn't know how or when. As for numbers, they figured that Bromley would employ about a dozen men to guard the event. And that estimate might even be high—he needed only four or five men, at best, to carry out the execution. It wasn't as though they were executing a king.

The plan was to overwhelm them. Cayle had enlisted more than fifty men to assist in the rescue. Finding fifty willing men had not been difficult. As angel Burford had prophesied, there were a lot of men eager to take a measure of revenge against Bailiff Bromley.

Something caught Thomas's eye. He peered into the distance beyond the hill. A lone horseman paused on high ground, just long enough to be seen, then disappeared behind the ridge.

At Cayle's signal, the rider would come toward the execution site, casually at first. His approach would serve as a timing devise, like the fuse of a bomb. The other parties in the rescue effort would time their moves based on his approach. When the rider was a hundred yards distant, Felice would scream for mercy and pretend to faint.

This was where Cayle's superior numbers figured in. They would storm the mound and overpower Bromley's guards and the executioner. Thomas and Cayle would follow behind them and free Howel just as the rider reached the mound. The two of them would help Howel onto the horse to make good his escape. Then, Felice, Thomas, Cayle, and the others would slip away in the confusion.

Thomas studied the guards atop the execution mound. They were of average height and weight. Larger than he, but not as large as Cayle. The experienced revolutionary had told Thomas not to worry about the guards—his men would take care of them. Thomas was to concentrate on freeing Howel.

Still, Thomas worried.

All around them, the crowd was in a festive mood. Men laughed and slapped their knees as they swapped farm and animal stories. Women complained about their children, complained about their husbands, and shared the latest gossip. Little children ran among the legs of the adults like they would trees in a forest, squealing and playing hide-and-seek.

Thomas heard a ripple of excitement coming from the back edge of the crowd. He turned to see what was causing it. A cart approached. In it was a large man, heavily bound and on his knees. Howel. A black-hooded executioner stood over him. Bailiff Bromley rode in triumph beside the cart on a large war horse. The parish priest followed close behind the cart with a dozen armed men trailing behind him. The cart rumbled slowly toward the execution mound.

Catching sight of her father, Felice shuddered. She whimpered. Thomas placed his arm around her. It didn't seem to help. The closer the cart came to the execution mound, the more disturbed Felice became. Thomas turned her away so she couldn't see. She buried her head against his chest. Her shoulders shook with sobs.

Placing his head next to hers, he whispered. "No matter what happens, I will always love you."

Felice raised her head. Tear-glazed eyes met his. It was the first time since Thomas's return from Rome that they had been this close, this intimate. Felice didn't say a word. She didn't have to. They both knew. They had always known.

"God in heaven, I don't believe it!"

Cayle's cry separated them. Thomas looked up.

Kendall! He was riding with his father's men. Felice shook her head, finding it equally difficult to believe that Kendall would be counted with his father in this matter. Thomas too couldn't believe it. But before he had a chance to say anything, Cayle cried out again.

"Something's wrong!"

He glanced beyond the mound. Thomas followed his gaze.

The horseman had reappeared. He rode back and forth nervously as though he was pacing.

"Not yet! Not yet!" Cayle muttered.

Thomas checked the cart's progress. The oxen had slowed as they began to ascend the mound.

While Cayle's attention was fixed on the rider, Thomas kept his eye on Kendall. The bailiff's son dismounted, handing his reins to a boy. He seemed intensely interested in the crowd. His eyes scanned slowly from the edges toward the middle.

"Put your head down!" Thomas whispered.

"What now?" Cayle cried.

"Kendall. He's looking for something. Probably us."

"I knew I should have dispatched that boy when I had the chance," Cayle muttered.

"By the time he sees us, it'll be too late," Thomas replied.

Atop the mound the cart with the prisoner came to a jolting halt next to the wooden post. The executioner assisted Howel to his feet, climbed out of the cart, then turned to help his prisoner down. Thomas thought the executioner's courtesy odd. In a matter of minutes he would attempt to kill the man, yet now he was concerned lest the condemned man stumble and fall?

Howel faced the crowd and Thomas got his first good look at him. He had to fight back a surge of rage. Howel was dressed in a filthy, stained serge tunic, little more than a sack. Bits of straw and clumps of dirt soiled it; not only it, but his hair as well. The man's arms and legs were discolored with not a few red stripes. His face was blue with bruises. One eye was black and swollen shut.

Thomas heard a gasp beside him. Felice got a glimpse of her father. She trembled in Thomas's arms.

"I don't like it," Cayle said, still pondering the rider's unusual activity. "Something's wrong. Something's definitely wrong."

Thomas turned to see for himself. No sooner had he done so than the rider spurred his horse down the hill at a gallop. He rode straight for them, shouting, whooping, waving his arm over his head.

Cayle cursed. "No! Not yet, you fool!" He glanced all around him. His men had not yet moved into position.

"What is he doing?" Felice cried. "Did you give the signal?"

"Of course I didn't give the signal!" Cayle spat.

Their element of surprise dissipated with the growing murmur of the crowd. Soon everyone's attention was on the approaching rider, including the guards and Bromley. Even Howel turned his head to see who was stealing attention away from his execution.

"Signal the men!" Thomas cried.

"They're not—" Cayle stopped himself.

Solitary figures appeared in strategic locations. This was the signal the men were in position and ready to attack.

Cayle took charge. "Thomas. Get to Howel any way you can. We may have to get him out of here on foot!"

Thomas nodded, merely in recognition that he'd heard the order. He had no idea how he was going to carry it out.

Cayle signaled his men with a shrill whistle.

As the rider approached, his whooping turned into words. "Trap! It's a trap! It's a trap!"

The warning came too late.

Standing confidently on the mound of execution Bromley brandished his sword. His face red, his neck taut, he pointed to three distinct places and shouted, "Now! Now! Now! Attack! Attack! Attack! Attack! Attack!"

Flaming arrows crisscrossed high overhead. The bailiff had planned a signal of his own.

From a ravine hidden behind the execution site mounted soldiers poured forth like bats from a cave. Hundreds of them, swarming, encircling the execution mound and the spectators, cutting Thomas and Felice and Cayle off from all support, flushing Cayle's men from their positions, routing them, scattering them in every direction.

The rider had broken off his approach and was being pursued by half a dozen soldiers on horseback. Cayle's men had been completely neutralized. Thomas and Cayle exchanged glances. It was just the three of them now.

Thomas turned to Felice. "Leave! Get out of here! Meet us back at the camp."

Felice shook her head. "I'm not—"

"Don't argue with me! There isn't time!"

He was right, there wasn't time. Not for an argument and not for a rescue. Before he and Cayle could take a single rescuing step, a line of guards on foot encircled the mound, separating the spectators from the execution site. There must have been fifty of them. All chance of breaking through them vanished. Bromley had thought of every contingency.

Except one.

His son.

Behind Bromley, Kendall drew his sword. He charged the executioner. The hooded man, his attention drawn by Kendall's yell, turned to intercept him. Kendall planted his foot in the man's chest and sent him flying. Reaching behind the prisoner, he clawed at the ropes.

"Oh, Kendall!" Felice gasped.

Thomas stood with the rest of the crowd, all dumbfounded, as Bromley's son attempted to free Howel.

"I told you he wasn't evil!" Felice said excitedly.

"Be ready," Cayle said, "this may be our chance."

Thomas was way ahead of him. If Kendall could free the ploughman, maybe Howel could cause enough distraction for them to act. Thomas didn't even want to think about how they might escape. One thing at a time.

Howel was glancing over his shoulder. His muscles flexed as he tried to break free of his bonds. But it wasn't to be. Kendall couldn't free him quickly enough.

The next instant, his rescuer flew backward headfirst. With one hand, Bromley had the boy by the hair, with the other he held his sword across the boy's neck. Howel made a move toward them, only to be knocked back by one guard while another assisted the executioner to his feet.

Order was restored atop the mound.

A frustrated cry escaped from Thomas's lips.

"So, I have a traitor in my house," Bromley said loudly. "Strange how that doesn't come as any surprise."

Kendall was stripped of his sword. His head jerked back at an awkward angle, he glared at his father but said nothing.

Dragging his son to the execution post, Bromley shoved the boy's face against it. "Is this what you choose over me?" he screamed through clenched teeth. He was shaking with rage. "You would side with an ignorant ploughman over your own father?"

His cheek smashed against the stake, Kendall managed to mutter, "I have no father."

This enraged Bromley even more. With his forearm he smashed his son's face against the post again. He took a step back, looked at his dazed son, then smashed him again. Kendall slumped to his knees, still leaning against the execution post.

Standing beside Thomas, Felice watched with horror-stricken eyes. Her hands were raised to her mouth. She wept for Kendall. He'd done this for her. To redeem himself.

Unexpectedly, Kendall shoved himself away from the post, catching his father by surprise. He rolled through his father's legs, knocking him over like a bowling pin. Kendall lost no time. Once more he shoved the executioner aside and grabbed at the ropes to free Howel.

The next instant, Kendall's eyes flew open wide. Startled. Shocked. They fluttered as the strength and life drained from him. He slumped to his knees. His mouth dropped open as he gazed down at the steel blade that protruded from his chest.

Then, Bailiff Bromley withdrew his blade from his son's torso.

"Oh, Kendall!" Felice whimpered. She covered her face with her hands. Her shoulders shook with sobs.

Thomas stood dumbfounded, as did Cayle and the rest of the crowd as the macabre drama played out before them.

The bailiff had stunned even himself. He watched as his son fell face forward onto the ground. He staggered a few feet, as if pulled by the weight of his blade. After a moment or two, the bailiff rallied.

"Tie him to the post with the heretic!" Bromley ordered, his voice low and heavy with authority.

The priest held his prayer book against his chest as though his life depended upon it. He shook so hard the bottom of his clerical robe could be seen quivering from a good distance away.

The executioner moved Howel to the pole and bound him. Then, gathering the boy in his arms, he did his best to hold the boy in place while tying him. The limp weight of the boy was proving to be a problem. He looked to a couple of guards for help.

"I'll hold him," Howel said.

The executioner stared dumbly at him, puzzled by the offer.

"No trick," Howel assured him. "I'll hold him while you tie us both."

The executioner hesitated. He looked to Bromley.

The bailiff stared back at them stone-faced. With a flick of the back of his hand he indicated he didn't care. Howel's hands were untied and Kendall was placed in his arms. Then the two of them were tied to the post.

Thomas and Felice and Cayle looked on with disbelief as preparations continued for the execution. Their rescue plan had been scuttled; their forces were scattered; Kendall, in a surprise rescue effort, had failed and was dead. The guards were stronger, better armed, and outnumbered them.

Thomas had never felt more helpless in his life.

Bailiff Bromley stepped forward to address the crowd. The man showed no sign of emotion over the death of his son. Holding a piece of paper in his hand, he read from it.

"Let it be known by all here present, that this man, Howel, a ploughman of Fearnleah, did deliberately and maliciously violate the law which forbids persons from possessing sacred texts. Furthermore, that he assisted in the translation of these texts into the vulgar language, an act which is strictly forbidden."

Bromley turned to the parish priest of Fearnleah, who was still ashen white and trembling. Bromley said something to him that Thomas couldn't hear. But the priest heard and he fumbled frantically to retrieve something from a pouch. He produced a handful of cloth strips which he gave to Bromley.

The bailiff held the strips over his head and cried, "These strips of cloth bearing forbidden sacred text were found in this man's possession. When questioned, he did not deny they belonged to him. This evidence testifies against him."

Thomas turned to Cayle. "We've got to do something!"

"What can we do?" an exasperated Cayle replied. "There are too many of them!"

Bromley gave way to the priest who moved in front of the condemned man. With a shaky voice, he said, "For all these many years, I have known you to be a just man and a good and kind father. However, you have violated the laws of God and England and for this offense, you are condemned to die."

"Thomas? Don't let it end this way," Felice cried.

Thomas took a step toward the mound. Cayle grabbed his arm. "What are you doing?"

"I'm going up there to get Howel."

"And get yourself and us killed too? Would Howel want that?"

The priest continued, "As you prepare to meet your judge, give glory to God and renounce this heretical translation perpetrated by a student of the devil himself, John Wycliffe. Confess your sin, my son, that God may have mercy on your soul."

The crowd hushed. Would the huge ploughman make a tearful confession? Would he curse God, the King, the bailiff, and all the spectators for killing him? Would he plead his innocence and beg mercy? These and a hundred other responses they had witnessed at public executions. This was the moment of high drama. This was the reason for their coming.

The condemned man cradled the dead boy in his arms. He returned the stare of the crowd. Then, unexpectedly, a hint of a smile appeared and grew steadily until it erupted in a full-blown belly laugh.

Howel's reaction was so unexpected, it was eerie. Deep, hollow laughter wafted over the shocked crowd. Some of them shuddered and hid their children's eyes, thinking the ploughman mad. The condemned man lifted his eyes to the sky.

He shouted, "'Come unto me, all ye that labour and are heavy laden, and I will give you rest.'"

The bailiff shot a glance at the priest. Was Howel quoting Scripture? He suspected as much but didn't know for sure. He wanted confirmation. The priest affirmed his suspicions with a nod.

Howel addressed the men and women who had come to watch him burn. "The first time I heard those words," he said, "was the day my brother died. And now I pass them along to you on the day I die! Listen to it! It is God's invitation for every man!"

"Silence him!" Bromley shouted.

The executioner fumbled around the cart looking for something with which to gag the prisoner. He found nothing.

Howel shouted, "Here's another one. 'The Lord is my shepherd!' Do you know where I learned that? At my house! My own hand wrote the first letter! Think of it! God's words in my own—"

Bromley had taken the matter into his own hands. As he'd done the day of Howel's arrest, he did again now. Fistfuls of cloth strips were stuffed into Howel's mouth.

Felice turned to Thomas. "I'm going to remove my hood."

"What? No!"

"I'm not going to let my father die alone, thinking we've abandoned him."

Thomas gripped both her hands to prevent her from doing it. "If you remove your hood you will soon be up there with him!"

"Maybe that's the way it should be," she replied.

"Felice, think about your father! How will he feel seeing you lashed to the post beside him? He hid you and tricked Bromley to keep you safe! Don't throw that away!"

Her hands relaxed.

Bromley was addressing the crowd again. "Let this man's death serve as an example to all who would embrace or promote the heresy of John Wycliffe."

He ordered the fire to be set.

Three men stacked kindling branches around the base of the post up to Howel's knees. The executioner was handed a torch. Without wasting a moment, he circled the post, lighting the kindling at various points.

"Please, God, no," Felice cried.

Thomas pulled her close to him.

The flames took hold and multiplied, leaping as high as the condemned man's waist. Howel looked down at the fire all around him. He squeezed Kendall tight and laid his cheek against the top of the boy's head.

The crowd grew excited. Their level of frenzy grew in proportion to the fire.

The flames rose to Howel's chest. Lifting his head, he managed to spit the cloths from his mouth.

Moving his head from side to side to duck the flames, he shouted, "If it is a crime for an Englishman to read the Word of God, then I would rather die than be an Englishman!"

"Silence him!" Bromley shouted.

"The flames embrace us!" Howel cried. "I welcome them! I will light the land for but a short time, but there is a light spreading across England that will never be extinguished! And that light is the Word of God!"

Bromley was ranting. "Shut him up! Shut him up!"

But the flames were too high, the fire too hot. The executioner could not get close enough to prevent Howel from speaking.

A flash of pain crossed Howel's face. He moaned. His eyes rolled upward. They fluttered, but only momentarily. He was struggling to keep his senses intact. He laid his head against the burning boy in his arms. "Forgive me, Kendall, for thinking you were anything like your father."

"Do something!" Bromley raged. "Silence him!"

Howel cuddled the dead boy in his arms and said, "We will enter heaven together."

Felice's knees buckled. When Thomas found it difficult to keep her standing, Cayle moved to her other side. Together, they held her up.

She mumbled almost incoherently, "Take him, God, please take him. I cannot bear to watch him suffer."

The crackling and popping of the fire was loud now. The flames extended well above the post. Howel and Kendall could be seen only intermittently between the sheets of flame.

Howel lifted his head. Slowly, almost regally. His eyes were still clear. He looked straight at Felice. It was as though he knew exactly where she would be standing.

"Don't weep for me, my beloved," he said.

"I love you, Father!" Felice whispered.

He looked at Thomas. "My son, don't let the lamp flicker." A flame covered his face.

At that moment, Thomas's eyes were opened, and he saw beyond the flames.

He saw Peter, crucified upside down.

He saw row after row of Christians covered with pitch, lighting Nero's circus.

He saw the tombs of the martyrs, buried deep in Rome's bosom.

And he saw Howel, a ploughman, a commoner—a man who had heard the Word of God in his native tongue, and who, like those who had gone before him, was willing to die for what he knew to be good and true.

"What can one man do?"

"Did you say something?" Cayle asked.

Thomas took Felice in his arms, turning her away from the mound. The flames were high. Howel could no longer be seen.

"I was just thinking of the question Lord Harborough kept asking, 'What can one man do?'"

"Give me ten men like Howel," Cayle said, "and I'll change England."

Thomas lifted Felice's chin until their eyes met. "Never have I known a man as wise and strong as your father," he said. "As God is my witness, I will not rest until every man, woman, and child in this land knows Holy Scripture as your father knew it."

Felice managed a weak smile. "Take me home," she said.

A NOTE FROM THE AUTHOR &

The idea for a series of novels set during the time of the appearance of the early English versions of the Bible came to me as I was thinking of the men and women today who risk their lives to smuggle Bibles into various countries. The stories these adventurers tell are awe-inspiring—and their belief in the power of the Bible to alter the course of lives and nations is humbling.

And what of those who risk their lives to possess this contraband? They face prison and death sometimes for a single page of Bible text.

How strange this seems to us. The Bible as contraband? Even stranger is the thought of a country without the Bible. Our problem is not that we don't have God's Word; our problem is choosing which of the many English versions to read—not to mention deciding about study notes, red-letter editions, hard cover, soft cover, or leather cover; pictures or no pictures; maps; size; gold-leaf edges, and whether to have our names embossed in gold on the cover.

How far we've come since those first English versions. And how much we've forgotten about those early English translators and those who first read the Bible in English. They have more in common with the smugglers and the prisoners than they have with us.

We haul our Bibles around all too glibly, having forgotten the price that was paid so that we might have the privilege of reading a Bible in English. The purpose of this series of novels, then, is to refresh our memories by portraying the lives of people like us who were not as fortunate as we are to live in an age when the Bible is so freely and readily available. It is my prayer that, after reading these novels, you will be unable to pick up your Bible without offering a silent prayer of gratitude for those who have gone before us, who thought safety and health and life itself was not too great a price to pay that believers might have a Bible in a language they understand.

A few historical notes regarding *Glimpses of Truth*:

John Wycliffe spent most of his adult life attempting to bring about reform within the Roman Catholic Church. What is most amazing about his effort is that he preceded Martin Luther and the Protestant Reformation by nearly two hundred years. While most of his struggle took place in academic, political, and ecclesiastical arenas, it was the work he accomplished in the small village of Lutterworth during the final two years of his life that was most significant. For it was here he completed his greatest work—an English version of the Bible.

While he was not the first man to translate Scripture into English, his translation marked an epoch in the development of the English language. Whereas Chaucer is recognized as the father of English poetry, Wycliffe is recognized as the father of English prose.

Probably the most compelling evidence of Wycliffe's continuing impact is an odd event that occurred thirty years after his death. Roman Catholic officials were still so incensed over the impact of Wycliffe's work that they ordered his bones to be exhumed and publicly burned. His ashes were then scattered over the River Swift at Lutterworth as a warning to those who would embrace his translation and teachings.

So then, if Wycliffe's version is such wonderful English, why did I substitute for it, in this novel, text from the King James Version?

While Wycliffe's version was revolutionary for its time, it is still Middle English and extremely difficult to read. Those of you who have struggled through unrevised versions of *The Canterbury Tales* know what I'm talking about. The vocabulary, structure, even the letters themselves appear foreign to us.

In this story I wanted to capture the wonder the English peasants must have felt the first time they heard God's Word in their own language. I attempted to recreate this by juxtaposing Latin text (which they didn't understand any more than you do) with the King James Version. Produced in 1611, this version retains an old English feel with beauty and readability.

One other note about Wycliffe's version. It was a very literal translation. He retained Latin constructions and word order, which made it difficult to read. Even he recognized this, and later versions of the Wycliffe translation attempted to improve its readability. His assistant at Lutterworth, John Purvey, is credited with this revision. In this novel, Thomas Torr is also given this task.

Whenever one reads a historical novel, the question inevitably rises, "Which parts are historical and which parts are fictional?"

With the exception of John Wycliffe, all the major characters of this story are fictional. Thomas, Felice, and Howel represent the peasant class. Bailiff Bromley and Kendall represent a rare middle class, neither peasant nor nobility. Lord Harborough, of course, represents nobility with his ties to King and Parliament. Bishop Pole and the cardinals in Rome represent ecclesiastical authority. And Cayle represents the growing unrest among the peasants, which led to the Peasant's Revolt of 1381, referred to in this story. Political life in England during this time was a precarious balance of all these elements.

Of course, references to the English King and the Roman Catholic Pope and their political worlds are based on actual history.

As for the events themselves, they are largely fictional. I have attempted to recreate what life was like for the common Englishman. Since they spent their days from sunup to sundown merely trying to survive, they did not keep written records. Most accounts of this time record life among the nobility.

I did my best to portray settings historically. The celebration of Christ's Mass (Christmas), the choosing of the Lord of Misrule, the making of books in a scriptorium, the houses and meals, Rome and Saint Peter's, medical treatments, and worship—all these things have been drawn from historical accounts (see the "Historical Annotations and Bibliography" section, which follows).

One area of study that has enriched me and has become a personal joy is that of the chant. Its structure and message are inspiring. And its ability to lift a person's heart and mind heavenward is phenomenal. When writing the worship scenes I played this music to inspire me. My fear is that my limited abilities have not done it justice.

As I already mentioned, all things related to John Wycliffe are historical. With the exception of any personal comments he makes to Thomas, I drew from his writings to communicate his position. The account of his death is based on historical records. As for the sermon he preached that day, we have no record of the text. The text I use in this novel, however, is an actual sermon of his, though I don't know for certain the date on which it was preached.

Lutterworth is a real village. A scriptorium was housed there, as portrayed in the story. But because there is no record of how this particular scriptorium functioned or was laid out, I portrayed it from general accounts of how a scriptorium was operated.

Wycliffe's itinerant preachers, the Lollards, are a matter of history. It was they who sealed the success of the Wycliffe translation by taking the Scriptures to the English countryside. As for the rumors that they and the Wycliffe translation incited the peasants to revolt, this too is historical—historical, unsubstantiated rumor.

To conclude on a personal note: on September 6, 1997, as I was writing the first draft of this book, I took a break to watch the funeral of Princess Diana, held at the historic Westminster Abbey in London. During the ceremony, Tony Blair, the Prime Minister of England, read from the Bible. His passage was 1 Corinthians 13.

Naturally, everyone's thoughts were focused on the untimely loss of the charismatic and beloved princess, and on the two young sons she had left behind. As the Scripture passage was read, however, I couldn't help but notice that the Prime Minister was reading publicly from an English version of the Bible. I was struck by the fact that there was no outrage, no alarm, not so much as a sneer or raised eyebrow in reaction to what he was doing.

This complete absence of hostile reaction is testimony to the men and women of God who died martyrs' deaths for doing what the Prime Minister of England today does so casually. These courageous Christians of ages past did not live to see this day, though I'm sure, as the writer of Hebrews says, "they dreamed of it from afar." Their victory is complete, their reward is sure. And we are the beneficiaries of their pain and sacrifice.

JACK CAVANAUGH
OCTOBER, 1998

AFTERWORD
THE HISTORICAL BACKGROUND OF
JACK CAVANAUGH'S BOOK OF BOOKS SERIES
BY WILLIAM E. NIX

THE BOOK OF BOOKS series by Jack Cavanaugh covers nearly three centuries—from John Wycliffe (c. 1328–84) to King James I of England (1566–1625). During those years, people experienced dramatic changes that parallel our own times. Forces, often remote and mysterious, challenged standards of authority, tradition, belief, and values. Social allegiances, class structures, and family relationships were changed throughout Europe.

When Wycliffe was born, men and women reasonably hoped they were creating a serene civilization that would endure for centuries. Religious vitality had transformed society. Great works of art and architecture complemented the profound philosophies that had developed in the newly emerging universities. Dualistic heresies had been suppressed, and the papacy was universally accepted as the head of a common Christian religion. Europe was relatively prosperous, and the great nations were at peace. But the appearance of tranquility was an illusion. The achievements, though splendid, were not stable. All was not well with the world.

Nature itself had a profound impact on life during these centuries. Between 1100 and 1300, Europe reached its maximum level of expansion during a period of "optimum climate." But in about 1300, Europe entered a cyclical climatic change that lasted nearly 500 years. By 1400, the average monthly temperature had dropped about 1 to 1.5 degrees centigrade. Around 1550 another average temperature drop resulted in the "little ice age," which persisted until the nineteenth century. Though the change may have been all but imperceptible to humans, the growing seasons were significantly altered and rainfall increased. The cooling climate, especially in northern Europe, caused the tree line to move lower in mountainous regions, and tilled fields at higher levels were abandoned. Important food sources were displaced, the sea route to Greenland became unnavigable, floods were rampant in Holland, fish migrated from the Baltic, and even the substantial wine industry in England disappeared. All because of the climate.

Dramatic changes in population growth affected the territorial interests of the newly emerging nation states. By 1300, the population of Europe was two and a half times what it had been in 1000, pushing limits of existing technology and patterns of soil exploitation. After 1300, this growth first leveled off and then declined sharply as the result of widespread famine and epidemics in Europe from 1313 to 1317. Then Europe was struck by one of the most catastrophic scourges in human history—the Black Death (1347–50).

The Black Death (probably bubonic plague) originated in China, spread across the heartland of Asia along the caravan routes, and entered the Crimea. Merchants carried it on to Constantinople and Italy. It swept across Europe over the next two decades and, endemically, for generations. By 1400, the population of Europe was reduced by one-third to one-half its pre-plague level. And although after 1450, the trend began to reverse, Europe was not again as densely populated as it had been in 1300 until the seventeenth century.

While previously the Roman Catholic Church had been the only institution to reach into every local community, in the century following the Fourth Lateran Council (1215), moral laxity and corruption among the clergy became widespread as it did in society in general. Papal power declined and secular rulers reclaimed lost prerogatives.

In 1295, Kings Philip IV of France and Edward I of England struggled to gain the upper hand in their long-standing rivalry. Both rulers sought funds by taxing the clergy within their domains. When Pope Boniface VIII forbid the clergy to pay such taxes without papal consent, Philip challenged the assertion of papal authority in 1301, and even though Boniface issued the Bulla Unam Sanctum (1302) as a response, the pope was unable to enforce his claims.

The succeeding pope, Clement V (1305–14), dominated by Philip IV, was consecrated and enthroned at Lyons in southern France. He moved the official papal residence to Avignon instead of Rome (1309). Although Avignon was not a French city at that time, the popes were completely under French influence until 1377—the so-called "Babylonian Captivity." When the Black Death spread to Avignon (1347), half of the College of Cardinals died in a few weeks. Finally, Pope Gregory XI returned the papacy to Rome in 1377, but he died the following year, and contentious rivals immediately claimed the papal throne. The "Great Schism" (1378–1414) engulfed the church in further turmoil.

France and England were deeply shaken by the events of the fourteenth century. Dislocations of the population by death and mass migrations into towns and cities caused new problems. Administrative structures survived as political units, but at times neither France nor England could preserve law and order. Edward I of England was preoccupied with a war against the Scots when the French king, Philip VI, "confiscated" the duchy of Gascony. Edward reacted by declaring war on the "so-called king of France" and launched the devastating Hundred Years' War (1337–1453). The Black Death then swept across France in 1348 and was carried to England in the autumn of that year before raging through the rest of the British Isles in 1349. The better range, striking power, rapid-fire capability, and tactical use of the English longbow enabled the English to overpower the heavily armored feudal armies of France and to effectively end the first phase of the wars at the Battle of Poitiers (1356).

Panic caused by famine, epidemics, and the Black Death drove the people to emotional instability. Bloody peasant rebellions and the senseless civil and religious wars took place after the plague. The practice of witchcraft, almost unknown in the early Middle Ages, also reached new heights as desperate men and women sought answers for the troubles that befell them. Although secular philosophies were prominent, this was not an age of worldly cynicism about religion. Mysticism, both orthodox and heretical, became commonplace. Many people entered regular and informal religious communities. Some brought God's Word into the vernacular languages, such as the Lollards, John Wycliffe, John Purvey, and William Tyndale.

The second phase of the Hundred Years' Wars, initiated by Henry V, added to the already heavy burden, as England lost everything it had gained in the first phase and more. But an even more severe trial followed the end of the war when the restless nobility and professional soldiery returned from France to plunge the country into the Wars of the Roses (1454–85) over rival claims to the throne. Finally, Henry VII, claimed the throne by right of conquest and a dubious hereditary claim. After nearly 150 years, war, pestilence, bloodshed, violence, plots, and counter-plots had sickened and exhausted the people and killed off most of the leaders among the nobility.

Christopher Columbus rediscovered the New World in 1492 just as the population of Europe was beginning to hold its own. Sponsored by Ferdinand II and Isabella, then occupied with expulsion of the Moors from Spain, Columbus reopened boundaries that provided opportunities for new levels of prosperity, but not without difficulty. Spain and Portugal appealed to Pope Alexander VI to settle their new territorial disputes in the New World. He drew a line of demarcation (1493) that was revised by the Treaty of Tordesillas (1494). The agreements disregarded the interests of Europe's other contending rivals.

Meanwhile, Henry VII (1485–1509) proved himself one of England's ablest rulers. His children were married to leading royal families in Europe. Prince Arthur married Catherine of Aragon (1501). When Arthur died (1502), lengthy negotiations resulted in Catherine's betrothal to Prince Henry (1503). Princess Margaret married James IV of Scotland, and Princess Mary married Louis XII of France. These steps secured Henry VII as England's legitimate monarch. When Henry VIII (1509–46) came to the thrown he had a full treasury, a united nation, an efficient administration, and his brother's widow for a wife. England, with only half the population of Spain and a fourth that of France, compared well with them in governmental efficiency and military might.

Popes had honored Louis XI as the "Most Christian King" of France and Ferdinand II and Isabella as the "Catholic Kings" of Spain. Henry VIII received the title "Defender of the Faith" from Pope Leo X (1521). Still, none of these monarchs acknowledged papal claims to appoint higher clergy, tax clergy in their realms, or appeal ecclesiastical cases to Rome. These issues surfaced under Henry when Catherine lost four children before princess Mary was born (1516). Henry sought a way to set Catherine aside. He desired a male heir. Emperor Charles V, nephew of Catherine, dominated Pope Clement VII, and he delayed action on Henry's request. The matter was then referred to universities in England and Europe, a few of which sided with Henry. He summoned Parliament (1529) to deal with the question, and Lord Chancellor Thomas Cromwell persuaded Parliament and the clergy to acknowledge the king as "Supreme Head of the Church in England."

With the question of final authority decided, Henry divorced the first of his six wives. Parliament then issued a series of statutes severing all ties between England and the papacy (1533–34). Henry dissolved the monasteries and confiscated their lands (1535–39). He sold the lands to nobles, gentry, and merchants to raise revenue for war with France. The process bound a whole new class of landowners to the English crown and the new religious situation. Henry was determined to remain doctrinally Catholic and determined to suppress heresy, whether Lollard, Lutheran, or Anabaptist. His break with Rome was practical and political, not doctrinal. He approved the Ten Articles (1536) but later repudiated Protestantism. The Six Articles of 1539 reaffirmed Catholic doctrine under threat of severe penalties.

In 1538, Henry approved distribution of a new translation of the English Bible to the churches, although the "Great Bible" was not issued until 1539. It was approved by Thomas Cromwell and Thomas Cranmer, first "Protestant" Archbishop of Canterbury. Miles Coverdale produced the Great Bible. It was a revision of Thomas Matthew's (pen name of John Rogers) revision of William Tyndale's Bible. Beginning with the second edition (1540), the Great Bible carried a preface by Thomas Cranmer, and was therefore call "Cranmer's Bible." Five other editions were published (1540–41), and it was still officially appointed to be read in the Church of England at the time of Henry's death (1547). The Bishops' Bible (1568), a revision of the Great Bible, was generally found in churches until 1611.

Henry's sickly son was only nine when he became Edward VI (1547–53) of England. Under him the government moved rapidly toward building a church that was moderately Protestant in doctrine and ritual. Cranmer gathered the most ancient liturgies of the Catholic Church and translated them into majestic English as the Book of Common Prayer. The new Protestantism had not yet taken root when Edward died and was succeeded by Mary, his devoutly Roman Catholic eldest sister.

Mary I (1553–57) tried to return to the religious situation of 1529. She abolished all the anti-papal legislation and returned the church to papal obedience. Mary outraged English patriotism by allowing three hundred Protestants, including Thomas Cranmer, to be executed for heresy in three years. Protestants took refuge on the Continent. Some went to be with John Calvin in Geneva, where they made another English translation of the Bible—the Geneva Bible (1557, 1560). It became the favorite personal Bible across England until 1611. When Mary married Philip II of Spain, arrogant son and presumptive heir of Charles V, patriotism and Protestantism became indelibly identified in the public mind.

Elizabeth I (1558–1603) ascended to the throne amid cheers of relief. The religious scene was revisited, and Elizabeth accepted the title "Supreme Governor" of the church. She insisted that the revision of the Articles of Faith and the Book of Common Prayer be acceptable to moderate Catholics and Protestants alike. Independence from Rome was a dominant theme during her reign, though she refused to pry into the personal beliefs of her subjects. Under Elizabeth, England clearly adopted a conservative form of Protestantism that looked on Presbyterians with suspicion and on Baptists with contempt. Many in Parliament sought to "purify" the church. They met with Elizabeth's firm resistance, and unyielding protagonists who refused to comply were arrested. The Anglican church settled between the Catholic minority who wanted to return to Rome and the Puritan minority who wanted to build a more radically Protestant church.

By 1603, when the Tudor line ended with Elizabeth's death, England had seceded permanently from Rome, removed the threat of aristocratic violence, withstood the Spanish Armada (1588), and achieved peace with Spain. Only their own king could attack their beliefs or undermine the property rights of its privileged classes. More prosperous than ever, Englishmen began to establish colonies in the New World. But this delicate Tudor balance was destroyed by the Stuarts, when James VI (1567–1625) of Scotland came to the throne in 1603.

James, the only son of Henry Stuart, was born in 1566 to Mary, Queen of Scots. Mary was executed by Elizabeth, and the baby (James) was raised as a Protestant by regents who ran Scotland. James became convinced that the Presbyterian system of church government would destroy royal control over the church and destroy the monarchy itself. As he moved into his new realm of England, James I (1603–25) was met by Puritans who presented the "Millinery Petition" (1603). They sought relief from their "common burden of human rites and ceremonies," which James agreed to discuss at the Hampton Court Conference (1604).

James was disposed to adopt a mediating position and approved minor changes in the Book of Common Prayer. When John Rainolds (Reynolds), Puritan President of Corpus Christi College, Oxford, suggested a new translation of the Bible, and his stern opponent, Richard Bancroft, Bishop of London, reluctantly concurred, James ordered the work be begun. A strong body of revisers was formed to produce the King James ("Authorized") Version (1611) using the Bishops Bible (the 1568 revision of the Great Bible) as its basis. Then the name "presbyter" came up at the conference. James confused the English Puritans' term with the Scottish Presbyterians, declared that in Scotland he had learned "no bishop, no king," and threatened to "harry" dissenters out of the land.

Although James had praiseworthy aims—peace with Spain, tolerance for the Catholic minority in England, union of England and Scotland, and a strong but benevolent monarchy—he soon ran into difficulties in three areas: religion, finance, and foreign policy. Unlike the Tudors, he did not inspire confidence as a political leader. Rising costs brought him into conflict with Parliament, which refused to grant him money for his extravagant court. His foreign policy, especially toward Spain and France, antagonized the Puritans. By his own authority, he increased customs duties, which angered foreign traders.

Roman Catholics who felt they were in a dangerous situation went into exile in Spanish Flanders. At Douay, they organized the English College (1568), moved it to Rheims (1578) in France, and returned to Douay (1593). While in exile they translated the Rheims-Douay Bible into English (1689, 1609/10). This work was actually completed before the King James ("Authorized") Version.

As Jack Cavanaugh, in his Book of Books Series, places "real people" into their historical settings to interact with one another in events that are larger than life, we are both entertained and informed. Jack Cavanaugh is an outstanding practitioner of the writer's craft, portraying details of flesh and blood people caught up in the canvas of sweeping events that are far beyond them. His sense of balance and perspective, broad background and intimate detail, adventure and reflection are combined in a most unusual and profound way.

WILLIAM E. NIX
DALLAS, TEXAS
JANUARY, 1999

Jack Cavanaugh's new series, Book of Books

Glimpses of Truth is the first in a series of compelling historical novels—filled with danger, romance, and adventure—that traces the people, their sacrifices and commitment, and the events that brought the Bible into the English language.

If you liked *Glimpses of Truth*, you'll be sure to want to grab up the rest of the books in this four-volume series.

Coming in Spring 2000!

Beyond the Sacred Page

Book two in the Book of Books Series, the story of the Tyndale version

Softcover: 0-310-21575-7

We want to hear from you. Please send your comments about this book to us in care of the address below. Thank you.

ZondervanPublishingHouse
Grand Rapids, Michigan
http://www.zondervan.com

A Division of HarperCollins*Publishers*